עת לבנות

A TIME TO BUILD

עת לבנות

A TIME TO BUILD

ESSAYS FROM THE WRITINGS
OF
RAV DR. JOSEPH BREUER זצ"ל

Published for

THE RABBI SAMSON RAPHAEL HIRSCH
PUBLICATIONS SOCIETY

By

PHILIPP FELDHEIM, INC.
"The House of the Jewish Book"

New York

These essays were published originally in the following Feldheim books:

A Time to Build I, 1975
A Time to Build II, 1981
A Time to Build III, 1983
Jewish Marriage, Source of Sanctity, 1982

© Copyright 1995
FELDHEIM PUBLISHERS
Jerusalem-New York

POB 35002
Jerusalem, Israel

200 Airport Executive Park
Nanuet, N.Y. 10954

ISBN 0 87306 734-7

Printed in Israel

לזכר נשמת

מרת מרים בת הח"ר יעקב צבי ע"ה

מאת בעלה הח"ר שמשון

בן מוה"ר לוי יוסף זצ"ל ברייער

ובנותיה

Table of Contents

IV. Jewish Marriage

V. Israel

VI. Holocaust

VII. Yomim Nouroim

VIII. Pessach

IX. Prophets

X. Organizations

XI. Miscellaneous

Preface

In the Torah world the name "Rav Breuer" is synonymous with a way of life which embraces authentic Judaism and rejects compromise as a solution to the challenges presented by a world hostile to Torah adherence. This stand has been criticized as a rigid ideology of religious isolation, incompatible with the requirements of "modern" orthodox Judaism. In truth, it is an ideology which safeguards the Torah way of life in our time.

Rav Breuer's concept of the true Jewish *Kehilla* as the life-blood of the Jewish organism has come to be generally accepted as the successful road towards a harmonious, sovereign Torah community. The creation of his own *Kehilla*, with its schools and numerous institutions, inspired large segments of orthodox Jewry which have come to view the *Kehilla* as the major guarantor for the spiritual survival of our People.

Rav Breuer's wisdom and patience, the sterling quality of his *p'sak din*, his matchless presentation of Tanach and Talmud, and his tireless and fearless drive towards the uncompromising perpetuation of Torah principles, have left an indelible mark.

For many years, Rav Breuer wrote extensively on the concept of *Torah Im Derech Eretz* in its contemporary application. The power of his word — spoken or written — is reflected in this collection of fifty-seven essays from his writings.

THE RELEVANCY OF THE TORAH
IM DERECH ERETZ IDEAL

I.

God's Torah obligates us to the never-ending, unadulterated fulfillment of its precepts (V. 4, 2.). It makes allowance for the temporary neutralization of a law (Yebamoth 90) if such action helps to secure the strengthening, salvation and survival of God's Torah (such as Elijah's sacrifices on Mount Carmel at a time when sacrifices were prohibited outside of the Sanctuary). Cases of this nature are mentioned in the Talmud (Brachot 54, Yoma 69, a.o.) under the title of *Horo'as Sho'oh,* referring to measures taken in certain circumstances to strengthen the Law of Torah.

Rav Hirsch's concept of *Torah im Derech Eretz* — shared by his rabbinical contemporaries and disciples — is too well known to warrant renewed discussion in these pages. He viewed it as the only possible way in which the sons and daughters of our people were to prove and maintain themselves as proud members of the Nation of God, in ideology as well as action, in the midst of a cultural surrounding of an entirely different orientation. The life of the Yehudi in the business world, equipped with all available skills, as well as the life of the academician (as teacher, physician, lawyer, engineer a. o.) were to be elevated to a true *Kiddush Hashem.* Or should these professions be left to those who are estranged from Torah Judaism?

Rav Hirsch and the proponents of his ideology were fully aware that their approach to Jewish education and professional training would also claim victims. They regretted this deeply but they saw no other way. They were equally cognizant of the disapproval of their course by rabbinical leaders in other countries. The following is characteristic for Rav Hirsch's thinking: to an inquiry which reached him from one of the countries of Eastern Europe regarding the nature and acceptability of the Torah im Derech Eretz precept, he replied that the question would have to be decided by the local rabbinical authorities (in the East).

A point to ponder: how many victims may have been claimed by the rejection of the Torah im Derech Eretz ideology?

II.

Certain circles which found it difficult to remain unaware of the greatness of Rav Hirsch maintain that his demand of Torah im Derech Eretz was but a *Horo'as Sho'oh* essentially prohibited for the Torah-true Jew and only found necessary for the salvation and strengthening of Torah. It is claimed that its validity, as that of every *Horo'as Sho'oh,* is limited to the conditions of life prevailing in the time of Rav Hirsch.

Anyone who has but a fleeting insight into the life and work of Rav Hirsch will realize that his Torah im Derech Eretz formula was never intended by him as a *Horo'as Sho'oh.* "Our school must be governed by the spirit of Torah im Derech Eretz; *at no time and circumstances* may it give up these principles (of Torah im Derech Eretz education)", thus he states firmly in a draft of by-laws for his Kehilla. Or shall we listen to Rav Hirsch in his famed polemical essay against the Breslau Seminary (Coll. Writings, Vol. VI, p. 392-3): "Ever since we have begun to make our modest contribution to the Jewish cause by speech, pen and deed, it was and is our wholehearted endeavor to present and advocate the most intimate union between Judaism — total, unadulterated Judaism — and the spirit of all *true* science and knowledge . . . we maintain that our whole future, with all ideological and social problems the solution of which is eagerly awaited by mankind, belongs to Judaism, full, unabridged Judaism . . . because we can view the welfare and future of Judaism only in the framework of the most intimate union with the spirit of *true* science and knowledge of every age, we are the most outspoken foes of all *false* science and knowledge, foes of every attempt, in the guise of science, to lay the ax to the roots of our Jewish Sanctuary . . . for if there were no alternative and we had only the choice between Judaism and Science, then there simply would be no choice and every Jew would unhesitatingly make his decision . . . rather to be a Jew without science than Science without Judaism. *But, thank God, this is not the case . . .*"

Does this Hirschian demand for Torah im Derech Eretz bear the slightest resemblance to a *Horo'as Sho'oh?*

III.

Let us for a moment assume that the Torah im Derech Eretz precept was indeed a *Horo'as Sho'oh* (which it decidedly was not): there is a type of *Horo'as Sho'oh* which remains valid for an indefinite period of time if the conditions which brought it about last for many centuries. This is borne out by the following: it is common knowledge that the Torah prohibited the written documentation of the *Torah Sheb'al Peh* (II 34, 27; Gittin 60). Pressing circumstances and the increasing dispersion of our people, posing a severe threat to the survival of the "Oral Teaching", led to the writing of Mishna and Talmud, a *Horo'as Sho'oh.* As the conditions which resulted in this emergency measure continued to prevail throughout the ensuing centuries until our own time, this *Horo'as Sho'oh* became a permanent institution — and thus was born our immense Torah literature.

We ask: are the conditions which led Rav Hirsch and the rabbinical leaders to the supposed *Horo'as Sho'oh* of Torah im Derech Eretz any less valid in our own time? Are they not rather more acute and far more pressing? Is it any less vital for our contemporary youth to comprehend "Judaism from within", to imbue themselves with the consciousness of the true meaning of being a Jew and of the lofty nature of their people's God-willed convocation to which they are to dedicate their lives in loyal devotion? Is it any less important in our time that our youth, *equipped with thorough Torah knowledge,* strengthens its un-shakeable determination to help the Divine Will to rule over their lives in surroundings poisoned by atheistic and materialistic slogans? To absorb of cultural values only that which is worth-while and noble and to accept only those scientific theories which fit in the framework of the Divine Science — such Torah im Derech Eretz should be any less needed in our time?

We would have every reason to be grateful to Divine Prov-idence if it were to send us a Rav Hirsch in our confused age in order to guide our sons and daughters with his Torah im Derech Eretz ideology on the only possible road of survival; in order to strengthen them in their fight against the dangers which lurk in the world that surrounds them; in order to demonstrate that be-fore the Torah im Derech Eretz precept which proclaims the rulership of God's Torah in the life of the Yehudi, all phantom Judaism, masquerading as so-called reform and conservative Judaism, are revealed in their miserable meaninglessness (which will finally cause Torah-true rabbis and organizations to abstain from their treasonous course of recognizing the types of so-called Judaism as acceptable "movements" within Jewry). Would that we had a Rav Hirsch and the Torah im Derech Eretz formula to help the *Jewish State* rising on holy soil in our time to achieve *its only possible permanence as Torah State!* Is it conceivable, against this background, to consider the Torah im Derech Eretz precept, a *Horo'as Sho'oh* designed to satisfy the need of an era *long past?*

IV.

Times may have changed. But the problems have remained essentially the same. We must solve them along the course as it has been charted for us. Are we really certain that our children will remain true to their calling if we create for them an artificial ghetto?

Half-heartedness and compromise are never acceptable but they are virtually fatal in the area of education. Only an *unwavering, straight forward* course will lead to success. We neither look for nor require the agreement or approval of those who prefer a different course. Their criticism does not touch us. We certainly respect the ideology of other circles provided their course is also an unmistakably consequent one.

As for us, let us do our best to promote and fulfill the Torah im Derech Eretz ideal in its true spirit and let us protect it from regrettable misuse and misinterpretation.

*   *   *

A personal footnote: on the day before he passed away, my father s.z.l told me: "I am firmly convinced that the way shown by Rav Hirsch s.z.l. will be *Mekarev haGeulah*". A sacred testament.

OUR WAY

Can one talk of a German Jewishness? In the sense that the Divine precepts of the Torah, as laid down in the Written and Oral Law, are equally binding for all parts of the Jewish people, the term "German Jewishness" is as unjustified and misleading as the expressions "Hungarian Jewishness," "Polish Jewishness," "Lithuanian Jewishness." Wherever the Galuth has dispersed the members of our people, they were united by the same ideals of sanctity to which they were to dedicate their lives.

Divine Judaism embraces all of life in all its manifestations placing on it the stamp of the Divine Will. This Will obligates us to the most minute adherence to the lawful ordinances by our spiritual leaders which they formulated for the protection of the Divine Law and its realization in our lives. While Halacha and Minhagim have caused differences in practices which assumed significant proportions in the various parts of the Jewish world, they have never in the least endangered the unity of our people which is derived from God's Torah. Still, temperament and taste, as far as admissible within the framework of the Torah Law, have not been without influence on the way in which Mitzvoth are practiced and have also shaped the character of the various Torah institutions. It is in this sense that we may perhaps speak of a "German Jewishness."

Thinking of New York which has become the melting pot of Jews from all parts of the world it becomes quite evident that none of the various elements are willing to give up one iota of their characteristic Jewishness, be it Ashkenazic or Sephardic Jews, Lithuanian, Hungarian or Polish Jews—with or without the Chassidic stamp. Each of these groups have organized themselves for the purpose of fostering and perpetuating their characteristic type of Jewishness.

This also holds true for the Jews of Germany. This trend lead to the creation of our Kehilla. Its by-laws which are based on those of the Kehilla whose name it carries bear testimony to its determination to maintain the sacred aspects of a true Kehilla, on new soil and under radically different circumstances, along the road charted by the great Rabbinical leaders of Germany. This is its fundamental statute:

> "The K'hal Adath Jeshurun has set itself the task to further the fundamentals of Judaism, Torah, Avodah, and Gemiluth Chassodim, and to create for itself those institutions which are required for the realization of these precepts. The fundamental Law of this Kehilla is the Religious Law as handed down in Torah, Talmud and Shulchan Aruch. It is the highest authority for all decisions and measures by the Kehilla; they are valid only if they do not contradict any part of the Religious Law. The Divine Service of our Kehilla follows the Minhag Ashkenaz."

While the by-laws of our Kehilla do not refer to its intent to maintain its German-Jewish character, this intention became evident at the very moment of its inception.

Physically, the Kehilla's German-Jewish character is immediately visible in the Synagogue. Extensive chapters in the Shulchan Aruch stress the vital importance of cleanliness, order and dignity in the Synagogue. Thus, these aspects in themselves have little to do with a specific "German Jewishness." The same holds true for our posture during the Tefilla. The Halacha is silent on the preference of a stationary versus a moving position in regard to the intensity of kavonoh during the Tefilla. The sainted Ari hakodosh, and with him many of our Torah Greats, assumed stationary positions during the Tefilla—and they were certainly not German Jews.

The melodies of the Tefilla and the Niggunim of the Keriath Hatorah are warmly familiar to the members who originate from Germany and who would not wish to miss any part of their accustomed service. Whether this type of Divine service pleases other circles is a matter of contention. The same holds true for other types of Divine Services. This is a question of taste over which one cannot argue. One thing is certain: it has nothing whatever to do with Jewishness.

Our Synagogue possesses a choir which, however, does not take any part in the actual Tefilla. The Torah-true Kehilloth in Germany also had their choir which finds its incomparable predecessor in the great choir of the Levites in the Beth Hamikdosh. When Rav Hirsch was once asked why he had a Synagogue choir, he replied gruffly: "Leave me in peace with your Meshorerim (used to accompany the Chazan in the Tefilla) whose religiosity is often quite doubtful. My choir consists of members and children of my Congregation; it is part and parcel of the Kehilla and its melodies enhance the dignity and sanctity of our Divine Service." If we did not have our choir, we would sorely miss it.

It is a self-understood fact that our Synagogue was constructed and equipped in accordance with the rules of the Shulchan Aruch. The so-called Almemor rises in the midst of the Congregation. The separation of men and women is strictly carried out. In our Synagogue the lawful separation (Mechitza) is established by a high women's gallery which is topped by a tall trellis. These measures correspond with the requirements of the great Rabbinical leaders of Germany. This required separation finds its halachic source in the arrangements which were made in the Beth Hamikdosh for the Simchath Beth Hashoeva (See Midoth, Ch. 2, Sukkah 51) when the men were placed downstairs while the women were placed on a gallery "to enable them to see from above" (Rambam, Hilch. Beth Habechiro, Ch. 5). If Synagogues of certain countries featured the custom to use curtains also for a women's gallery (instead of a trellis) it goes without saying that this custom must also be continued in those of our local Synagogues which are also dedicated to the perpetuation of other former customs. We may add that he who is not satisfied with the combination of gallery and trellis and rather prefers a thick curtain should also demand of his wife to cover her hair with a full cloth turban rather than with the customary "Sheitel." For half-hearted measures are never in place. (As to covering of women's hair, we may also look towards our great Rabbinical leaders of Germany. Our Kehilla has every reason to be proud of its women whose overwhelming majority lives up to this law in the manner approved by our Rabbinical leaders).

This holds equally true of weddings in the Synagogue. In Hungary weddings in the Synagogue represented a decided trend towards Reform against which the local Rabbinical authorities justly fought. This, however, was not the situation in Germany. Leading German Rabbis have performed weddings in the Synagogue. Thus, there is no reason for our Kehilla to refuse weddings in the Synagogue.

In reality, all the aforementioned aspects which are chiefly evident in the Synagogue still do not justify the term "German Jewishness". We would prefer finding its justification in the ideological devise of "Torah im Derech Eretz". Our Kehilla strives ceaselessly to live up to this great precept in the life of its members and in the education of its youth. For it is the great heritage of its great Rabbinical leaders in Germany.

At first glance, the program of "Torah im Derech Eretz" appears to be in complete contrast to the so-called "Chassidic Jewishness"—which has also lately become a catchword. However, this is true only when a distorted view is mistaken for the true picture. This applies to both aforementioned concepts of Jewish living, both designed to chart the course towards the fulfillment of God-willed tasks in our lives.

Generally, the superficial student deduces from the "Torah im Derech Eretz" precept, as expounded by the great Rabbinical leaders in Germany, the necessity of acquiring secular knowledge, i.e. the training and proficiency in worldly cultures and professions. Actually, "Torah im Derech Eretz" implies infinitely more than a mere synthesis between Torah and secular knowledge. It views the Divine Torah as God's gift of mercy to His people, whose very existence is shaped and completely dominated by it. To be a Jew thus means to chart one's course of life in purity before God, i.e. to conceive of life as possible only under the rulership of the Divine Will and to be ready at all times to subordinate family and social life to its purifying and sanctifying guidance. The Jewish man must submit all his thoughts and actions, all phenomena of life, all that serves to enrich his sphere of knowledge and perception before the tribunal of Torah in order to accept from its hand that which may stand up before its truth and judgment.

Admittedly, "Torah im Derech Eretz" is also concerned with "Parnassa" and the preparation for it. Yet it is in this area of economic sustenance that God's Torah aims at the domination of the prevailing Derech Eretz in order to turn it into a Kiddush

Hashem. Consequently, in a broader sense, Derech Eretz embraces the "earth way" of the Yehudi who must seek self-perfection in all his actions and strivings under the rulership of the Will of God.

"On all your ways perceive Him" (Mishle 3)—have Him before your eyes and analyze yourself whether you are able to stand up before Him. This great Jewish maxim of life mirrors most exactly the reflection of the "Torah im Derech Eretz" precept.

Is there a contradiction between genuine Chassidism and the "Torah im Derech Eretz" principle?

Let us be realistic: it is a fact that the Rabbinical leaders in a number of countries refused to permit the study of secular knowledge. It is equally true that in this country even Chassidic circles recognized the necessity of a secular education and acted accordingly. Thinking of Eretz Israel, the Chassidic leadership there must also be aware of its responsibility in helping to provide trained teachers, physicians, lawyers, engineers and farmers for the Jewish land. If Torah authorities claim for themselves the leadership in Jewish life, they cannot possibly leave these vital professions to an element which refuses to conform to the Torah principles proclaimed by the Torah leaders. This being the case, what separates genuine Chassidic Jewishness from the genuine "Torah im Derech Eretz" Jewishness? Nothing at all.

One should not confuse Chassiduth with the so-called Chassidic movement which began in Poland in the 18th century. The latter met the needs of the Jewish masses who lived in terrible misery, and thus spread rapidly. Tefillah was projected into the foreground from which flowed strength and faith in God; dances and songs induced enthusaism and joyfulness; the stress on human and humane qualities increased the self-respect of the impoverished. Thus, without a doubt, Chassidism saved these

Jewish masses. However, the resulting frequent neglect of Torah
study lead to justified protest by Torah giants and caused a
regrettable inner rift which was subsequently healed when a great
Chassidic leader returned the study of Torah to its rightful
central position.

Genuine Chassidic Jewishness strives for Chassiduth which
in itself is a lofty achievement on the ethical ladder which the
Yehudi must attempt to climb. This is demonstrated for us by
R. Pinchas ben Yair (Abodah Zarah 20b): Our highest duty is
Torah and its study; this leads to carefulness which in turn leads
to active striving; to guiltlessness; to purity; to holiness; to modesty; to the fear of sin; and finally, to Chassiduth. Accordingly, a
Chassid is a Jew who gives himself in limitless love to the Divine
Will and its realization and to whom the welfare of his fellow-
men constitutes the highest source of satisfaction (see Hirsch,
Chorev, Ch. 14). Thus, in the Talmudic era, the title "Chassid"
was a mark of highest distinction—and this is what it should be
today.

The so-called Chassid who confines his Avodah to prayer
does not deserve this title as this "Avodah of the heart" does not
call him to the Avodah of life where he must practice and apply
the precepts of Chassidus.

He does not deserve the title if he is particular regarding
the Kashruth of his food but fails to apply the precepts of conscientiousness and honesty to his business dealings.

He does not deserve his title if his social life is not permeated by love and the deep interest in the welfare of his fellow-
men; if he does not shun quarreling, envy or even abominable
lashon hora; if he does not earnestly strive to acquire those
midoth for which Rav Hirsch (in his Chorev) calls so eloquently.

Certainly the mere exhibition of a certain type of clothing
or the type of beard worn or even the adornment of long side-

burns do not entitle the bearer to the title of honor—Chassid. These may be marks of distinction—but they must be earned to be deserved.

Even study of the Zohar does not necessarily signify the attainment of Chassidus. If this were so, only a few chosen ones would be eligible.

Yet the deep faith and trust in the Chassidic leadership is surely justified for these Torah leaders personify in their very mode of life the precepts of Chassiduth.

Doubtless, the so-called German Jewishness with its "Torah im Derech Eretz" demand can stand up proudly before genuine Chassidism: to live up to the "Torah im Derech Eretz" precept in its true meaning is to follow the path upon which Chassiduth greets us as the crowning glory of life. Thus, Rav Hirsch, and with him the great Torah leaders in Germany, were exemplary Chassidim sent to us by Divine Providence.

DEDICATION ADDRESS

Delivered at the Dedication Ceremony of the New Synagogue
of K'hal Adath Jeshurun, New York City, 24 Ellul 5712 —
September 14, 1952

למען יזמרך כבוד ולא ידום "so that the honor may sing to You, a
Song that will never be silent." ה' אלוקי לעולם אודך "God, my God,
for all time to come I will pay You homage." These words, this
vow conclude the solemn hymn מזמור שיר חנוכת הבית which we
have just heard.

Amidst joyous songs we entered this site, joyous songs fill
this exalted moment. For truly—we have every reason to give
joyous thanks to ה' Who has stood at the side of our Kehillah,
שהחיינו Who has given it life and helped it to surmount the vicis-
situdes of our time; וקימנו Who has given our Kehillah the
strength to overcome all difficulties and tribulations והגיענו לזמן
הזה to celebrate this festive event. Surely, we have reason to gaze
upwards to Him with grateful hearts הטוב והמטיב, Whose goodness and love have enabled our Kehillah to achieve this momen-
tous goal.

Our gratitude, the deeply felt thanks of our Kehillah go to
all its men and women who have shared with magnificent devotion בלב שלם ובלב חפצה in the building of this Sanctuary. Our
gratitude goes to our Kehilla's generous friends and especially
to the women of both Chevros who actively shared in the
furnishing and decor of our Beth Haknesses. Above all, we
convey our profound sense of appreciation to the members of

the Administration and the various committees which support
its work—all joining together in the spirit of selfless sacrifice in
order to complete this great task, שלם ה׳ שכרם.

ברכת הטוב והמטיב Compelling as we feel the urge to pronounce
the ברכת שהחיינו, at this time, several of our Rabbinical greats
doubt whether even at special moments like this the שהחיינו or
only הטוב והמטיב should be spoken as a complete, full B'rocho.
The following consideration gives credence to these doubts.

When the second Zion Sanctuary, after many obstacles but
constantly encouraged by Chaggai's and Zecharyah's words of
admonition, was finally reconstructed by those who had
returned from exile, the Prophet Zecharyah addressed the following message to his people in the name of God: כה אמר ה׳ צבאות
אשר ביום יוסד תחזקנה ידיכם השומעים בימים האלה את הדברים מפי הנביאים
בית ה׳ ההיכל להבנות "May your hands be strong as you perceive in
this hour these words from the mouth of the Prophet: Know, on
this day ביום יוסד בית ה׳ צבאות only the founding stone of the
House of God, of the House of ה׳ צבאות has been laid; now it is
your task ההיכל להבנות to erect the Fortress of God, God's
House." This means: You think that you have already built the
House of God? Not at all. Today you have laid the founding
stone for the House of God; now you must erect God's Sanctuary and guide it towards completion. Thus spoke Zecharyah.

In the same vein came the great message of admonition
from the Prophet Chaggai as he addressed his people in this
hour. While the second Sanctuary had been built, it rose as a
modest structure compared to the glorious construction of the
first Zion Sanctuary. And we read how bitter tears were shed in
remembrance of past glory. But the Prophet admonishes: do not
shed tears, do not display weakness — חזק, חזק, חזק, three times
he repeats his plea: be strong, ועשו carry it out, for כי אני אתכם, I
צבאות ה׳ am with you.

But, why? Does not God's Sanctuary stand erect? And now
ועשו? Yet, if God's Sanctuary is to rise proudly on holy soil ועשו
את הדבר אשר כרתי אתכם בצאתכם ממצרים, then you must continue the

labor, you must realize the challenging task which God proclaimed to His people in the hour of redemption. Carry out this task ורוחי עומדת בתוככם, foster this spirit in your midst, אל תיראו go to work, fearlessly and proudly.

The message of the Prophets culminates in the call for the same task that 'ה set for His people when they were about to erect God's Sanctuary in the desert. עשו לי מקדש This House of God is to rise as a center of קדושה from which My people shall draw the sanctity of their lives, so that ושכנתי בתוכם My שכינה, the blessing of My proximity will forever dwell in the midst of this nation. This also holds true for the Zion Sanctuary on God's sacred soil, in God's land. Sanctification of all of life—Jewish people: the people of God; Jewish land: the land of God; Jewish state: the state of God—all this had to become reality if the Zion Sanctuary was to fulfill its mission.

The Sanctuary fell in ruins because it failed to imbue the life of our people with the spirit of sanctity. The painful realization of this failure is the bitter theme of our Prophets' words. היכל ה' היכל ה' Yirmiyahu exclaims in bitter disappointment: what good is your constant talk about God's Sanctuary — היכל ה' המה you, yourselves, should be the Sanctuary of God, the Sanctuary which is to rise in your daily lives.

When the second Sanctuary was built on God's soil, the same Prophets who had fought consistently against obstacles that were standing in the way of the reconstruction concentrated on the main task of educating the people to become fully conscious of the responsibility placed upon them by this great event. It is quite immaterial whether this Sanctuary was lavish or modest—thus the Prophet Chaggai admonishes לי הכסף ולי הזהב נאם ה' צבאות "Mine is the silver, Mine is the gold." I demand not gold and silver from you, they do not bestow sanctity on the Sanctuary—but חזק ועשו את הדבר וכו' carry out the Divine precepts for which this House of God has been erected.

In the same vein the Prophet Zecharyah meets his people at the time of the dedication of God's Sanctuary and presents them with this Divine Message: תחזקנה ידיכם, strengthen yourselves, equip yourselves with power, be aware that it is you who places the real founding stone for the House of God in this hour. Be ready now to construct the היכל, the real Sanctuary, the sanctuary of your homes, of your lives.

Even this admonition of the Prophets failed to be heeded, failed to be realized by the people. And so, the second Zion Sanctuary toppled in ruins, buried state and land and brought unspeakable Galuth terror over our misery-stricken people. Yet through all Galuth periods there sounds the Divine call as issued through the Prophet Yecheskel: כה אמר ה׳ א׳ כי הרחקתים בגוים וכ׳ הפיצותים בארצות ואהי להם למקדש מעט בארצות אשר באו שם "Even if I have sent them far away among the nations and have dispersed them in all lands—I wish to find My מקדש מעט wherever the Galuth finds My people . . ." Build for Me houses of worship and of study, build them for Me as מקדש מעט that they may prove themselves to be building bricks for the blessed future secured by God for our people.

Permeated by this consciousness we celebrate this festive hour. יום יוסד בית ה׳—It is a day which symbolizes the love of הי״ת for our Kehilla which helped it to become a further foundation stone for its sanctuary. We recall in this hour that ברכה בשם ומלכות is being pronounced when a building has been finished. This construction is far from being completed. With God's help we shall continue to build and continue that which our previous בית הכנסת helped us attain—as we expressed it this afternoon when we bade farewell to our old home. We shall continue to grow in strength מחיל אל חיל in order to work at the true completion of our sanctuary. With God's help this building will rise in beauty when the light of Torah—for which we kindled the נר תמיד in this festive hour—shines ever brighter in all our houses; when all our houses consider themselves as centers of Torah living and dedicate themselves to the full realization of the Torah precepts; when in all our houses למוד התורה is treated as the highest, holiest task for young and old; when God's holy Shabbos spreads its sacred glow over all our houses, over all our lives. All this, our social relationships, our daily work, must be lived under the dominance of משפט and צדקה, must be able to stand before God in honesty and love. The requirements of כשרות, of טהרה and צניעות must elevate our houses as the requirements of קדושה and טהרה must inspire and sanctify our married lives. The בית המדרש of our school must play the essential role in preparing our children to mature into proud, strong, uncompromising Yehudim.

Then, then we shall be ready to pronounce the B'rocho בשם ומלכות. Then all will come true for this בית הכנסת of which the Psalm sings which we just heard, of God's blissful proximity in our lives which alone guarantees our salvation from darkness and devastation, God's proximity to which alone we owe our sustenance and strength.

If all this is true for our בית הכנסת, then all sacrifices which we have brought for the erection of this building and towards the construction of our school will surely bear rich fruit.

The festive joyfulness which permeates this hour of celebration is justified because we are determined to meet the great challenge presented by this בית הכנסת. "To You, oh God, the honor shall sing" we have just heard למען יזמרך כבוד, and ולא ידום "a song that will never be silent" . . . What is meant by this? Of God's Sanctuary in the desert it says in the Torah: ונקדש בכבדי "This Sanctuary receives its sanctity through My honor," meaning those who are honored through God. Men, Jewish men are they who are inspired by the knowledge ואתה כבדי ומרים ראשי that "You, oh God, are my honor. You lift up high my head as I dedicate my life to Your service." To You, my God, I devote my whole being, to Your Honor my life shall be consecrated. Such a life becomes a source of honor and pride for God, ונקדש כבדי it is the honor for which God longs. למען יזמרך כבוד If we offer this solemn vow, then ולא ידום the song of our lives will never be silent, for its melody resounds through our entire God-serving existence. To You, oh God—so vows the Psalm, so we promise in this solemn hour—to You we shall pay homage at every moment of our lives.

Yet it is neither festive psalms nor festive speech that bestow קדושה upon this sanctuary. It is the first תפלה which we are about to pray that fills this House of God with true קדושת בית הכנסת. The Psalm verses which introduce our תפלת מעריב tell us clearly what it is that the תפלה will help us attain. שיר המעלות Hear, to which lofty heights the תפלה is designed to elevate us. הנה ברכו את ה' כל עבדי ה' bless God, dedicate your total lives to Him, live up to your task as true servants of God. From this House you are to draw the strength to remain upright in the midst of nocturnal plight. If such strength is to emanate from the תפלה and from this House of God, שאו ידיכם קדש then you must raise your hands in sanctity up to God, then your daily labors must be worthy before God and only then will you truly "bless God." יברך ה' מציון then infinite blessing will flow for you from the Zion of the Torah to which this בית הכנסת is dedicated. Then you may confess in every situation and circumstance of life: ה' צבאות עמנו משגב לנו God is with us, He raises us high above all that threatens to tear us down; ה' צבאות אשרי אדם בוטח בך because we secure for ourselves God's proximity by virtue of the Divine guidance, we have the right to accept from God's Hand all that His wise counsel decides for our lives. ה' הושיעה we long for Divine assistance; המלך יעננו ביום קראנו as long as we worship God as the Master over our lives, as the Guide at every phase of our existence—God is near to us, infinitely close, and we may rejoice in the knowledge that God hears when we bring our תפלה up to Him.

May these great, precious values of Torah living become ever more the loyal life companions for us and our children —

ה' הושיעה המלך יעננו ביום קראנו

THE SPIRITUAL LEADERSHIP
OF THE KEHILLA

A Kehilla is healthy—provided it lives. There is pulsating life in the Kehilla if its membership is fully aware of the eternal values of this its most precious possession; its members support their Kehilla joyfully, ever eager to promote its healthy growth and development.

The Kehilla needs and counts on the active support of everyone of its members, young and old. The youth, especially, possesses qualities which are desirable for the Kehilla: energy, enthusiasm, initiative. Yet it is also characteristic for youth's receptive nature that it tends towards new trends, new customs and modes; frequently, the motives may be traced to the attempt of imitating others or to an—unjustified—inferiority complex. The older generation, on the other hand, possesses experience, maturity, calm judgment. It tends—and it is often reproached for it—towards the traditional, that to which it is used.

New trends are not always desirable, and the old ways possess values which must be nurtured and cultivated. A mutual complementation through close cooperation between young and old—which will alleviate undeniable shortcomings on both sides—is a vital necessity also in the life of the Kehilla.

A unified leadership is certainly required. In our Kehilla

such leadership is provided by its Rabbonim. They represent and interpret the ideological principles which give our Kehilla its characteristic stamp. Their co-workers are aware that in this area a unified approach to all basic problems is a vital necessity. We respect but do not accept the attitude of others who do not share the philosophy of the educational training program of our Kehilla. Youth is often drawn in various directions and we can understand that it is easily swayed to accept that which is prevalent in other circles. In itself this gives certainly no rise to fears of our youth's turning its back on the specific character of our Kehillah.

There are certain practices which might be interpreted as a deviation from the characteristic atmosphere of our Kehilla. We are concerned with the custom which calls for vigorous "Mitzve dancing" during the festive wedding meal but does not provide an opportunity for a single Dvar Torah (either under the Chuppa or during the meal). This practice directly contrasts with the admonition of our Sages which characterizes any meal, particularly a festive one, as a "meal of the dead" that is not accompanied by Words of Torah (P. Aboth III, 4).

Another development gives rise for more serious concern. While the growing number of young men in the Kehilla who are eager to broaden their talmudic background is a source of real satisfaction, it does not per se provide the spiritual and character education if study is limited to the Talmud and the other Torah sciences are being neglected. The serious study of Tanach, Tefillah, Jewish Ideology and Jewish History, keeping pace with one's growing maturity, is an irreplaceable source from which we all, in every age and especially in the youthful stage, may draw an inexhaustible wealth of *ideological values* which form the eternal reservoir for the strong Yehudi who is proudly conscious of his Divine Judaism.

To repeat: the profound importance and lofty significance

of Talmud study cannot be stressed enough. But it is wrongly
applied if this means neglect or even elimination of the vast
realm of other Torah areas.

Incidentally, for the cultivation of genuinely Jewish
Midoth, among them modesty which keeps far away from con-
ceit and arrogance, the spiritual traffic with our Sages of the
Talmud may be highly recommended.

Some of these manifestations add fuel to the occasional
talk of various "trends" within our Kehilla. Even if this were the
case, it is of little concern in a healthy Kehillah where the spiritual leadership is in full command. It defines and represents the
principles which give our Kehilla its own stamp in clear and
concise firmness and labors ceaselessly to bring these ideals
closer to the understanding and perpetuation by our membership, especially the youth.

Our Kehilla may be proud of its heritage. This does not
imply that it must slavishly hold fast to all that which the great
leaders זצ"ל to whose guidance our Kehilla owes its prosperity
considered necessary (even if it is no less necessary in our age).
Pride in our heritage does not mean that all that for which these
great could take resposibility must necessarily continue to
decide our conduct in unchanged form. Growth and development in all areas is a sign of healthy progress in the Kehilla. Let
our course be determined by the spiritual leadership to which
our Kehilla offers its trust and confidence: with a high sense of
responsibility it carefully weighs the measures which serve best
the total interest of our Kehilla.

We live in a turbulent time, shaken by revolutionary thunder. In no small measure its effect is felt in our Jewish temporary
age. All signs point to a period of transition. Little wonder that
our Kehilla, too, is not unaffected by the reverberations of
change. We must be all the more grateful in the knowledge that
the fundament upon which our Kehilla rises is of proven firm-

ness and that it will continue to support and give strength to us all, young and old, who join together and work together in the common striving for להגדיל תורה ולהאדירה.

ADDRESS AT THE FOUNDING MEETING
OF THE SISTERHOOD
March 20, 1940 (1st Nissan 5700)

It is with sincere pleasure that I welcome the founding of a women's organization in our midst. No knowledgeable person will fail to understand the need for such an organization.

We realize that our times demand a joining together of our women—and, no doubt, our Kehillo will benefit greatly from it.

Indeed, our Kehillo is built upon our homes,—and it is the Jewish woman who puts the stamp of a special character on our homes. The success and the blossoming of our homes is truly the work of her hands.

This was so at all times. But today, in a time of such great upheaval and unspeakable suffering, we must stress this point more than ever.

In the forthcoming Seder nights we will be speaking of את בתינו הציל, "salvaging our homes." The violent storms which have for so long tossed our people about have made the saving of our homes the foremost and most sacred of our concerns. For, if we save our Jewish homes, then all is saved, regardless of how much we have lost. So long as we know that our Jewish homes have been salvaged from the flood waters of catastrophic events, we need not feel destitute nor let the forces of weakness crush us. Jewish tradition teaches us that "the preservation of our homes" is the achievement of our women.

We can thank God's mercy for having been able to build our homes on new—though alien—soil. It is only because of our women that our work will succeed.

Our men face difficult problems. We cannot minimize these awesome problems. The road to פרנסה is not easy; numerous obstacles confront us,—and when the fate of the שבת is at stake, we must be ready to sacrifice and suffer self-denial.

Many a home knows anxiety and dire need. But our Jewish homes should radiate love, happiness and blessings.

ברכה, שמחה, אהבה, according to our Sages, are those special gifts that come to our homes through the quietly devoted work of our women. Wherever these gifts are found, the husband will draw new courage and strength, qualities he needs in order to travel the Jewish road of duty with patient and steadfast good spirits.

This is to be the case for our homes—be they ever so modest and unassuming. When the hands of women light the candles for שבת, darkness will give way to never fading light.

The road to פרנסה is beset by crushing burdens. Every step of the way is a struggle against elements which are the sworn enemies of everything Jewish, of everything good and pure. Our Baale Batim would be in mortal danger if they were not able to drink from the eternal fountain of God's Torah, those eternal sources of purity which guarantee the survival of our homes.

Wisely our Sages comment: It is the woman who lights the way home for her husband when he returns from the house of learning.

Our homes are to be Jewish homes in the true sense of the word. They must be places of sanctity, as marriage is sacred and the table the altar of the sanctuary. The Sages comment significantly: The Jewish woman is the priestess of her house, for she meticulously tends to the כשרות of her table and the טהרה of her marriage.

Our women face enormously difficult problems when they consider the education of their children in a new, alien and differently oriented land. But, be it ever so alien and different, our women will have only one care and that is, that their sons and daughters will be able to cope with their surroundings, and mature into strong and uncompromising Yehudim. את בתינו הציל—here, too, our women are to prove themselves as the preservers of our homes.

I have given you only a few of the important points describing the great problems which our women are expected to solve.

Uniting our women into this organization is a commanding necessity today. Our Sages have always put great trust in our women. Their courage and strength must therefore be constantly supported and sustained. It is the new surroundings into which our women are placed that make such great demands on their time, their strength, on their energy and on their psychological resources.

The expression "the treadmill of every-day life" is heard quite often. Wearisome and tediously petty details make up the day's work. While this is true, it really should be looked at from a different perspective.

Therefore, it is doubly important that our women get together, consult and stimulate one another in the framework of pleasantly agreeable and friendly meetings, where they can leave behind the confines of their daily responsibilities. They will be enriched and their knowledge will be broadened by Shiurim and lectures, and they will become aware ever anew of the great ideal to which they dedicate their life's work.

In addition to Shiurim and lectures, your organization will consider projects which have always been the prerogative of women. We are referring to the duties of צדקה and גמילות חסדים, the care of the sick and of those needing help.

And now our thoughts turn to our Kehillo: Our women need the Kehillo; our Kehillo needs its women. The Kehillo expects and counts on their cooperation. Our Sisterhood is called upon to offer suggestions affecting the welfare of the Kehillo and will cooperate in preserving the decorum during services in Shul.

And when, with God's help, our Kehillo will come to build its own מקוה, as well as the school which is so urgently needed for our children, our Kehillo can be certain that you, the Sisterhood, will always be ready to help.

Although for the time being we only have a Talmud Torah, the Sisterhood should promptly begin work on the establishment of a Kindergarten.

I confidently expect that our Sisterhood will grow and prosper.

Take up your work by uniting in peace and harmony. Put aside anything that might endanger this harmonious work. Never forget for a moment the great and vital goal for which you are working: For the future of our homes and of our children, and for the strengthening of our Kehillo.

May God's blessings reward your work.

OUR TEFILLAH B'TZIBBUR

The institution of our choir dates back to Germany where it was part of most of the larger Congregations. Similarly, the style and intonation of our *Shlichai Tzibbur* as well as the *Niggunim* are those with which we are familiar. Congregations in Eastern Europe knew no choir and their *Chazanut* bears an entirely different quality from the one to which we are accustomed. Thus it is perfectly natural that our choir and *Chazanut* may not necessarily expect an understanding attitude from circles which prefer so-called "Meshorarim" to a choir and which are used to a different kind of *Chazanut*.

This, however, is an undeniable fact: while it is true that the Divine Service in the *Beth Ha Knesseth* preserved *through* the centuries its character as laid down in Talmud and Shulchan Aruch (and thereby our *Tefillah* has proven to be a bond of strength which united all parts of our people at all times despite its dispersion throughout the world), it is equally true that the various *minhagim* resulted in differentations not entirely insignificant. The same applies also to *Chazanut*: the Sephardic *Chazanut* is different from the Ashkenazic one, and even within the Ashkenazic one, which also includes the Polish style, there have evolved certain differences.

There is no justification to the oft-repeated criticism that our service lacks the *Hislahavut*, the fire, the warmth of emotion. The expression of feelings is largely conditioned by the emotional background and temper of mood which are different in different people; or it may be a matter of taste which traditionally cannot be debated. Equally unjustified is the claim that the institution of the choir is an innovation which must therefore be refuted. By the same token one could take issue with the system of so-called "Meshorarim" which were introduced in Poland, Germany, and other European countries during recent centuries and which, as "Singer", or "Bass" (thus the family name "Singer" "Bass"), accompanied the *Chazan,* even during the *Tefillah,* in a more or less tasteful manner.

We have to accept the idea that *Niggunim* (Melodies) which have found a permanent place in a *Kehillah deserve* the same respect with which it has to treat its other *Minhagim.* The institution of the Synagogue choir must be considered from the same viewpoint. Let us sketch briefly the period of its birth and the motives which led the great Rabbinical leaders in Germany to install the choir as a permanent part of the Divine Service.

It was at the turn of the 18th and 19th centuries, the period of the French Revolution with its effects on the Western-European realm. A new era seemed to have dawned which swept away many of the prejudices and social injustices which afflicted the human society. The hour of redemption also came for a Jewry heretofore excluded from the great pulse of cultural life. The doors of the Ghetto opened and the brilliant rays of an unexpected young morning penetrated the medieval night in which inhumanity and hatred had imprisoned the Jews for so many centuries. The great dream was — emancipation, i.e. the acceptance of Jews in the Western-European cultural world with the simultaneous recognition of their equality as citizens of the state in which they lived. While not immediately attainable, this lofty goal seemed concrete and close enough to warrant a major battle which promptly began. It developed that the rays of this rising sun of emancipation blinded many a Jew whose imagination was stirred by the possibility of penetrating all areas of cultural achievements which for centuries were blocked to the sons and daughters of the Jewish people. The first opportunity to obtain possession and power in the economic field, freed from the bond of social injustice; the first chance to attain an honorable degree of equality in social life — this created havoc in the minds of many Jews who came to regard the Judaism of their birth, the Judaism of their fathers and mothers handed down to them as a God-willed task and destiny of life, as an unbearable burden which required only a courageous decision to shake off forever. Naturally, there arose "leaders" who offered themselves to their brothers and sisters as guides to the "new era".

In these circles there was agreement on one point: Judaism must be reformed, it must be fitted to the "Zeitgeist" (as they called it) in order to enable its adherents to cope with the coming emancipation with its unlimited possibilities. Among these circles there were two types of leaders: Conservatives and radicals. Of Judaism the radicals wanted to accept only that which could stand up before the demands of the time. They characterized as insignificant ceremonial laws of Torah such fundamentals as the Shabbos with its work prohibition which stands in the way of any business career; dietary laws which complicate the social contact with one's fellowmen; and finally even the Milah. All that found grace with these "leaders" were the moral and ethical demands of the Torah which they considered important ingredients of Judaism, and last but not least the institution of the mixed marriage which they welcomed as an effective means to establish interfaith unity. Little wonder that true Judaism found itself completely stripped of content by such radical reforms and that many Jewish sons and daughters who entrusted their future to such guidance regarded baptism as the required "entrance ticket to the realm of Western-European culture". This then was the road of the Reform.

The conservatives were more careful and chose the road of gradual development. Their goal was to gain the confidence of the masses who were unwilling and "not mature" enough to accept a radicalistic solution. Thus the reformist demands of the conservatives centered upon an era which showed undeniable defects and which lent itself readily to attempts of reform. This was the Divine Service in the Synagogue. The Synagogue had to be cleansed from the foul-smelling odor commonly associated with the term "Judenschul"! The Synagogue had to be infused with order, dignity, and solemnity, which lead to true devotion. Thus the "Meshorarim" were replaced by the choir, the Derashoth by the sermon in the German language. It was but an incidental beginning that in the process certain parts of the *Tefillah* were eliminated, such as *Bameh Madlikin, Yekum Purkan, Piyutim*. Soon more parts of the *Tefillah* followed suit which were replaced by prayers in German. Finally it became almost a patriotic duty to cut out from the *Tefillah* all prayers which lend expression to our longing for Zion and Yerushalaim, for Moshiach and Geulah. It was considered an act of ingratitude to fail to see in emancipation the ultimate end of the Galuth. It was only a question of time before the orthodox Jewish masses would gradually become receptive to the aims of the radical reform, i.e. desertion from Judaism. It was a process which developed rapidly.

Torah-true Western-European Jewry would have been smashed to pieces by the storm of events had not Divine Providence sent men as leaders who took up the heroic struggle against the forces which failed so miserably to recognize the impact and significance of their time and which betrayed the sacred heritage of their people. This is not the place to trace in detail the work of salvation performed by the great Rabbinical leaders or to analyze their success in saving Western-European Torah-Jewry from complete annihilation. Suffice it to state that they knew how to unite men and women, sons and daughters, in Kehilloth where, with the light of their spirit and the fiery glow of their soul, they proclaimed the eternal greatness of our Divine Judaism which bestows the God-willed imprint upon the lives of its adherents and obligates them to faithful fulfillment of every single one of Torah's laws and demands from the written and oral teachings unto those laid down in the Shulchan Aruch. The Rabbinical leaders explained to their Kehilloth the position of the Jewish people as the people of God among the nations; they interpreted for them the tasks the Jewish people is called upon to solve in Galuth; they reiterated the truth that emancipation has never meant emancipation away from Judaism but represents a renewed test of our people's readiness to fulfill its God-willed convocation also in times of prosperity and success. They expounded the idea that the Jew may well absorb the cultural values of contemporary society so long as he is ready, at all times, to subordinate himself to the majesty of God's Torah-truths and prove himself an uncompromising Jew in whatever position of life he may find himself.

While these leaders freed the Divine Service in the *Beth Haknesseth* from undeniable defects which developed in the course of time and which often violated precepts laid down in the Shulchan Aruch, they never touched the *Tefillah* itself, not even the *Piyutim* (unlike the Kehilloth of the East) although unfortunately they are no longer understood by many Congregants. To intensify the atmosphere of sanctity and dignity they introduced the choir in the place of the "Meshorarim", usually consisting of members and children of the Kehilla. The choir does not take part in the actual *Tefillah*. Its chief purpose is to lead the singing of the Congregation. Thus the introduction of new melodies is less important than the growing familiarity of the Kehilla with the tunes sung by the choir enabling the members to accompany the singing. When the Rabbinical leaders chose to present their sermons in a manner befitting the taste of their time, their real aim was to enflame and inspire the hearts and minds of their disciples to maintain faithful loyalty towards God's Law and its demands on our Jewish lives.

All these measures were not concessions to the Reform but — being in complete accord with the Law of Torah— served to neutralize and nullify reformistic aspirations by demonstrating the impurity of their motives and the senselessness of their design (comp. Hirsch, Ges. Schr., Vol. I, p. 448).

The Kehilloth of these great leaders understood the meaning and intent of these measures realizing that they served to strengthen their deserved reputation even in the ranks of the Reform.

Yet this is the same Rav Hirsch who, in an attack of unparalleled fury, lashes out against the emptiness and self-deception of so-called Houses of God and of a so-called Divine Service if they comprise the totality of Judaism and fail to encompass the Divine Service of life. He writes passionately of the old "Judenschul" which, in its plain simplicity and even with its proverbial "disorder", he vastly prefers to the temples with their architectural features and the aesthetic beauty of their "Divine Service" (comp. Ges. Schr. Vol. I, p. 94 ff). This is the same Rav Hirsch who, in flaming words, condemns a Synagogue order which dared to violate the Jewish Law by organizing a "new order" designed to undermine the Judaism of Torah (comp. Ges. Schr., Vol. II, p. 343 ff.).

The dream of the heroes of Reform ended in utter catastrophe. Divine assistance has brought us to this country and has helped us to attain unity in our *Kehillah*. Our *Kehillah* proceeds on the road charted by the great Rabbinical leaders in Germany. This road lead to the salvation of Western-European Torah-Jewry. It will do so again in America, in the face of a reform movement which found an all too fertile ground in this blessed land of freedom. An even greater threat to Torah Judaism emanates from the moderate reform movement which goes under the name of "conservative Judaism". As a certain protection against these dangers our great Rabbinical leaders s.z.l have equipped us with weapons which have proven their invincible power for all time to come.

"GLATT KOSHER — GLATT YOSHOR"

The conscientious and minute observance of the laws of Kashruth belong to the sacred obligations to which we are to live up if our Jewish houses are to rise in purity before God and His Torah. Supplying our families with totally reliable foods is one of the major tasks a Kehilla has to fulfill.

We may note with satisfaction that the supervision of our meat products from the time of Shechita until they reach the customer meets all the requirements of total Kashruth. This enables our Rabbinate to assume full personal responsibility for the reliability of our Kashruth.

The concept "Glatt Kosher" refers to certain situations when an animal is rejected because of an existing "Sha'aloh"— generally involving the lung—even if the halachic decision would be favorable. Just as all ethical strivings should extend beyond the prescribed boundaries—"lif'nim mi'shuras haDin"—so the practice should be adopted to declare only such meat as kosher that has not been involved in any kind of "Sha'aloh" (comp. Chulin 37b). Such practice would indeed deserve the title of "Glatt Kosher."

A further comment: "Kosher" is intimately related to "Yoshor." God's Torah not only demands the observance of Kashruth and the sanctification of our physical enjoyment; it also insists on the sanctification of our social relationships. This requires the strict application of the tenets of justice and righteousness which avoid even the *slightest trace of dishonesty* in our business dealings and personal life.

God's Torah not only demands of us to love our neighbor in that we concern ourselves with his welfare and property, but it insists further on a conduct of uncompromising straightness ("Yoshor") which is inspired not only by the letter of the law but is guided by the ethical principle of honesty which, then, would deserve the honorable title of "Yeshurun."

"He fears God who walks in uprightness" (Mishle 14:2).

We would welcome a campaign to link a drive for "Glatt Kosher" with an equally intensive one for "Glatt Yoshor." This objective is given hopeful expression by the Prophet Zephania (3:13):

> "The remnants of Israel will not do iniquity, nor speak lies, neither will a deceitful tongue be found in their mouth."

NER TOMID

The dedication of a Ner Tomid in our Synagogue on the occasion of the seventy-fifth Yahrzeit of Rav Hirsch זצ״ל gave fitting expression to the importance which this great bearer of light has for our Kehilla. In all houses of God a Ner Tomid illuminates the ארון הקדש in which our sacred Torah rests. It proclaims the silent yet eloquent admonition that it must be God who leads us with His sacred Will through life; that it must be God who illuminates our path of life. The Ner Tomid commemorates the Menorah in the Divine Sanctuary of which it says: להעלות נר תמיד, that its light may shine forever upwards (Ex. 27, 20). Similarly, the Ner Tomid in our Houses of God looks to men who consider it their life-convocation to guide and lead their people with this light on its path through life. Such bearers of light were granted to our people since Moshe Rabbenu throughout the millenia of its history: they were men sent by God who fought against the night which threatened to engulf wide segments of our people; men who, with Divine assistance, illuminated with the Divine light of Torah "the dark streets," האירו לרבים מבואות אפילות (Midrash to Psalm 50, 23). With the full dedication of their lives to the Divine Ner Tomid, these great leaders have secured for themselves their own "Ner Tomid," the impact of their personalities for all time to come.

Why has our Kehilla dedicated the Ner Tomid to this great bearer of light, to this Prince of Torah among the many Great of our people? A brief analysis of his interpretation of the Ner Tomid of the Menorah in the Divine Sanctuary will supply the answer to this question.

The Menorah with its seven flames of light teaches us how to shape our spiritual and intellectual existence, symbolized by the light, if it is to unfold on the soil of God's Sanctuary. The main part of the Menorah in the Hechal consisted of a center shaft upon whose summit the light burned in a westerly direction, turning towards the Holy-of-Holies which contained the ארון with God's Torah. From this center shaft emerged side arms to the right and left which initially branched outward but then strove upward and on the summit turned their light from the right and left towards the light of the center shaft. What is the meaning of this arrangement? Man's spirit manifests itself as the penetrating intellect and as the will which leads to moral action. The Judaism of Torah demands that our spirit turn above all towards the ארון of the Torah; that our spirit recognize God from his Torah; that our spirit with its will dedicate itself towards the service of God: thus our perception must be above all knowledge and recognition of God; our will leading to moral action must be above all service to God. To such Divine recognition, to such Divine service calls the light of the summit of the center shaft which is turned towards the ארון of the Divine Law.

As the seventh day of creation bestows with its God-proclaimed Shabbos the mark of Divine Creation upon the six days of creation of the world of nature, so the center shaft of the Menorah sends out six arms towards the right and left which appear to lead away from the center stem but actually turn their summit light towards the light in the center. Judaism of the Torah expects that we turn our spirit towards the world and its multitude of facets, recognize and perceive them and conquer them. But these six arms with their flames of light emerge from the center shaft and are rooted in it: ראשית חכמה יראת ה', all knowledge of the universe, all study and research must be rooted in the recognition and knowledge of God; it must be borne and imbued by it. Truth is that which stands up before the ruling Throne of Torah. Our will may only dare to conquer the realities of life if all our strivings are dedicated to the service of God. If our knowledge and perception of the world emanate from God's Torah, then all six lights will send their rays towards the center light; then every newly gained knowledge of the world will enrich our knowledge and recognition of God; then every law of nature which reveals itself to our probing mind will proclaim ever more triumphantly God's Omnipotence. All so-called "secular" knowledge subordinates itself as auxiliary science to our true science of life, the science of Torah. If our worldly endeavors are permeated by the striving to dedicate in servitude all that we achieve to God and His sacred Will, then the six lights of the Menorah will send again their rays towards the middle light; then all we strive for and achieve on earth will be Divinely-hallowed service of life.

To Rav Hirsch this was the essence of the demand of Divine Judaism. With this תורה עם דרך ארץ in the true sense of the word, he led the heroic fight against the powers of tragic estrangement and, with God's Menorah in his hand, charted for the sons and daughters of his time the path of salvation illuminated by the Divine light—and again in his days there were fulfilled the words of the Prophet העם ההולכים בחשך ראו אור גדול "the people that walked in darkness lived to see the great light" (Is. 9, 1).

The battle is not yet concluded. Neither in this country nor in the Holy Land. More than ever Rav Hirsch must be our leader. Our Kehilla owes its development and its fame to his guidance. In ever growing numbers our people drink from the inexhaustible source of his Torah wisdom. His Ner Tomid our Kehilla dedicates to him.

Of the course which he charted for us Mishle (4, 18) says significantly: ואורח צדיקים כאור נגה הולך ואור עד נכון היום "The path of life of the Tsaddikim like the brilliantly shining light—burning ever brighter unto the day destined long before" — To this bright dawn of our God-willed future his life was dedicated.

Thus for this Great there comes true the word of wisdom (Berachoth 18): צדיקים במיתתן נקראו חיים "Tsaddikim live on even when
they are no longer with us on earth."

THE MISHEBERACH FOR SILENCE

"He who has blessed our forefathers, Avrohom, Yitzchok and Yaakov, Moshe, Aharon, David and Shelomo—He may bless him who guards his lips and neither speaks during the Tefilla and Keriath Hatorah nor indulges in loose talk. All blessings of Torah and Prophets may come upon him—may he have healthy and upright children—may he inherit both worlds: the good of this world and the perfection of the future world, Amen."

This Misheberach was written by the great תוספות יו״ט three hundred years ago with the proviso that it should be read each Shabbos in all Synagogues. This must puzzle the probing reader. Evidently, there was no need to compose a special Misheberach for honesty in business dealings, truthfulness, or conscientiousness in keeping the marriage—and dietary laws. Why, then, the need of public recognition of dignified conduct in the House of God? Even if the Shulchan Aruch were not to demand such conduct with all the earnestness at its command; even if it were not to condemn the violation of dignified conduct in the Synagogue as a severe transgression—would not the most elementary sense of decency cause us to avoid scrupulously every talk during the Tefillo and Keriath Hatorah as an abominable desecration of the Tefilla and the sacred site of worship? There must have been good reason for the great teacher of the law to move him to ordain this Misheberach. The undignified talk in the Synagogue, strictly prohibited by the Law of Torah, seems to have been an old evil which unfortunately continues into our own times.

So-called Reform Judaism has managed to erase this evil with commendable energy. However, at the same time it has also thoroughly erased the sacred, precious heritage of the fathers and mothers of our people and used this occasion to put an end to the contemptible "Judenschul." There is, in any case, no talking in the Reform Synagogue, "devotion and dedication" prevail there. It is not that the Reform rabbis possess more power than the Great of our people, but this "reform" corresponded admirably with the feelings of their followers. Henceforth, there was to be no more cause to be ashamed before the Christian church. While the devotees of the reform temples may feel the same appetite for talking as their orthodox brethren, they can surely be expected to be doubly disciplined in the Synagogue in view of the fact that their religious life is more or less confined to the Synagogue. Why not, after all, bring a small, inexpensive sacrifice to the religion!

Regrettable as it may be that the important rules regulating the conduct during the Divine worship were not generally obeyed in times gone by, there is an explanation for this puzzling negligence which, while it may not serve as an excuse, will at least help us to understand its background. Our ancestors did not seek God in the Synagogue. In the light of true Judaism, they attained Divine proximity in their homes and business activities by virtue of a life which assumed the character of a continuous service of God. Thus it came that they felt "at home" in the Synagogue. Moreover, for many the Synagogue offered the only opportunity to get together and thus the ground was laid which led to conduct unbecoming the dignity of the surroundings.

That our rabbinical leaders were deeply concerned with this state of affairs is borne out by the fact that the above-mentioned Misheberach was introduced by the תוספות יו"ט because of his deep-rooted fear that the cruel slaughter of hundreds of thousands of his contemporary fellow-Jews in Poland might have been related to the desecration of the Houses of Worship by loose talk! Alas, our own time offers more than enough ground for self-reflection on this sad subject.

Let us preserve our "Judenschul" with all the precious values it bears for us. We need not look to the church or to our Torah-estranged brethren in order to learn the importance of dignified conduct during the Divine Services. To us all that matters is that the same Law demanding such conduct also shapes the entire scope of our Jewish lives.

Consider this: the more serious the demand of dignified conduct in the Synagogue appears in the light of the Torah-law, the larger looms the responsibility for each of us, especially in our days, who violates this rule. All we achieve is that we discredit our "Judenschul" in the eyes of our gentle fellow-citizens and give those who indulge in open warfare with the Shulchan Aruch cause to the—not quite unjustified—criticism *that we, ourselves, do not follow the Shulchan Aruch.* "And they call themselves "orthodox" . . . "! *Would this not, God forbid, result in tragic Chillul Hashem?* (Chasam Sofer, Resp. Or. Ch. 31).

The Misheberach for Silence has not taken root in its original form because of the probability that poor conduct in the Synagogue might merely be a passing phase. However, the Misheberach on Shabbos bestowing the blessing on the Congregation includes this significant hint in the following words: May God bless all those "who dedicate the Synagogues only for *prayer* and enter them in order to *pray."*

It is a sad commentary on our times that this stress on the sole purpose of the Synagogue—prayer and Divine Service— seems to be necessary even in our days.

INDIVIDUAL TASTE — TRADITIONAL CUSTOM

The very title of this essay indicates the existence of many facets of life which depend on the prevalent taste and thus cannot be subjected to a generally valid evaluation. For taste is a matter of individual subjectivity. This applies to areas of physical taste, such as food: that which pleases one may be rejected by another; favorite dishes of one's youth may find little appreciation with one whose parental roots stem from a different soil. The same is true in the world of fashion although here individual taste is far less decisive. Most people are content to be ruled by the whims of fashion and willing to relinquish their individual judgment. As long as the prevalent fashion remains "harmless", there may be no harm in bowing to its dictatorial requirements. However, when a higher Law — and to us this is the Law of Torah — must invoke its veto, the dictates of fashion become immaterial. When it comes to the question of how to dress, Jewish women and girls will adhere to modern fashion only as long as their Jewish conscience permits it. As for the men and boys, if general custom should prescribe the elimination of the head covering, they will at all times be conscious of what Jewish custom expects of them.

Evaluating experiences of joy or sorrow is also a matter of subjective judgment inasmuch as they result from particular emotions and customs. No other language contains a wealth of terms for happiness and joy comparable to that offered by our holy tongue. Thus, we need but refer to Rav Hirsch's profound interpretation of *somach* (related to *tzemach,* to grow) as the inner joy; of *sos* (related to *tzitz,* the bud breaking open), the joy which seeks outward expression; and finally of *gil* (related to *kol*) the loudly jubilating joy. Let us ask ourselves whether the inner joy or the measured expression of joy with which we react to an experience do not deserve the same approval that is generally given to loud and boisterous celebrations of joyful events?

Judging from the description in Mishna and Talmud, *Simchath Beth Hashoevah* was certainly a joyful event of public festivity directed by the great leaders of our people. Similarly, King David gave his people a most impressive demonstration of the joy which permeated his being at the occasion of the return of the Holy Ark of the Covenant (Sam. II 6). What these loud and emotional expressions of joy had in common was that they were the overflowing outpouring of Jewish souls filled with truly holy joyfulness.

The same holds true for expressions of sorrow. The pain which remains locked in the heart and finds its outlet in the quiet tear is surely no less felt than the sorrow which manifests itself by wild sobs. Here, too, the individual temperament is decisive. While the Prophets, Mishna and Talmud generally do expect mourning to be emotional, they accept its validity only when it is genuine. If this is the case, then it is only proper to reserve judgment based on individual taste and attitude.

In this connection, it may be fitting to refer to the widely practiced custom of accompanying the Tefilla with more or less pronounced physical activity. While this is an ancient custom, it has always met with mixed reactions by the spiritual leaders of past centuries. In the final analysis, it is the concentrated dedication (*Kavanah*) which gives true prayer its character. It must be left to the personal and emotional attitude of the individual to determine whether the calm, dignified position at prayer as recommended by the Rabbinical leaders of every section of Jewry, is more conducive to concentrated dedication than the more mobile posture. (Comp. Orach Chaim 48, Mishna Berura ib.).

Consequently, one's posture and position during the Tefilla should not merely be guided by the example set by other circles within Jewry.

It follows that festive events likewise cannot be measured by a generally valid yardstick. This applies particularly to wedding celebrations which should be held within moderate limits (as is true for all "affairs", including Bar Mitzva parties). Here, especially those circles which — as it is put — "can afford it" should take the lead by setting the example. — We wish everyone a "beautiful" Simcha. But its "beauty" is not measured by the amount of money spent on the affair.

Wedding ceremonies are frequently subject to varied Minhagim which should be maintained and which should command the respect of all parties concerned. We will leave it to the reader to decide whether lack of punctuality and general disorder may be labeled as "Minhag" (in any case not an attractive one). Whatever the verdict, let us not renounce our customs to which we are used and which appeal to our taste, especially in the case of wedding ceremonies and celebrations, just because they may not be acceptable to other circles.

To repeat: stormy expressions of joy are natural and genuine provided they are rooted in temperament and custom. Nothing is more unnatural than trying to wear a cloak that does not fit. Our conduct should always be guided by self-respect and — good taste.

THE ROLE OF THE YOUTH
IN THE KEHILLA

It seems hardly necessary to emphasize the importance of youth in the Kehilla. The future of the Kehilla is tied closely to the youth on which it depends for the vital process of rejuvenation. The very first prerequisite is the training towards uncompromising Judaism. This task, certainly a most difficult one, begins at earliest childhood. The foundation laid by parents and home is strengthened and developed by the school which depends for its success on the harmonious interplay between school and home. The diversity of intellectual and emotional trends creates many a problem for both teacher and parent and requires from both the utmost tact and understanding. The type of atmosphere and society created by school and home is of inestimable significance in its effect on the life of the Kehilla. For Judaism must not only be studied, but—lived. In home and school our children are to experience Judaism at an age when they still do not grasp the full impact of their duty to recognize themselves as sons and daughters of God's Nation. It is the great task of the school to implant this realization gradually in our children, borne and inspired by study and knowledge. In this sense "the fear of God is the beginning of wisdom" (Ps. iii, 10).

In addition to house and school, the success of education

depends to a very large degree on the surroundings, on the society. Often one good friend is able to achieve results where school and home proved powerless. And just as often the opposite is the case. "Much depends on the society" (*Sota* I, 4). This is true even for early childhood.

Our houses rise in the midst of the Kehilla. Fathers and mothers recognize their positions as members of their Kehilla in the clear realization of the values they derive from the Kehilla as their obligation towards its progressing growth and development. Together with school and home, the Kehilla plays a tremendoulsy significant role in the education of its youth. Parents take their children to "Shul," an old-Jewish, sensitive term for our בית הכנסת: The House of God in which the congregation "assembles" is to be truly a School of Life for the parents as well as for the children. The rich sources of the Jewish Year reveal themselves to the soul of the child in this center of prayer. Here, every morning and evening invites to the gathering before God; from here the sanctity of the שבת at home derives its true wealth; from here emanates the heightened festivity of each יום טוב; here the ימים נוראים fill even the young with serious thoughts; here the youth shares in the mournful compassion inspired by תשעה באב; here the youth takes part in the joy to which שמחת תורה and פורים entitle and celebrate together with their elders the solemn proclamation of the חנוכה-week.

Yet these impressions and experiences will only prove fruitful for the education of our children if they recognize and accept the "Shul" as a site of sanctity. Every conscientious Jew is called to live up to the great admonition which greets him from the height of the ארון הקדש: דע לפני מי אתה עומד, "Know before Whom you stand" (*Berachoth* 28b). This proclamation makes it a self-understood duty for every parent, father and mother, who are seriously concerned with their children's education to conduct

themselves in a manner which will not belie the great demand of
דע לפני מי אתה עומד.

The Kehilla looks to the youth and beholds its own future.
Year after year of growing maturity increases the task of the
home, the school, the Kehilla. Every young man, upon his
eighteenth birthday, receives the right to vote and, at the age of
twenty-five, may be elected to serve in the Kehilla administration. What a wealth of educational work must be performed by
the Kehilla, if it may expect its 18-year-olds to acquire the
maturity of judgment and the stabilty of Jewish character which
will enable them to do their full share in the development of the
Kehilla! How successful must this education be, if the Kehilla
expects to entrust the responsibility of administering its sacred
tasks to the young man of twenty-five!

Our youthful members are thus called upon to vote in any
referendum or election, submit suggestions and proposals and
work for their adoption through a majority vote of the members
present. Finally, the youth is expected to participate in the election of the representatives of the Kehilla (Trustees) as well as
that of the Rabbi.

With this procedure, the Kehilla supplies its youthful
members with a prerogative which is clearly decisive for the
development and very existence of the Kehilla. The question
arises whether eighteen-year old Kehilla members possess the
intellectual maturity, the objectivity of judgment which alone
guarantees that their right to vote does not turn into a weapon
of caprice but helps to advance the welfare of the Kehilla.

It is well known that the Mishna (*Aboth* 5, 24) has fixed a
far more advanced age for the maturity of intellect and judgment. Yet the Mishna is surely not of the opinion that below the
age of forty there does not exist a state of intellectual maturity,
or that below the age of fifty there does not exist the objectivity

of judgment which marks the mature advisor. The same is true if the Mishna assigns the striving for achievement to the twenty-year old and talks of the firm strength of the man of thirty. The Mishna merely wishes to see men in these respective stages of life at the height of striving and strength. If the same Mishna demands the building of the Jewish house from the eighteen-year old, it must have surely taken for granted that the young man of eighteen, even at his youthful age, is fully aware of the grave responsibility bestowed upon him by the task of building a Jewish house. Only he whose mind has been nourished by spiritual values and who is imbued with an overpowering determination to live up to the demands of Jewish life may be considered fit to attempt the building of a Jewish house at the age of eighteen. By bestowing on them the right to vote, our Kehilla thinks of those of its eighteen-year old members who have acquired the basic prerequisites for the founding of their houses, even though the circumstances of contemporary living seldom allow the eighteen-year old to marry. The right to vote is based solely on this youthful maturity. How can it be achieved?

From earliest childhood our youth must be trained to walk the Jewish path of life. We referred previously to the all-important role played jointly by house and school and the achievement of this goal. Our children must live Judaism in their homes and in school. It is the school's specific and lofty task to introduce the children to Torah-Judaism through its sacred sources; to teach them the awe of God's mysterious Omnipotence as Creator as evidenced in the realm of nature and all its phenomena, and to recognize God's creative Will which alone provides the existence of mankind with meaning and content; to train them to perceive the course of man's history which lead to the selection of the Jewish people, and to challenge them to follow the development of our nation from the era of the forefathers to its miraculous redemption by God from Egyptian bondage; to demonstrate how the Jewish people realized its task as the nation of God who revealed His Will at Sinai; finally, to implant deeply into our children's minds and hearts the firm conviction that only faithful realization of the Divine Torah, as laid down in the Written and Oral Teachings—their authentic transmission throughout the millenia being the guarantee for their Divine origin—decides the fate of our people for all time to come. From Torah and the Prophets' admonitions our youth shall draw the knowledge that our people received its land only as the Land of God, that its state can endure only as the State of God, and that our Galuth bears the seed of our ultimate redemption. Our youth shall learn the pride of being part of the Nation of God whose future is assured through the life of every upright individual, however modest his station, a life which received its true significance by its wholehearted dedication to the Divine Will. If circumstances force our youthful members to spend their formative years in non-Jewish cultural surroundings, they will make certain to accept only those values which can stand up before the ruling Throne of Torah, for they know that firmness alone safeguards their uncompromising Torah-Jewishness in every walk of life.

This, in general outline, pictures the spiritual trend of character formation which we desire our youth to achieve in order to train them to attain אמונה which will help them to prove themselves as מאמינים בני מאמינים. Yet, spiritual character formation is meaningless if it is not supplemented by the development of the moral character bearing the imprint of the Divine Will. God's Torah guides us towards the lofty goal of moral perfection which we must strive to attain in ceaseless labor. This perfection sanctifies our lives (קדושה), permeates our sensual desires with the nobility of purity and, through the precepts of justice and love, conquers selfishness and greed, envy and hate, and the evil hunger for power.

In many cases, the assumption that our eighteen-year-old youth has already attained this Jewish character would appear to be a self-delusion. For the Jewish path of life is beset with struggles and challenges which are generally not mastered at the age of eighteen. Here, God's Torah proves to be the most potent guide on the road to spiritual and moral fortitude. The deeper our youth plants its roots in the soil of Torah the stronger will it resist life's stress and storms. Once the school has laid the groundwork for thorough Torah knowledge, the way of our youth must lead to the Yeshiva, to the Beth Hamidrash. אם פגע בך מנוול זה משכהו לבית המדרש—thus pronounce the Sages in an admonition of eternal truth (*Sukka* 52): ugliness and evil find their masters only in the Beth Hamidrash! Irrespective of one's individual mental ability, no one may absent himself from the Beth Hamidrash. God's Torah provides life-nourishment for each of us to prepare and strengthen ourselves for our Jewish way of life.

School, Yeshiva, Beth Hamidrash, are the sacred centers dissipating the educational values and training which are to form a Kehilla-youth upon which the right to vote may justly be bestowed at the age of eighteen. Yet there is one additional prerequisite upon which this right is conditioned.

The impact of the community and the particular atmosphere it creates is a powerful factor whose importance for the Jewish character development cannot be stressed enough. The community educates; so does the social togetherness in school and house of learning. This educational source is the unity within the Kehilla. As previously analyzed, the Beth Haknesses of the Kehilla becomes already to the young child a familiar and beloved place of worship where his youthful soul, as part of a great Congregation, receives its first impressions of the Kehilla.

That which means so much to the young ones, the Beth Haknesses must become to an even higher degree for our youth. *The youth must not be absent from the Beth Haknesses of the Kehilla.* Particularly in the years of growing maturity, the youth must be made aware of the vital significance of the Beth Haknesses and, beyond it, of the Kehilla. Youth must learn to esteem and love its Kehilla.

Courses and lectures must be employed to familiarize our youth with the character of a true Kehilla, with the task it is called upon to fulfill and with the high significance of the Kehilla as a vital and pulsating cell within the organism of the Jewish people. Such familiarity must be the basis for the youth's right to vote.

The Kehilla should have statutes outlining the tasks it must solve and expounding the rights and duties of its membership. In addition, the statutes should define the position of the Rabbinical leader and representatives of the Congregation who are entrusted with the welfare and furtherance of the communal interests. From these statutes the youth will draw the conclusion that it is neither the Rabbi nor the Board of Trustees with its numerous sub-committees which form the Congregation but that it is above all the support and sense of responsibility of *all* its members which safeguards the healthy development of the Kehilla. This positive attitude to the Kehilla and its values can, may, must be implanted in the youth of eighteen if he is to cast his vote for the welfare and the future of his Kehilla.

Admittedly, this right to vote, even with all the necessary prerequisites, is not entirely immune to a partly justified criticism. One quickly tends to accuse youth of a lack of modesty, of conceit and self-adulation, of a lack of respect for its elders. While this may be true in a few cases, it must not be allowed to result in a negative evaluation of the question of youthful cooperation in Kehilla work. In the hour of the Sinai covenant,

Moshe Rabbenu counted on the youth, bearers of the future (*Ex.* 24, 5), a youth "implanted" in the soil of Torah (*Ps.* 144, 12; *Pesachim* 87a), a youth accepting the dignity of old age as a command of the Torah (*Lev.* 19, 32) and fully aware of the respect it owes the mature judgment of the "elders" (*Deut.* 32, 7). Whenever this is not the case, the prophet predicts the symptoms of inevitable decay, a time when "youth usurps the power, frivolously rising above its elders" (*Is.* 3:4–5). If this happens, the following remark of the Sages assumes full actuality: "if the elders tell you to tear down and the youth tells you to build, tear down and build not, for that which the elders tear down serves the reconstruction, but that which youth presumes to build bears in truth—destruction" (*Megilla* 31).

Yet it is youth which claims for itself vitality, energy and the enthusiasm which are of such great importance for the life of the Kehilla, if young and old work together in harmonious union. Let us remember that the Sages bestow the term זקן not necessarily on the man old in years, but also upon the youth who is permeated by the truth of Torah.

Even if the right to vote seems rather early for the eighteen-year old youth, the vote at a more advanced age would in no way be more beneficial for the Kehilla if the conditions which we have outlined were not fulfilled. The bestowal of the right to vote on its eighteen-year old members constitutes a vote of confidence by the Kehilla to which the youth must live up in its attitude towards Kehilla work. Thus prepared, the Kehilla may confidently choose its representatives from the ranks of its youth upon the completed twenty-fifth year, in accordance with the statutes.

SCHOOL AND HOME

There is little that is really new in the field of school-home relationship. Yet it seems entirely in place to reassert the actuality of "old truths" which are frequently ignored or even forgotten.

School and home complement each other. For this reason the constructive cooperation between school and home is of utmost importance. In a spirit of goodwill parents must devote their wholehearted interest to the school to which they entrust their children. It does not mean that they are not entitled to submit requests, suggestions, even criticism of school procedure— all this is welcome *provided* that the contact is made with the proper authorities (administrators or teachers) and that the required respect is maintained at all times.

If the student complains at home of an incident in school and the parents, as adults, recognize the complaint to be without foundation, they will not hesitate to reject it. If they are in doubt they will listen quietly to the complaint and will carefully avoid voicing any judgment or opinion in front of the child. If necessary they will make contact with the school authorities. They will never allow remarks by the child which are disrespectful of school, school authorities and teachers. They will scrupulously suppress any negative or destructive criticism of the school and its personnel in front of the child. For would it not be a betrayal of their all-important role as parents were they to cause their own children to lose respect of and thereby confidence in the school and its teachers? Respect and trust are the vital ingredients of the healthy relationship between the students and the principal and teachers. On them depend discipline and the positive attitude towards the curriculum.

Frequently the school will seek the assistance of the home if the student's conduct and effort are unsatisfactory. For the school depends greatly on the influence and guidance emanating from the parental home. By the same token the school must scrupulously avoid any action or approach which might in any manner serve to weaken the child's respect of and trust in the parent.

By helping to promote the child's respect and love for the school, parents in reality help themselves. For the issue is not only the child's conduct and achievement in school. It is often desirable, even vital, that the home request the help of the school in order to improve the child's attitude and relationship at home. Parents will have themselves to reproach if their own negative relationship to the school and its teachers and the inevitably resulting deterioration of the child's respect for school deprives them of the invaluable help the school is able to offer them when problems arise at home.

To repeat: in their own interest and in the interest of their children parents will scrupulously avoid any critical appraisal of the school and its staff in front of their children. In their children's interest they will wholeheartedly support the work of the school, will refrain from tearing down its reputation by irresponsible discussions at street corners and at social gatherings, will refrain from building up minor incidents into major issues, and will confine their criticism to the proper channels, in the proper light, and in the proper manner. These appear to be self-understood requirements—yet it seems necessary to impress them again and again on the consciousness of the parent body.

EDUCATION FOR STRUGGLE

Education in general, and Jewish education in particular, is geared towards struggle. Conquest of egoism is the goal of all education towards which the educator—and self-education—must strive incessantly. Every child comes into the world as a tiny egoist, knowing only himself and the satisfaction of his needs. This is the animal in man. Only when the soul in man and the spirit serving it, governed by a higher will, assume the guidance of man's actions, will the animal fade away and man will rise to become a truly human being. Jewish man can only rise to become a true man if he accepts the supreme leadership of God, Creator and Master of his life, who proclaims His creative Will as Law upon the life of Jewish man (Yech. 34, 31).

To be a Jew means to be a fighter. "Who is a hero? He who fights himself" (Aboth 4) and battles victoriously against all that the Divine Will does not wish to find in the Jew: lust and greed, tightfistedness and dishonesty, jealousy and hatred, and all the numerous demoniacal products of egoism.

To be a Jew means to be proudly conscious of one's God-willed task of life and of one's consequent allegiance to the people of God and its mission in the history of mankind. This pride can only be achieved in battle, through self-education. He who has been successful in this task is immune against the materialistic lie, the scientific theories (those which stand in opposition to the

Divine Truth); immune against a Bible criticism which falsifies and mutilates his Divine Book although it is proclaimed in the press and study halls as the inviolable result of "scientific" research. That which is preached today as truth is being followed on the morrow by a new "truth"—but "the Word of our God stands firm for ever" (Isaiah 40).

Who would deny that the life of the Jew is surrounded by dangers. His minority position among the nations spelled danger from the outset. "Look onto Abraham, your father, as the solitary one I have called upon him" admonishes Isaiah (Ch. 51), the faithful of his people, for all time to come. Fight for God's Shabbos even if it is being denied and ignored by all the world and even if it complicates the economic existence of the Jew. This is and was true at all times.

Dangers? They lurk everywhere. Not only those which were mentioned. There are also the dangers of the street, of literature, films, radio, television—certainly triumphs of man's ingenuity and technological progress but, alas, frequently misused. Propagated by the forces of advertisement, the lure of sensuality turns much of this "progress" into vile products of decadence which abuse the standards of cultural refinement and which call for abolishment by government agencies concerned with the future of our country's youth. Protection against these dangers? A radical elimination of the benefits of our era's technological achievements is certainly not warranted. Programs must be carefully selected and parents must set a good example for their children.

Above all, there is the admonition of this profound word of wisdom: "He who is met by ugliness, pull it into the House of Learning" (Sukka 52). In the centers of Torah we gain the strength to equip ourselves for the battle against the dangers which threaten our Jewish way of life. And last, but certainly not least: "Be on the lookout for (the right) companionship" (Nedarim 81). The influence of the society in which one lives is all-important, to the good or bad. One good friend—and we have gained a fellow fighter.

The Jew—a fighter. "I will render you as the sword of the hero" (Zech. 9). This is how the Prophet wishes to see us all.

MESSAGE TO A GROWING YOUTH

The Holy Book of God has rested in your hands since your earliest childhood. It was handed to you by your parents and your teachers so that from its pages you might learn what path your life should take. It guides you through life. It has helped raise you and has trained you to be mindful of the consequences of whatever you do. It answers your questions and you rejoice in the fact that God Himself is your Teacher and Guide. Not everything in it is clear to you. The Words of God present many a puzzle. But you know that it takes a lifetime to delve ever deeper into the thoughts of God. And you feel proud that even when you were still very young you were already permitted to read a book over which very old and wise men still pore studiously and reverently.

God calls you to His service; this you see from every line of His Book. His holy Will commands, and you obey. For you are a creature of God and your life would have no meaning for you unless you were able to tell yourself that God has called you into being because He needs you. And therefore you hearken to His Word so that your whole life may always be in accordance with His Will.

The Law of God commands you throughout life, for you are the servant of God. "Be complete with God, your God" (Deut. 18:13); you may be truly satisfied with yourself only when you can honestly say that every instant of your life has been such that it can readily meet with God's approval. The aim of your whole life should be to come ever closer to this goal.

You heed the commands of God and you shun the things He prohibits. You let yourself be guided by the many faithful guards which He has placed at your side to warn you and remind you to remember God. Thus His Shabbos calls you to Him and reminds you: Do not forget that the world you are living in is God's, and that He is your master. You put on Tefillin and bind the symbols of God's law around your arm: it is to Him that you dedicate your energies; you fasten them to your head: you wish to delve ever deeper into the thoughts of God and fill your mind with Divine truths.

You want to be truly human—God requires it of you, and then you will be the most glorious of all His creatures. But you become a real human being only if you can control yourself—self-control is the trait that raises you above the beast. A free and divine will lives within you, for the soul which God has breathed into you is divine. God demands that your body be a worthy vessel for your divine soul, and this it can be only as long as you are in control of your physical forces. You have been trained along these lines from early childhood. You eat and drink only that which is permissible by the Law of God. Thus the food you eat is worthy of you. You are human, divinely human. You see how the beast follows its animal instincts. But you do not eat like the beast—you eat as human beings should, for you are in control of yourself. You serve God even while you eat.

Indeed your body does resemble that of the beast, but God tells you that *your* body must be a worthy container for your pure soul. It is up to you to see to it that it does not descend to the level of the animal. If you are a real human being you have no reason to be ashamed of your body. Adam and Eve were naked "and they were not ashamed"; they did not need to be ashamed as long as God's Word served as the supreme guiding light in their lives. It told them what "was good and bad" for them, and they obeyed its directions. It was only when they disregarded the Word of God and allowed themselves to be led by the desires of their hearts that shame overcame them, for then they really had to be ashamed of themselves. For man, if he obeys only his lust and sensual impulses, is worse than the beast. Henceforth, man was to cover his body in modesty. The first human couple received its clothes from God. These garments are meant to admonish and question him constantly: have you advanced sufficiently, do you live in such a way that you need not be ashamed of your body? Can you control yourself?

You will understand, then, why God attached symbols to the ends of your garments as reminders telling you, as it were, "Follow not the call of your heart or your eyes." Accept the Law of God for all your days and let it alone be the force that directs your heart and that serves to guide your eyes. Be truly human!

Nay, more: not only your garment, but also your body bears the symbol of God. The Torah calls it a "Sign of the Covenant" (Gen. 1:11). Every Jew who is determined to live as a Jewish man must bear it. Whosoever does not bear it, loses his right to be called a Jew. You, too, bear it. You bear it with pride. And you have a right to know what this most sacred symbol of God means to you for your whole life.

*   *   *

Ever since you first began to read the Book of God, you have known that it is not the stork that brings the children. Why should you not know that it is to your parents that you owe your life? "Rechem" is what the Holy Scriptures call the mother's womb. The word has another meaning—compassion. Remember this one word whenever you feel the warm love your mother gives you, whenever you sense the sweet compassion that only she can show for your needs, great or small. For this word means to tell you that your mother carried you in her womb before you were born. There you lay protected and were nourished by her blood. There you developed until you were ready to start life on your own. You are part of your mother, and whenever she looks at you, she thinks of this and she gives you loving care and self-sacrificing devotion. And you, in turn, are to look up to your mother with reverent humility because, when she bore you, she placed her own life in danger. As a child you read the line in the Bible that says of the mother , "in resignation shall you bear children" (Gen. 3:16). The mother knows that her life is endangered when she bears a child, and yet she resigns herself to her sacred vocation as a mother and puts you into the world so that you, too, shall follow your own divine calling. Thus she herself fulfills the call of God, cares for you, nourishes you and worries about you. She is the guardian of your childhood and the guide of your youth, and she is proud and happy once she sees you on the way on which you will find your place in life that God demands you to take. Can you then even begin to understand the unbearable pain that must tear her soul if all her sacrifices would turn out to be in vain?

Your eye cannot be blind to the unsearchable wonders of God's Nature. The Torah has opened your eyes for you so that you may recognize God. Have you ever placed a seed into the soil and watched a delicate plant or even a strong tree sprout forth from it? You may well have asked what it was that made such a tiny seed break forth into such miraculous growth. Your parents, your teachers were unable to explain it to you. You were awestruck by the wonder-working power of God. But this you were taught: that there are tiny seeds in each flower which must be fertilized before a plant can develop from them. In other words, pollen from another flower must fall on it and only thus pollenized will that seed have strength to grow into a plant or even into a mighty tree. This pollen lies in the anther; the wind carries it to another flower and there it passes through the pistil to the seed. The seed thus fertilized is placed into the soil and there it undergoes a process of development until the day it breaks forth and sees the light of day.

And now look up to your mother, look up to your father, and then remain still, and lock up in your heart the precious, holy secret of how you came into being, and whoever tries to cheapen it for you in a vulgar and slighting fashion will find a poor listener in you. With every uncouth word that such a person speaks to you he insults your father and dishonors your mother—would you stand for that?

You cannot poke fun at things that are sacred; you cannot treat them lightly. You do not ever pronounce the name of God, but you feel its sanctity even when you merely think of it. God has called your development within your mother's womb a "sacred" thing (Ex. 13:2). You dare not speak of it in a light vein and whenever you think of it you are moved by feelings of sacred awe and grateful love.

If a school mate of yours should come to you giggling and jeeringly asking you whether you know "where the babies come from," you will give him a look of contempt and turn away from him without even answering his question, for he was about to cheapen and vulgarize something that should be precious to both of you.

*   *   *

"Work on your perfection. Become ye. perfect" (Lev. 11:44)—thus the Law of God calls unto us and bids us to remember it throughout our lives. This simply means: "Serve Me ever better, devote all your strength to Me and My Will with your might. All the forces within you shall be sanctified unto Me, and they will be sacred if only you will be able to channel them properly and use them in accordance with My Will." The. same forces and drives that exist in the plant and in the beast are also found in man. But man possesses a divine soul which is capable of comprehending the Will of God and of freely subordinating all his faculties to it. Herein lies the difference between man on one hand, and plant and beast on the other. A free man who channels all his powers in paths that are in accordance with God's will is the most divine creature on earth.

The beast pursues its desires, sustains itself, reproduces, and thereby serves the Will of its Maker. This is also true of the plant. But something more is expected of you. The word of God directs your attention to the powerful laws that control the drive to reproduce, which is inherent in all of nature. It is only "after their own kind" (Gen. 1) that plants and animals can reproduce. A deep mystery surrounds the law of nature which makes plants fructify only plants of the same kind and similarly mates animals only with others of the same family.

You, a human being, would have to feel shame when contemplating even the minutest growth, the very lowest beast, unless, you too, will regulate your own forces and desires in line with the Will of God. God must reveal His Will to you to enable you to subordinate yourself freely to Him. Only then can you be truly human and may proudly look down upon the. rest of the world of Creation. For while the world at large serves the Will of God by immutable laws laid down for it which it must automatically follow, you obey by the strength of your own free will. Henceforth you will know that you can be a true human being only if you can control yourself and govern your desires and thus comply with God's call to "perfect yourself".

It is not your intellect that distinguishes you from the beast. You must show your superiority to the beast in the way in which you conduct yourself. Your mouth which receives your food and drink is at the same time the instrument of speech provided by God. Be sure that you need not feel ashamed when you sit down to eat. Your meal, too, shall be sacred unto the Lord.

Do not be greedy, do not incessantly run after pleasure. The more a physical desire stirs within you, the harder you must work to control yourself. Thus you train the forces that make you a human being and, if the Word of God demands of you to see to it that your "purity" remains unimpaired, then you must train and develop this force within you. As long as you possess purity, you will never sink down to the level of the beast. You will struggle and you will emerge victorious.

But once you cease to struggle and allow your lusts and desires to dominate you, the divine spark within you will grow fainter and fainter until it will all but have died away—and you will be "unclean", you will come to resemble the beast and all your knowledge and intelligence will no longer serve to separate you spiritually from the manger from which the beast gets its food. Your conduct will become beast-like and then you will be a beast. That is the meaning of the solemn warning that is so often repeated in the pages of the Torah. Do not allow yourself to become unclean; work on your purity.

The love which attracts man to woman is sacred in tne eyes of God. It is the mysterious force which calls man to his holy task to dedicate himself to the blessing of God: "Be fruitful and multiply" (Gen. 1:28). God wills that man and woman unite in marriage in order to build together a home in which God shall dwell. Their home is dedicated to God, for His Word reigns supreme there, and children are born to them in accordance with His holy Will. It is for this sacred purpose that man preserves his strength. The Word of God knows of nothing more sacred. At no other moment does man rise more divinely above the beast than at this instant. Can you then understand how horribly degrading it would be if man were to sink down to the level of the beast—and that happens whenever God departs from their marital union. God does remove His presence if His Law is disregarded, if, instead of His Law, those forces would rule supreme that drag man into dirt and bestiality.

"Conduct thyself before Me, walk in perfection before Me," thus said the Lord when He made His eternal covenant with Abraham. "Devote thy whole life to Me, do not hide anything from Me; see to it that all thy faculties are dedicated to My service." And so you will understand why God stamped the symbol of His covenant upon that part of man's body which is most closely associated with sensuality, for that part, too, is consecrated to God. The faculties of your body serve the Divine Will and you may stand proudly before your God and need not be ashamed of your body. There is no other creature on earth that can do what you are able to do: lift up your faculties freely to the Lord and say: let me dedicate myself and all that is in me to Your holy Will.

There will undoubtedly be struggles, but you will be prepared for them and win in the end. You scorn lust even though your desires tempt you, for you know that you can be truly human only if you control yourself. And you do not want to be a beast.

You want to be a decent person. That does not only mean that you must not be at odds with those around you; you must also be decent and honest with yourself. You will attain this goal if you watch yourself and keep your mind pure and clean. Do not occupy your mind with things that would fill your thoughts and your imagination with vulgarity.

This holds true particularly when you get ready to go to bed at the end of the day. Recite your nightly prayers—never forget them. Recite the "Shema" and call to mind your Jewish task in life as set for you by God. Read the Psalms which hold up God before you, for He wants to guide you through life, through troubled and happy hours alike—and then lie down and recite this Berachah before you fall asleep: "May God lay the bonds of sleep upon my eyes and slumber upon my eyelids. May it be the Will of God that I lie down in peace and rise again in peace, that my thoughts will not trouble me nor bad dreams or evil imaginings befall me; let my rest be perfect before Thee." With these last words you offer a tender prayer that God may help you use your faculties to devote them to His holy Will.

But if you feel that you do not seem to be able to master these feelings that plague so many young people of your age, do not be discouraged or ready to give in to them. Feel free always to confide in your parents frankly and openly. They are there to help you and to advise you at times when you need their assistance and support. You can hardly give them any greater happiness than the knowledge that you trust them. Be truthful and open with them, and you will never regret it. At a crucial hour when the forces of sin threatened to overcome him, the image of his father appeared to Joseph and kept him free from sin—thus our sages tell us. Do not avoid your parents but rather seek to come closer to them so that they may assist and reassure you.

If you would rather unburden yourself to an older friend, do so, or seek out a teacher in whom you will be able to confide —and you will see that everything will seem much better and easier once you feel that there is someone upon whom you can count for help and guidance in your problems.

Do not feel that you must be ashamed because you have such thoughts. The only thing of which you would have to be ashamed would be lack of will power on your part.

Remember that your parents and teachers were young once too and went through much the same struggle as you do now. Why, then, would they not be willing to listen to your problems with understanding and give you the benefit of their experience?

They expect you to come to them openly and ask for their help and advice. Try it—you will never regret it. You will feel more at ease. They will give you good counsel, and you will follow it.

They will advise you to go about your work with energy and zest and to see to it that your time is well occupied so that you will have no time for loafing or for thoughts unworthy of you. If you have spent a full day in hard work you will go to bed tired, but you will be satisfied with yourself, too. And then you will sink into restful sleep and awake to face the new day with refreshed and renewed strength.

Your parents and teachers will guide you to the Source of Life, to your Divine Law, so that you may take more strength and support from it. You will then come to see the great purpose for which you have been called to dedicate your life.

They will suggest that you strengthen your body so that your physical strength may benefit your moral strength as well. You will achieve this end by exercising, swimming and other physical activity.

Whenever you become discouraged and are ready to give up hope, then your parents or teachers will show you that you are not as weak as you think. Try to master yourself in other ways at first. Control your anger. Do things that you do not particularly like to do. Try sometimes to keep from eating food that you like very much. And when you can record such small victories in your daily life, you will find to your pleasant surprise that you are not so weak after all. Then you will extend your efforts to other spheres and you will succeed in the end. Then you may truly feel proud of yourself.

Watch your friends and choose them carefully. You are imbued with Jewish pride; this means that you are proud of your Jewish calling and you will not allow the things that are sacred to you to be dragged down into the dust. Just as you will never allow anyone to make fun in your presence of a law of God, so will you never tolerate ugly, vulgar language. Whoever enjoys that sort of twisted humor can never be your friend.

Take care that such an attitude will not take root in your circle. It is always only a few—thank God—who try to get the attention of others by such means. You just do your share and you will find many friends who, like you, are not going to stand for ugly conduct.

Why, you would have to be ashamed of yourself if you could not stand up for what is right. After all, you do want to be known as an educated person. But education is not limited to acquiring knowledge in the various fields of learning. With all the knowledge in the world you can still be crude and uncivilized. Only he who works not only on the training of his mind but is also anxious to keep on improving his character may say that he is "an educated man."

For this reason you practice the laws of God day after day. They awaken your energy and steel your mind. You will have need of this energy when it comes to turning your back upon all things vulgar and contemptible.

God wants to "dwell in your midst" (Deut. 23:15), thus says the law; your "circle shall be. holy." God avoids the nearness of those who cover themselves with filth and take pleasure in indecency. Do not banish God from your side; be decent!

*   *   *

When God handed the first clothes to the first human couple —clothes which shall henceforth remind you, too, to be human —He implanted at the same time a guardian within the breast of man, who is with him constantly in order to warn him when danger threatens and to give him courage and strength when he seems about to falter—this is the feeling of shame.

Shame is something you feel as soon as you go astray and act contrary to the Will of God. It calls out to you: What you just did was ugly, it was contemptible. And it warns you never to do it again. Tend this feeling within you; do not stifle it. And when you find that a friend of yours has lost that feeling of shame—avoid his company!

Be proud of your vocation. Do not say: I am only a child, after all who can talk of a "vocation" for someone my age. Once the Jewish girl has attained her twelfth year, and the Jewish boy his thirteenth, they are ready to think seriously of their Jewish calling. This demands all of your energy and devotion and may well fill you with justifiable pride. You increase your knowledge eagerly and industriously, for your mind wants to penetrate clearly into the world where God's wonders and the achievements of man fill you with awe and admiration. You steel your will-power which you will need in order to be able some day to fill the station assigned you by God.

You are still a child among children, cheerful and gay, but by approaching your duties with due seriousness you prove even now that you will be able to fulfill what may rightly be expected of you. Well or sickly, talented or not, rich or poor—you are determined to fulfill the Will of God with means with which He has endowed you.

*   *   *

Thus your school days pass, and when you are ready to set foot upon the world outside you will not find the change of pace too great. You will be more independent and free, but you will also be older and more mature. You will realize that you can only view the world clearly and objectively if you know the goal set for your life and work hard to attain it. You have known this goal since your early childhood; that goal is to serve with devotion the Will of God as set down in your Book of Life. You will regard the profession to which you will turn and to which you will devote your efforts only as a means to the end of filling your human "vocation" properly.

You will never be able to understand how men could subordinate their divine calling to their search for material gains. Does man really only live in order to earn money? Is life's only purpose to make it possible for man to eat, drink and be merry? When you meet people holding such a narrow view of life, you see before you fallen men who have misunderstood their divine calling. Like the beast, they subject themselves to the yoke of slavery and seek their food in primitive, animal fashion. Such people will be capable of sacrificing their human integrity for their lust, for they do not heed the Word of God which summons them to sanctity and to lifelong service. But you are regularly reminded by the weekly Sabbath that you are to be a servant of

God and that you are responsible to God for your very life, and that all your strength and achievements shall be subject to His judgment.

As long as you will hold on to the Torah you will not go astray; you will not be dominated by superficiality. You will always gather new strength from your Science of Life as taught by God and will view with increasing understanding the requirements God has made of you. You will not permit a single day to slip by without having drawn from the living waters of this source.

You will enjoy only refined forms of entertainment and pleasure and will avoid all contact with shoddiness and vulgarity just as you did when you were a child.

You are particular in the choice of the books you read and will exercise discretion in deciding which theatre or other forms of entertainment you will patronize. You will reject any literature which is not wholesome and edifying. You are not willing to sacrifice precious spiritual values for the spurious pleasure of one fleeting moment.

You will be glad when your material possessions increase and you rise in the profession of your choice, for now you will soon be in a position to set up a home of your own. Here you will provide a home for Him in accordance with His Will. You will marry as soon as you can, as soon as you will have the means to build this Sanctuary unto God, be it ever so modest. God does not require that it be magnificent and filled with splendor. God is interested only in the spirit that fills it, the thought that inspired its establishment, and He will hasten to bless and guard it.

All the strength which you have gathered since early childhood will now benefit your new home. Now that you have recognized by yourself your true divine vocation, you are now considered worthy to stand before God together with your wife who holds the same mature, serious view of life, so that He may assist you in bringing into being a new and strong generation. That which would otherwise be frivolous or even criminal has now become your sacred right and a way of fulfilling God's will.

You will find deep satisfaction in being able in manhood to look back upon a childhood and adolescence of which you will never need to be ashamed.

VOCATION AND CALLING

The choice of a vocation of our mature youth (we are initially concerned with our male youth) is unquestionably one of the serious challenges which confronts parents. Aware of their responsibility, parents realize that the success and happiness of their children are vitally dependent on the right choice of a profession which, obviously, should be compatible with their inclinations and talents. Fortunate the parents who succeed early enough in analyzing their children's talents and traits and are thus able to offer helpful guidance in their choice of vocation. Alas, the wrongly chosen profession often results in acute dissatisfaction or, worse, utter emptiness.

From such shipwreck of life our Judaism wishes to protect its adherents. It is true that life knows of "callings" to which one feels "called" upon when inner voices "call" for, and to, a certain activity in life which promises a higher satisfaction beyond the necessary material reward. Yet how insignificant is this call measured against the life-ennobling, life-shaping, life-pervading call to the Jew to attain his God-willed Jewish life calling. This call is *Kevah*, a way of life prescribed by Divine directive to which every other vocational activity is subordinated as *Ara'ie*, as temporary. He who follows this way of life in faithful obedience secures lasting wealth and true satisfaction for his life, however modest, even though his *chosen* profession may not be compatible with his natural talents and inclinations.

It is this true calling of life for which the parental home and the school hope to prepare our youth. Our school's path of education and training is that devised by Rav Hirsch s. z. l.: profound Torah scholarship is to be joined with the study of general areas of knowledge enabling the students to achieve competence in their chosen profession. As upright Jews they are to take their places in life, proud sons of the nation of God, inspired by the challenge and sanctity of their God-given life calling. — For this task no amount of Torah knowledge is sufficient. From God's Torah the character of the Jewish youth must receive its imprint (*Midos*) and the spirit to gain the insight to perceive the lofty calling for which the Divine Will has selected the sons of its people.

This means that the Jew must learn to view his Judaism against the background of its great world-historic mission; learn to strengthen his determination (*Emunah*) to prove himself as a conscientious Jew, forever aware of his true life calling, in the midst of an entirely differently oriented cultural surrounding in which he finds himself placed by virtue of his chosen profession.

Consequently, the Jewish life calling demands constant training and self-education. Not a day must be allowed to pass without occupation with the science of Torah (*Koveah itim La Torah*): "whether rich or poor, healthy or ill, young or old — this duty is incumbent upon everyone, as long as he lives". Only in cases of dire emergency may the twice daily Keriath Shema take the place of this duty. He who is unable to study Torah to the required extent must further all the more the Torah study of others (Sh. A. Y. D. 246). The realm of Torah science is so broad and extensive as to furnish food for everyone of us. Thus,

Torah study is incumbent upon the gifted as well as the less gifted ones. Caution is in place, however, in the application of such classification to the young of school age when the intellectual development is often a tedious process.

Students who have studied Talmud in the Mesivta with satisfactory results should be encouraged to continue their studies for at least one or two years in the Beth Hamidrash in order to achieve more proficiency in "learning" even while preparing for a professional career. If it is contemplated to continue one's Torah studies at another Yeshiva, only an institution may be recommended which follows the same ideological path prescribed by our Yeshiva and Mesivta for our students.

This, incidentally, brings to mind the oft repeated question whether it should not be welcomed if Bachurim express the desire to "remain in learning". "Remain"? Should not everyone "remain in learning"? Evidently what is meant is the exclusive occupation with Torah study. If this involves the student's full-time occupation with "learning" for a period of several years before embarking upon a professional career, such a decision should only be welcomed. We would have serious misgivings, however, if the decision of exclusive "learning" would exclude any thought of a practical preparation for the demands of life. Every profession requires training. This may not be possible at a more advanced age. (The chance of entering the firm of one's future father-in-law where further training is possible is not normally given to the average student). On the other hand, few possess the ability to become a Rosh Yeshiva. To be able to "learn" does not at all mean that one is able to teach.

In this connotation, the following Word of Wisdom comes to mind, albeit in a loftier, more far-reaching interpretation: "Thousands occupy themselves with the Written Teaching, but mere hundreds emerge who actually possess it; tens occupy themselves with the Talmud, but only one actually masters it — and thus muses Koheleth: "One man I found among thousands" (M. R. Koheleth 7).

In every case, the responsible officials of our Torah institutions should carefully determine, after a given period of time, whether the individual student possesses the qualifications to justify the choice of Torah study as an occupation, or whether it would not be necessary to suggest to him to concern himself with his professional training (while, of course, continuing to be *Koveah itim La Torah*). In many of the latter cases the school officials would do well not to rely on the self-judgment of the individual student.

Is it conceivable that the high praise which the Psalms (128) reserve for the head of the family who labors and cares for his wife and children would be directed only to the "less gifted" among our people? "Happy he who fears God, who walks in God's ways" — true fear of God presupposes *Limud Hatorah* in the firm desire to apply all Torah knowledge to a life devoted to the service of God; "thus he may enjoy (as 'ה ירא) the labors of his hands . . . happy is he, for his is the good"; — "love the labor" thus is the severe admonition of the Sages. (Pirke Abot, Chapter I).

"Torah study which is unconnected with practical work ultimately ceases to exist and results in transgression." This means: he who fails to pursue his *Parnossah* while studying the Torah is in danger of encountering economic difficulties which may not only force him to abandon his Torah studies but even, because of the lack of proper professional training, may cause him, in the quest for *Parnossah*, to violate the great precepts of straightness and honesty which must distinguish the bearers of

Torah if their lives are to serve the *Kiddush Hashem* rather than belie the validity of God's Torah (comp. Sh.A. Or. Ch. 156).

We most certainly need "Torah Greats" who dedicate their entire lives to Torah and who become a blessing for our people. Their livelihood requires — and justifies — organized support. Alas, these were always, and are today, the precious few. Among hundreds — perhaps one . . .

In this sense comments the *Mishneh Berurah* (ff.): "Not everyone will attain the lofty level where Torah study is the sole occupation; individuals may always qualify for this goal, especially if supporters come forward ready to guarantee their livelihood".

This was always the case in the history of our people. It was customary for the wealthy to turn to the spiritual leaders of the Yeshivoth requesting the selection of the most outstanding disciple as a future son-in-law of whom it could be expected that he would become a "great one in Israel". Frequently, he was promised full support of his family for a period of seven years to enable him to "learn" without the burden of economic worries. — This was often the way which produced the "great of our people." As often it was the women of our people who sacrificed everything to help their husbands to attain such greatness. Those, according to the *Mishneh Berurah*, were and remain but *Yechidim*, the few . . .

For the average person (and we stress: not only for the less gifted) there existed and continues to exist the lofty obligation laid down in the *Kesuvah* of his wife which the husband takes upon himself at the time of his marriage: "Be my wife in accordance with the law of Moshe and Yisroel: I shall work, honor, sustain and support you, as Jewish men are obligated to work and to honor, sustain and support their wives in truth . . ."

We need the greats of Torah. But we also need men, solid
Bnei Torah, who prove themselves as conscientious Yehudim in
every type of profession, thus striving towards the lofty goal envisioned by the faithful of our people: to serve with their lives,
before all the world, the sanctification of the Divine Will: *Kiddush Hashem*.

ON THE PATH TO LIFE

For those who uphold it God's Torah is a "Tree of Life" (Mishle 3); it helps us to live and determines the "length of our lives" (ibid 9). Faithful realization of its Divine demands promises life; death in life is the lot of him who denies it in life. "Life and death I have placed before you—choose life" (Deut. 30) calls Moshe Rabbenu's admonition into the future of each individual who counts himself as member of the people of God.

God desires to help us attain such a life. At the threshold of each new year we plead for His Divine assistance, זכרנו לחיים מלך חפץ בחיים.

Which is the path that leads to life?

All of us born of a Jewish mother are Jews by birth. Yet we must learn to *become* Jews, we must grow ever more consciously in our Jewish life convocation.

When we delve into the history of our people and review the proud parade of celebrated giants of the spirit who bestowed glory upon the Jewish name and who dedicated all their strengths to the attainment of the Jewish life convocation—let us never forget that there is no one who is born as a conscientious Jew, who had not to battle his way to Sinai, who does not view life's sole meaning and purpose in the unconditional acceptance of the Divine will of life and its full realization in our Jewish existence.

For the thinking Jew the path to Sinai does not reveal itself with mathematical logic. If it were so, Judaism would no longer be a moral challenge. Ethics and morality presuppose the possibility of being different, of a choice. The choice has been set by God from the moment when He placed man as a human being in His creation.

The passage of Korach forms a significant part of our Divine Book of Life: from the very beginning the Divine Will has recognized that there will be Jewish arrogance daring to deny God and His Will in frivolous demonstrations of unbridled rebellion.

Which is the course taken by a healthy Jewish education? He who is fortunate to have parents who are fully aware of their Jewish task of life finds himself placed early "with both feet" in Jewish living: he *lives* Judaism as a matter of course, he is not asked, Divine demands command his allegiance with forceful seriousness. Yet, with awakening maturity, the "why" and "wherefore" will move youthful lips; parents will welcome such inquiries which they regard as signs of pensive thoughtfulness. They will do their utmost to provoke them when they are not forthcoming. For in the same normal measure in which the healthy youth questioningly confronts all manifestations of his surroundings, Jewish life must similarly and profoundly stir his intellectual and emotional potencies.

Neither habit nor pious remembrance must be allowed to form the ties which bind the growing youth to his Jewish life convocation. Sad indeed would be the future if every new generation, instead of hoisting with joyous pride the weather-beaten flag of the Jewish truth of life in order to attain the palm of life's victory under its banner, would offer but tepid allegiance to the handed-down Jewish duties of life, their enthusiasm waning, their soul's fire extinguished, their senses dulled by the forget-me-not fragrance of childhood days long past.

Little wonder that so many turn their backs on Torah during the decisive years of their lives. This Divine Book requires an emotional attitude which must be carefully nurtured: for it forms the vital ingredient for the joyous and longing acceptance of Torah. Present the sated with the most delicious food and he will leave it untouched. Only he whose throat is parched with thirst will painfully long for water. Our Divine Book of life requires such hunger, such thirst. To awaken them is the task. Therein lies the secret of the successful influence on the youthful Jewish soul. Once this goal has been achieved, it can be securely left to the power of the Divine Word to tie for life the bond to its youthful bearers.

He whose soul has awakened to the mysteries offered by nature, history and one's own life in all their phenomena; he who has witnessed in holy fear nature's overwhelming wonders and perceived with King David (Ps. 19) the omnipotent language of the creative and purposeful Deity, he will conceive of his task as part of this Divine Creation and turn longingly to God's loving fatherly voice to learn the meaning of his God-willed existence.

"God's Torah, all-encompassing, answering the questioning souls" (Ps. 19)—of this Hymn of jubilation the barren Jewish soul which is sated by pleasure and possession has not the slightest conception. This glorious hymn may even move it to the most frivolous and contemptible blasphemy: "They are but precepts upon precepts, guidelines upon guidelines; a detail here, a detail there, causing one to stumble in life, to be broken, snared and caught" (Is. 28).

Jewish consciousness cannot conceive of God without attempting at once to anticipate His Will. For what would God mean to us if He were not manifested by His Will as revealed to us: The Divine Book is God's "Testimony" (עדות) for it is only through His Will that God speaks to us. From the lifeshaping precepts of His Will with which God bestowed meaning and justification upon human life we derive the blissful right to look towards Divine guidance which indulges our helplessness, leads us when we appear hopelessly lost, and protects our soul from the influence to which it would be perilously exposed. With childlike longing for the haven of security our soul fervently grasps the Divine Laws to let them guide it through the mysteries of life. This is what it means to offer boundless confidence, אמונה, in the Divine Guidance. To the barren Jewish thought this fiery word is reduced to miserable—"faith". Little wonder that this rootless flower will fall victim to the slightest provocation of the mocking mob!

"God's is the earth and that which fills it, and also the world of man and those that dwell in it" (Ps. 24) Your Divine Book of Life reckons with this fundamental recognition; in order to awaken it in you it leads you through nature and history that your soul may be permeated by their eternal enigmas and wonders which would overpower it if God were not to remove its unbearable burden. You will find life meaningful only because God interprets His universe for you as God's world—and infinite light penetrates the night of your existence.

When nature will have been transformed for you into a singularly lofty "Holy Mountain" (ibid.) as you are touched by the breath of the Divine creative Will; when you will perceive in mankind's shadowy path the traces of Divine Will, this Divine Book will calmly await the moment when you will be overcome by the all-consuming desire to draw ever more knowledge from it.

"Who may climb this Mountain of God—who may endure on its holy site?" (ibid.) This is the great question which fills your being and which demands immediate answer. Forever God's solitary Will hovers over all that is His and only frivolous folly would dare to live in God's world in defiance of this Will and bold usurpation of that which is God's.

Listen closely to your soul's pure voice, conscious of its Divine origin—and your "religious feeling" (as it is commonly called) will tell you that henceforth "your hands must remain pure, unblemished your heart; your life never to pursue nothingness nor devote itself to deceit"(ibid.)—

Emotions, no matter how profoundly felt, cannot save you from deceit, cannot find intuitively the Divine Will. God alone can present it to you. Then you must seek the course charted for you by the entity of your people in unbroken tradition; you must seek the Will of God where alone it may be found: in God's Torah as revealed to you.

THE TASK OF THE JEWISH DAUGHTER

In the first part of this essay (see "A Time to Build," Vol. I, p. 82), we investigated the significance of the two concepts ("Vocation and Calling") for the path of life to be followed by our *male* youth. Our *female youth* is no less challenged to practice *that* calling which it is called upon to follow: to prove themselves in life as true "daughters of Zion," a title which the prophets bestow upon those who are entitled to it by virtue of their faithful adherence to their God-willed life duties. The Jewish daughter has to be prepared for this calling upon which all measures of education and training are concentrated. If she is privileged to build her Jewish house together with her husband, lofty tasks await her in this calling: she is to be her husband's life companion (היא חברתך Mal. 2, 14), "guardian of the ways of her house," mother of her children; "as *her* husband he is known in public life"; "her children rise up and pay tribute to her, her husband praises her" (Mishle 31). Here is the most pertinent recognition and evaluation of the true calling of the Jewish daughter.

In former times the education of the daughters was entrusted mainly to the mother. She instructed them in the care of the body and taught them all that enriches feelings and emotions. "Teaching of love on her tongue" (Mishle 31)—"do not leave the teaching of your mother" (Mishle 1). These precepts are also inscribed upon the hearts of the daughters of our people.

With the advent of a "new era" which swept our people in its grasp, the establishment of schools for girls became a necessity.

The Task of the Jewish Daughter

99

Included in the curriculum were: Torah sh'biksav, Tefilla, Neviim, K'suvim, Pirke Ovos, Jewish History, Jewish world view and ideology (Hashkofo), the holy tongue. According to Jewish law the study of Talmud (Torah sh'b'al peh) is omitted. The Jewish communities of the East refused for a long period of time to accept the inclusion of such a curriculum and unfortunately, many girls were lost to Torah-Judaism. Eventually, Beth Jacob schools, founded by the unforgettable Sarah Schenirer and Leo Deutschlaender, met with general acceptance.

It is the great Chofetz Chaim זצ"ל who writes: "In the days of old when our daughters grew up in the protective atmosphere of the parental home, the instruction in Torah was not as important as it is in our time. Nowadays, it is our sacred duty to instruct the girls in Torah, Neviim and K'suvim, Pirke Ovos, Menoras Hamouar and similar texts, to ensure their upbringing as upright Jewesses (לקוטי הלכות סוטה).

The school for girls founded by Rav Hirsch זצ"ל, like the school for the male youth, functioned under the premise of Torah im Derech Eretz. For this was the only way which could promote the education of our daughters in the midst of a differently oriented cultural surrounding, to become proven and proud Jewesses whose minds, hearts and emotions are permeated by the firm desire to live up to their life duties in faithful fulfillment and to remain always conscious of God's first Sinai call, כה תאמר לבית יעקב, which was directed to the women of our people.

There are further reasons why the thorough training in the areas of general knowledge is of vital importance. Some girls strive towards a well-rounded general education, while others are interested in preparing for a specific vocation. In each case it may be expected that our female youth is eager to continue its Jewish studies after graduation from High School. The justification for the practical training towards a vocation cannot be denied. If it is our daughters' good fortune to be able to fulfill their God-willed task as wives and future mothers, the initially chosen practical profession may also be of help in their married life. When this is not the case, the chosen profession secures the independent standard of living which provides satisfaction in the loyal adherence to the tasks of life set by God.

Torah im Derech Eretz is the way of education and training for our male and female youth. Rav Hirsch זצ״ל never conceived of it as a הוראת שעה (as we established in another essay—see "A Time to Build," Vol. I, p. 17) and is thus no less applicable in our time. There is *one* area in which one might perhaps be justified, in a sense, to speak of a הוראת שעה—and it would still be eminently applicable in our time. We are thinking of the social contact between the sexes. In the spirit of the Divine warning of לא תקרבו לגלות ערוה, "do not come close to immorality" (Lev. 18, 6) our Sages demand the avoidance of any action which is liable to stimulate the senses. This also includes the separation of the sexes (Zechariah 12, 12), which applies in the same measure to young and old, married and unmarried. Yet this separation was never meant to be total; moreover, it would be unworkable in the framework of economic living. Thus, the Talmud reports that men and women attended lectures in the same room seated in separate rows (Kiddushin 81, comp. Rashi). The great rabbinical leaders to whom we owe the survival and strengthening of Torah-true Judaism, especially in Germany, neither practiced nor demanded a separation of the sexes in the strict manner in which it was applied in earlier days. They felt justified, even obligated, to apply their measures in an age when the supreme task was to educate the youth to become upright and uncompromising sons and daughters of our people, in circumstances completely different from those prevalent heretofore. (The Gaon Rav Y. Weinberg זצ״ל evaluated the wisdom of these measures in his שו״ת שרידי אש סי׳ ח׳).

If one is of the opinion that a total separation of the sexes is also required in our time, men should not be permitted to pay social visits with their wives (a practice which was surely not prevalent in days of old); neither should their daughters be allowed to be employed in business nor should men-teachers be permitted to be teachers in girls schools. —Of the advocates of total separation one should really expect a more rigid application of their view, unless they admit and are aware that even the demands of צניעות, by strict adherence to the eternally valid and required barriers (Kesuboth 72a), may depend on the customs of the time (משנה ברורה סי׳ ע״ה סעי״ק ב׳).

In the 67th chapter of the "Chorev," Rav Hirsch directs a moving message of admonition to "Yisroel's young men and women," basing his appeal on the applicable halachic laws. In that spirit, he demands the conscientious adherence to the אסור יחוד and the צניעות rules, in dress and hair covering which promote the Divine warning call of לא תקרבו וכו׳. The separation during the Divine Service through gallery and מחיצה was a matter of course. —Rav Hirsch approved of social activities involving families and their sons and daughters, but he strongly stressed the prohibition of לא תקרבו as a constant reminder of the limitations of social life. The two schools for boys and girls were housed in two separate but interconnected buildings where occasional joint assemblies and activities took place. These were measures which found their justification in the serious and challenging task to rear a maturing youth which, despite its special character, moved within non-Jewish and un-Jewish surroundings (unlike olden times) towards its eternal Jewish life calling. In such circumstances, the attempt to achieve total separation of the sexes (which, as pointed out, is not feasible) would have had the opposite effect.

And today? Can we prevent our youth from witnessing the progress of moral degradation merely by observing the clothing worn by girls and women on the street? Can we protect them from observing the immoral excesses of a decadent age? It would be sheer self-delusion if responsible educators were not cognizant of the fact that our youth cannot remain untouched by the sad effects of the disease. Silence would be a fatal sin of omission. We must help our youth. God's Torah leads the way.

Our youth must ever more clearly become aware of the lofty tasks to which God calls our people, everyone of us in the midst of mankind (ואתם תהיו לי ממלכת כהנים וגוי קדוש); aware and ever more conscious of the significance of קדוש השם and the warning of חלול השם; of purity and impurity (טומאה, טהרה), of the sanctity of life (קדושה) and the sanctification of enjoyment and possession (Deut. 12, 15), of the warning of lust (חמדה, תאוה) and immorality (זנות "do not come close to it . . ."); ever more conscious of the significance of clothing (צניעות, בושה, Genesis 2,25; 3,21; Numbers 15,37 ff.), of "sacred be your place of rest" (Deut. 23,15 מחניך קדוש והיה), of "wholly be with your God" (תמים תהיה עם ה' אלקיך)—all designed to train our youth to be joyfully and proudly determined to live up ever more to these Divine demands and admonitions, although the existing conditions make a total separation of the sexes impossible. We may then confidently expect of our young men and women that they will be cognizant at all times of the dignity their position demands and of their obligation towards the trust which we place in them.

Even with the prevailing new circumstances of life, the Psalm song (144) of a new Jewish youth must remain eternally young: אשר בנינו כנטיעים מגדלים בנעוריהם בנותינו כזוית מחטבות תבנית היכל "our sons carefully planted, growing up in their youth—and our daughters, even if modestly retiring, no less carefully reared—(both) an image of the Sanctuary."

SOURCE OF SANCTITY

Only a few short weeks still stand between you and your wedding day, a day you anticipate with the most pious emotions. You will not let yourself be attracted by fleeting pleasures of the moment, nor are you given to superficiality and thoughtlessness. And thus in your earnest search for the meaning of life and true happiness you have early recognized the treasure which has been put into your cradle at birth by virtue of the fact that you are part of the Jewish people. You were born a Jewess, the child of Jewish parents. As soon as your conscious self was fully awakened, you hastened to reach for your heritage, for the care of which your parents brought you into the world. Parents and teachers have stood at your side to assist you in facing life; they told you that God alone and only His Sacred Will can interpret life for you and give your life meaning and content.

And so you continued to grow into Jewish life: guided by God you cast your gaze upon nature and trembled at the secret of His miracles of Creation; taught by His Word you followed the sorrow-filled paths of the history of mankind and recognized the sublime destiny of the vocation of the Jewish nation.

The Jewish people is that segment of humanity in which the original purpose of Man is to find its realization as determined by God. It is a people which cannot conceive of a life without the guidance of God, which finds contentment and happiness, inalienable, unshaken by whatever blows fate might strike, in the knowledge that it has fulfilled God's purpose with every breath and with everything that life offers in material wealth and

103

spiritual values. The Jewish people is that section of humanity which has accepted the Will of God — while a deluded world scornfully rejected it — and whose further existence is conditioned by its faithful adherence to the Will of God.

And you understood the painful tragedy of Jewish history: Israel should have preserved its strength of leadership in order to be able some day to guide a desperate mankind along the path to the Paradise of Life it had forfeited — and instead, swept along by the frenzy of the nations, Israel forfeited its own Paradise. You have discovered in the Divine documents that shining goal which God's clemency has confirmed in writing to your people: dispersed among the nations, Israel is to find its way back to its true calling: casting off falsehood and pretense and taking up with ardent fervor the eternal heritage of the Fathers in order to impress a Divine stamp upon its life once more. Cleansed and rejuvenated, it may then confidently await the call of God to assembly. Jewish homes are the building bricks of which the Jewish future is made. As they establish their new home, the heart of every Jewish man and woman who give care and understanding to the practice of his or her Jewish vocation will be filled with the sacred vow to subject their home to the Will of God; to dedicate their combined strengths to the realization of His Will, to raise their children in accordance with His Will and thus assure eternal significance to their home.

*   *   *

As you were accustomed from earliest child-hood to ask yourself at your every decision, action or enjoyment of pleasure whether God's will would give its sanctioning approval, so will you also acquaint your-

self scrupulously with the important requirements by the
fulfillment of which alone your marriage will be able
to stand up before the all-seeing and examining Eye of
God.

You will pursue these regulations with all the
yearning of your Jewish heart, for they are designated
to govern your married life in accordance with the Divine Will. For in your heart there is a great and sacred
word which shall be a basic concept of your home, your
marriage: בית אל "House of God." This is the name
given in our Scriptures to Jewish homes, homes "wherein
God resides" where God's presence, loving and guarding,
dwells. You would not be a Jewess if you were not aware
of the fact that nearness to God can only be attained
through acceptance of His Will.

Together with your husband you will want to
serve God with your life in order that God may dwell
therein. But no human mind, however brilliant, will ever
be able to surmise the thoughts of God, and his most
sacred emotions would forever grope in the dark if they
would attempt, on their own, the discovery of God's
paths. "My thoughts are not your thoughts; your ways
are not mine" (Is. 55:8) — thus speaks Jewish truth.
It is the Will of God alone, which commands your
entire life, that will enable you to serve God.

You will have a "kosher" household, you will
keep the Sabbath holy, and observe the Law of God
in your personal and social life — would it not then be
inconceivably thoughtless not to have God's will shape
each aspect of your wedded life as well?

Your wedded life "as well"? Would it not become
forcefully obvious to everyone in whom there is still a
spark of Jewish truth that unless God's will rules *there*,

the Jewish home would cease to bear the characteristic of Jewishness? Marriage builds the home — and an ungodly wedded life will unalterably destroy the "House of God" and irrevocably banish the "presence of God."

Only if husband and wife consummate their marriage before God, if they accept God as a loving witness in their marriage and dedicate their life together to His holy Will — only then will they themselves stand consecrated, elevated and ennobled as "builders" for God. For they hand God the building blocks towards the construction of a future for mankind as intended by Him, and there is no relationship on earth which could come close in sanctity to the Jewish marriage. A "breach of faith" (Malachi 2) — a deplorable disappointment of expectations; an "abomination" against which human feeling revolts, for it is in opposition to all pure and healthy emotions; utter "desecration of the Sanctuary of God" (ibid.) — thus the prophet condemns a marriage relationship that cannot stand up before the Will of God.

*   *   *

But what is the basic *reason* for the individual laws which regulate married life?

Is this question at all justified? God speaks, His holy Will commands and man must respond with unconditional obedience. Whosoever makes obedience to His Will dependent upon the answer to this question, has already ceased to obey God; for it is then not God whom he obeys, but his own mind, which first approves and consents. To be sure, the Divine Law-giver has offered reasons for a number of His laws, and even if the Divine Word does not expressly demand it, we are still expected to investigate, in all humility, the Will of God. But just as the iron laws of Nature continue to exist and natural phenomena will go on (while the scientist laboriously tries to find explanations for them) even if their causes will remain forever hidden from the mind of man — just so every Divine word designated to regulate our lives is no less a law of nature. And, unless it would cease being the Law of God, it will continue to demand our inviolable and unconditional obedience.

Obey, fulfill, serve — and delight in the knowledge that you have complied with the Will of the Lord. You have been chosen to be enlightened now and then by rays of His own Divine light and thereby your perception of His Will becomes clearer — and you attempt to grope your way ahead in the infinity of Divine wisdom and truth — then thank God who in His grace bestows such wisdom upon man.

God must guide you if you are not to grope in the dark and go hopelessly astray: at what other time should this hold true if not in that moment in which Jewish men and women prepare to live on in future generations? God must guide them unless they are to destroy rather than build, to kill rather than give life. And even if the human mind were to comprehend entirely the mystery of the beginning of human life; if the eternal enigmas veiling the soul and its forces were revealed to him — even then only criminal audacity could dare rise up against the Will of God in open rebellion and lead the Jewish woman to venture even *one* step away from the path which God bids her go in order to reach that Sanctuary where, through the love of her husband, the hand of God, in benediction, places upon her brow the crown of the majesty of motherhood.

Your Jewish lips will not venture to use the words "petty," "unimportant," "insignificant" in connection with the Word of God where God commands your obedience. The last remnant of your Jewish conscience would be lost in you and every trace of the consciousness of the responsibility of motherhood gone, if you were thus to mock and blaspheme the sanctity of His Will and scorn the love of His father-like nearness — if you dared thus to gamble with the lives of your children, with the sanctity of your marriage and the future of your people.

You will certainly shun no expense, spare no efforts, where the welfare of your children is at stake. But could there be a Jewish mother — who would lay claim to such an ennobling title — who would as much as consider thoughts of trouble and sacrifice when there is a danger that she might become the murderess of her own children? Is this formulation too harsh? But does the plant not wither if even just one of the prerequisites for its growth and development is withheld from it? The Jewish marriage laws represent the instructions of the Divine Gardener for His human plants. Could there be a Jewish man, a Jewish woman, who would hesitate to meet His requirements conscientiously and readily and with unquestioning faith, lest they run the risk of heartlessly destroying with criminal hands the life of the "plant of God"?

Jewish truth regards life only as such when it is conducted in the service of God's intentions. It will not recognize a life in which the Will of God has no place. There is no thought that fills Jewish consciousness with such fear as does the possibility of being uprooted by God's hand, erased from the soil of God like an ugly, useless weed. Remember: כרת, the Lord Creator pronounced the sentence of "uprooting" in grim earnest upon the Jewish marriage that cannot pass His scrutinizing eye!

Before reading the text that will familiarize you

with all the details of the laws governing married life,
it is well to review the number of regulations which you
must follow before even the smallest piece of meat reaches
your table: not every animal may be used for food —
God alone knows which food the body can assimilate
without causing damage to the soul and its forces.
The animal that may be used for this purpose must first
be killed in accordance with strict directions laid down
by Divine Law — it is a sacred performance during
which a blessing must be recited. And then the animal
must be carefully examined for defects that might render
it "trefe." The next step is to make the meat "kosher" —
and how careful you are in following the rules for salting,
etc. — then follows the actual cooking during which
extensive precautions are taken to avoid any possible
mingling of "fleishig and milchig" — and all this just
so that you can serve that little piece of meat to your
husband and your children! But, no, that is not all! The
table which is entrusted to your care is, indeed, to be
God's table, a sacred altar and even if the precepts which
God prescribes for this purpose were multiplied a thousand
fold, you would still fulfill them all conscientiously and
faithfully; no effort or sacrifice would be too great for
you to preserve for your home the Divinely conditioned
Jewish character. And now the Word of God begins to
initiate you into the secret of the Divine Will which wants
to spread "purity" and "sanctity" over the house where
— in the words of the prophet (Mal. 2) — "the Seed
of God" is to be sown under the watchful eye of God,
because "children of the Living God" (Hos. 2:1) develop
and mature only on that ground which is saturated with
"purity" and "sanctity." And would you then not read
and re-read that code with profound emotions? You will
seek the advice of a wise mother or friend that they may
enlighten you where clarity is needed; you will anxiously

make sure lest you might have missed even one of the
precepts which you might therefore be guilty — God
forbid — of disregarding or forgetting; you will not rest
and feel content until you can say to yourself that you
may now venture to approach your wedding day as a
Jewish bride! This Law of God which has prepared you
for your wedding day will accompany you henceforth
throughout your life and will surround all the phases
of your marriage with its sanctifying regulations.

*   *   *

The laws of God which are designed to govern
our physical life are veiled in darkness. And even if
their reasons were hidden from us forever — is not the
mere fact that the Will of God desires to rule even our
sensual life and pleasure sufficient reason to warrant
our bowing to God in gratitude for His desire to be
near us when we partake of pleasure?

"Be complete with Thy God" (Deut. 18:13);
there is no force, not even the most sensuous one, which
may evade His Will which governs and fashions. And
if it be true that man rises in his true glory only when
he triumphs in freedom over his senses, then it is equally
true that there is no instant when the Jewish man may
feel a greater pride than when he is permitted to invite
the Lord to his table, to have God as a witness in his
marriage — and he feels His beneficial and sanctifying
nearness as soon as he lets His governing will guide him.

The Divine marriage laws are shrouded in darkness.
Could it really be any different? Does not eternal impenetrable mystery hover about the moment when the
seed is laid for the miraculous human plant? Both husband
and wife trust that this moment will bring with it all
the bliss and happiness connected with the blessing of

having children, and they entreat God to make their
child strong and healthy and receptive for all that is
noble and good, and they would certainly not want to
banish the presence of God at this moment, at a time
when He must be near and lend His support! With boundless gratitude they will take advantage of the Divine
privileges which are presented to them at that very moment.
"God wants to be united with the father and the mother
in order to bring human life into being" (Niddah 31) —
that is the ultimate reason for our Divine laws governing marriage.

*   *   *

In sensuous lust there is always the danger that
the animal in man may come to the fore and destroy
him. God wills it that man remain a pure, proud ruler,
serving only God. Thus His holy Will drives out un-
restrained lust and desire from among His people in
whose midst He has placed His sovereign Throne. For
this reason alone there must be a Divine marriage code.
Marital union is a service to God. It is a most sacred
and proud moment when husband and wife are called
upon by God to assist Him in the further development
of His mankind. But first the animal in man must be
banished completely if God's sanctifying nearness is to
participate in this moment.

טהרה (purity) is the Torah's name for the Divine
force which qualifies man for all that is exalted and
noble and which summons him to the free and joyous
dedication of his life to the service of God. This force
must be nurtured and strengthened and guarded against
all dulling and slackening. For, wherever it vanishes or
even is merely robbed of its ruling power, there טומאה,
impurity, increasing apathy, dull indifference and a super-

ficiality unworthy of man take root and will deaden
Jewish force and thus Jewish life itself.

The Divine marriage code serves the purposes of
"Taharah." Wherever this law prevails, "Tumah" can
never rise. But how could the Word of God ever call
the children of the People of God to "Kedushah" (Sanctity); i.e. to an ever closer approach to God, to complete
dedication to His Will; how could the law of God rely
upon the Divine forces within His sons and daughters,
if He were not absolutely confident that Jewish parents
would bring their children into the world in accordance
with the rules of "Taharah"?

If the misfortune befalls Jewish parents that they
must see their children go astray instead of finding in
them the strong bearers of those ideals for which they
were brought into the world, then there is only one thought
that can partially console them in their grief; that is,
if they can truthfully tell themselves that they had done
everything in their power to guide their children to the
right path of life. But what if the parents must stand
accused that they, too, are partly to blame for the degeneration of their children. Horrid and inconceivable is
the thought that at the moment when these parents were
called upon to assist in the giving of life to offspring,
they might have besmirched the human seed with the
poison of "Tumah" and thereby actually sacrificed the
future of generations to come — all for one fleeting,
irresponsible moment of sensual satisfaction!

*   *   *

Woe to the marriage where God and His holy
Will do not join in the moment of marital union; if
husband and wife do not dedicate their combined efforts

toward the realization of the aims of life as set forth by God! Who will then vouch for it that man will not use his strength rudely and egotistically and woman's personality be crushed into the dust under the boot of unchecked sensuousness! Do not deceive yourself: the beast in man is stronger than all the powers of civilization that fancy that they could stun or even conquer it. The beast retreats only before the sacred presence of God; the beast subordinates itself only to the governing influence of the Will of God. He alone succeeds in raising sensually-directed man to the rank of a nobleman dedicated to the service of God. It is in the ennobling of the urges of the flesh that the Law of God finds its ultimate triumph.

If, deep within your heart, you have prayed to God that He may send you the husband who will make you happy and together with whom you may strive for true peace in life, then pray, too, that your future husband should be a man who will bring unswerving obedience and fearful, sacred awe to the Divine marriage laws: for only where such obedience exists will God dwell and only God can bring the genii of "love and brotherhood, peace and friendship" — as enumerated in the blessing pronounced over every newly-wed couple — into married life.

As long as a Jewish husband observes the Divine marriage code, he will *love* his wife. For his love will not then be one of fleeting passion or passing attraction, but it will be that true love which is a joyous mutual devotion, a realization together of common ideals of life. And in the course of their married life — surrounded by a "hedge of roses" (Sanh. 37) of ever-recurring shy and sacred restraint, this love will find perpetual bridal rejuvenation. Each year of wedded life will add strength and intensity to this love, for such love receives in equal measure as it gives.

As long as the Jewish husband observes the Divine marriage code, there will be *peace* in his marriage; a peace which only God's nearness can impart to man. Or, to quote a word of wisdom (Sota 17): God weaves His Holy Name between man and wife and extinguishes forever the raging fires of dissension and enmity.

As long as the Jewish husband will come to his wife only by way of the Law of God, so long will his wife remain "sacred" to him, and the "tears of women" will never "wet the altar of God" (Mal. 2) — and the wife may feel secure in the blissful certainty that she will not be abused as a pitiful tool to unbounded sensuous lust: under the aegis of the law of God, to which incomparable homage is paid at the very instant of marital union, she rises up as the proud and equal "partner" of her husband (ibid.) to whom she lends strength for the fulfillment of the tasks which the "Divine covenant" (ibid.) requires of his life.

Jewish women! Observe the Divine marriage code scrupulously for your own sake! Will you speak of barriers, of burdensome bonds, when God, the loving, merciful Father, is ready to protect you forever from the chains of degrading servitude? None but the most superficial or shamefully ignorant person would be capable of such talk. Do not be so rash — by disregarding even one regulation —— as to force out one single stone from the sanctuary of freedom that is marriage, into which God has led husband and wife, for you may never know but that the very ruling you have chosen to ignore might be the all-important corner stone without which the whole structure will collapse.

*   *   *

You will scrupulously observe the laws with which God has sanctified and enobled the marriages of His people. You will fulfill them gladly and proudly. This joyous pride is the heritage of the mothers of your people. So long as you retain it, your marriage will remain forever young, for God will continue to dwell in your marriage. And men reach the most advanced age in youthful agility and sturdy strength — if God is near them (Ps. 92).

COVERING OF THE HAIR

You have promised to give your hand in marriage to a good and honest man in order to establish a Jewish home together with him. This decision did not come suddenly to you. The years of your youth that lie behind you have been years of mental and spiritual training for your future vocation in life. In marriage you will find fulfillment and the satisfaction which stems from devotion to the intentions of God. You are prepared to place all of your energies in the service of this most sacred of ideals and to fill to the best of your ability the station in which Divine Providence has placed you.

You do not enter marriage unprepared, for you do not want to gamble with your life. It is to the realization of the Will of God that you consecrate your life. It has always been your most fervent desire to perceive and understand that Will. You wish to be able to see ever more clearly the paths upon which God's Will guides you. You know His Law of Life and pledge to give it unswerving obedience.

For would it indeed be a Divine law of life if you were to obey or disobey it at random? Such an attitude on your part would mean that you would no longer obey God, no longer feel bound to a Divine code, no longer heed His Word; you would stand helpless in His great world, and would not know the purpose of your life. But you do want to live; you want to know the purpose of your life, and therefore you need the guidance of His Law and swear to it your faithful allegiance. On the basis of His Law you set up your home together with your husband; it remains dedicated to His Law; and it is in accordance with His Law, too, that you raise your children and convert your home into a sanctuary in which the loving Presence of God may dwell.

Will you cover your hair after marriage? I see a look of surprise in your face. I do not know whether you are astonished at what is being asked, or whether you just wonder that such a question even need be asked of you. I hardly think that this regulation could be foreign to you. You need only look around you and find Jewish women who cover their hair when entering into marriage. If, however, you were merely surprised that this question need be asked at all, then I have judged you correctly and I am sure you will pardon the question.

But what if the covering should disfigure you or cause you discomfort? I see you smiling and again I recognize you for what you are. For could such arguments influence you when it is a matter of following a sacred Jewish tradition or even a Divine Law? This is one point I must speak to you about and if it would be considerations of that sort that guide you, then I would know where my duty lies. Why, if this were really true of you, then you would indeed have cause to be ashamed of yourself. Life demands great sacrifices and frequently even the surrender of our dearest possessions, and the conscientious person does not hesitate for a moment as long as he knows that such sacrifices are required of him by the Will of God. And would anyone then hold back and hesitate to sacrifice considerations of vanity and convenience where there is a question of fulfilling ideal requirements? Jewish life expects of woman that she become a loving and understanding partner to her husband and a wise guide to her children. Indeed, it would hardly redound to the credit of the future Jewish wife were she to refuse to cover her hair because of such motives. What

would she then be able to tell her children some day if
they should reach for a razor blade in order to satisfy
their vanity; if they should feel that the Sabbath is a burden
to them because it runs counter to their convenience?

Are you familiar with that chapter in the Torah
(Num. 5) which deals with the measures Divine Law has
provided for dealing with a woman who has strayed
from the paths of unblemished morality and chastity,
from whose head the crown has fallen — a diadem which
the prophet (Mi. 4:8) calls צניעות and which sees
the highest glory for the Jewish woman in a life lived
"quietly and modestly walking with God?" Such a fallen
woman must come before the scrutinizing eye of God,
she must stand before the Priest in the Temple, and the
latter will remove the crown from her head — "he uncovers the head of the woman." "This is to teach you,"
comment the Sages (Kethuboth 72), "that Jewish women
never uncover their hair." Or, as Sifri (ibid.) formulates
the rule that is derived from this passage: "This is to
teach you that Jewish women are to cover their hair."
God expects that Jewish women will never uncover
their hair. By the act of having her hair uncovered, the
unfaithful is deprived of the right to bear this symbol
of Jewish womanhood. Jewish women will wear it proudly;
it is an Order with which God has decorated them. It
may not always enhance their beauty, but it will always
bring them honor. Has anyone ever refused to accept
the Order of the Garter with which the King desired to
honor him — just because its regalia does not suit his personal taste? Indeed, is it not the idea represented by the symbol
that lends dignity and beauty even to the most unpre-
tentious? And the prophet said: It is not the garments
which adorn the bride, it is the bride herself "who lends
grace to her garments" (Is. 61:10).

*   *   *

By covering her hair and thus wearing this mark of distinction as required by God, the Jewish woman declares herself ready to comply with all the demands which the Law places upon her. This symbol is quite ancient. — as old as the Law of God.

The mothers of our people, those glorious women who are the pride of our nation, who fully understood their vocation in life and upon whose selfless devotion to sacred duty the future of our people could safely depend — these women bore this symbol of dignity. What Jewish woman who truly understands her calling in life would not feel her heart beat more proudly at the thought that some day she too would be named along with those who conscientiously and with understanding took up the heritage left to their daughters by these women! The Jewish woman who covers her hair wears the visible token which ennobled the mothers of our people — and she will not prove unworthy of this token.

*   *   *

Of course it is just an outward sign and it may be worn by someone whose way of life is unworthy of the true significance of this sign. You yourself may know some women whose conduct is a mockery of this symbol, and, on the other hand, you are acquainted with others who do not wear it and yet their conduct is in no way inferior to that of any other conscientious woman. All this may be true. But would this not be true also of other Divine commandments? Is not the "Milah," too, merely an outward sign which should admonish the boy to grow up to be a man of moral perfection? And is the mark of "Milah" on a morally degenerated man not a gross mockery of all that "Milah" would have him be? But what father would fail to have "Milah" performed on his child for this reason?

*   *   *

But then you might say that the practice of covering the hair does not seem to be a custom followed by Jews only; it is the common heritage of the Orient, and thus it brings to mind the inferior position of woman in the East and the degradations that were associated with the harem.

I know that such a thought will never enter your mind. You are much too aware of the dignity inherent in the Jewish woman, of the position that is hers, of the realization that a Jewish marriage is something sacred and ennobling. You have carefully studied the Divine Books; the mighty words of the Prophets have resounded in your ears, and you would never enter into marriage so poorly prepared for this sacred calling. And even if upon superficial examination there might seem to be some truth in this argument — might it not be possible that two persons might engage in the same practice, but each for quite different reasons than the other? Does not the Oriental also pray and offer up sacrifices, does he not also have temples, priests and prophets — and, still, would you be so thoughtless as to consider identical certain phenomena and concepts which, while seemingly alike, actually represent ideas diametrically opposed to each other by virtue of the spirit in which each is performed?

*   *   *

The covering of the hair is to be the outwardly visible sign which shall show that the Jewish woman is ready to fulfill the ideals that she has been called upon to follow. Thus Jewish Law wills it. The woman who uncovers her hair "treats Jewish Law with utter contempt" (נקראת עוברת על דת יהודית, Kethuboth 72 Shulchan Aruch

אי"ה, Chap. 115). However faultless her own personal
conduct and her conception of life, she still could not be
spared this reproach. And it is sad indeed not to be able
to accord to a woman the full measure of esteem which
would be due her because of her great merits in life —
just because there was this one point to which she had
not given sufficiently serious consideration; had she been
consistent in her thinking, she would have come to one
conclusion only. And if she is blessed with children who
have grown up to dedicate their lives to the same ideals
she holds dear, then she may truly thank God upon her
knees that all her endeavors of education did not come
to nought because of this one inconsistency on her part.
For what answer would she have been able to give her
children had they questioningly pointed to that particular
place in the book of God which enjoins the Jewish
woman to cover her hair?

But wait — I am convinced that that Jewess,
that mother as I imagine her to be pure of heart, serious
of mind and profound in understanding — had she been
acquainted with that particular verse in the Law, she
would not have hesitated for an instant to bow her head
willingly and proudly to the call of the Law. For it is
ignorance above all, but also regrettable example, that
has alienated many a home from this sacred commandment.
The annals of history have yet to be written to prove
just how often the example set by only one Jewish woman
of importance was sufficient to cause this hallowed practice to vanish in the course of time from entire communities? But this fact would only serve to inspire dutiful Jewish
women to set a new example and to take up once again
this holy symbol with which Jewish Law has sought to
ennoble them. They will want to join hands across the
ages with the mothers of bygone centuries and millenia

who have shown them a glorious example of lives lived in service to God.

And even if their own mothers did not cover their hair, the daughters may be sure of their blessing and approval. For is there a happier feeling for parents than the knowledge that their children have surpassed them and have been able to achieve that which they failed to accomplish? Parents rejoice at the thought that their children have progressed from the point where they themselves had to leave off, and that their offspring have surpassed them, if that is possible, in active self-discipline. "We were not perfect," thus they would call to us from the eternal life, "be better, be stronger than we have been, reach for the good that you could learn from our example and do not let yourself be misled by our faults — we were not perfect." But what about "reverence" for the example set by our parents? Who would be so thoughtless as to apply this oft-abused term in this connection, this word that has all too often been used to serve convenience and self-deception so well? Do you also reverently cease your efforts for material gains at the point where your parents had stopped before you? Do you not, indeed, try to surpass their efforts wherever possible? Yet you would apply this false concept of reverence to your efforts towards moral advancement and thus endanger your own lives and the future of your children?

*   *   *

You are determined to cover your hair, because you know that you thereby obey Jewish Law, and it is your wish that all that Jewish Law commands us takes firm root in your home. But the more you familiarize yourself with the thought of accepting this particular law which is to designate you, also outwardly, as one of those

women upon whose strength God has founded the future
of His people — the more you will feel the urge to know
more about the motives which may have led the Divine
Law-Giver to expect His women to cover their hair.

Here, the words of our Sages come to your aid
and show you the way to better understanding. They conceive of woman's hair as "Ervah" (Berachoth 24 שער אשה
ערוה), as a "nakedness" the covering of which the law demands. And this thought will take you back to the beginning of mankind when God handed a garment to
the first human couple with which to cover their nakedness. Sensual urges had cost man his dearest treasures;
the Divine Word of Life had to make way for the whis-
pered insinuations of sensual considerations, the body tri-
umphed over the Divine soul and the soul felt ashamed
of the body. A poor light indeed is cast upon the first
woman here. She had forgotten her obligations which
had once brought her to man as "ezer kenegdo" — his
helpmate — that she might, jointly with him as his
equal partner, bring to realization a great Divine ideal
of life, a goal which no individual could ever achieve
alone. Broken was the bond of their marriage, a bond
which lent nobility and dignity to their lives only as long
as their life together would serve the fulfillment of
God's requirements. Dimmed was the light of life whose
guard should have been her most sacred concern. The
physical charms which she could regard as her pride and
glory as long as they were instruments of the Divine
soul were lowered to the animal level. And so they came
to be ashamed of their bodies. And God, His discipline
tempered by kindness, handed them garments to remind
them henceforth to let the body step back lest the soul
be robbed of its sovereignty. The Word of God applies
the term "Ervah" to any life that does not allow itself
to be governed by the Law of God, and wherever men

succumb to the lure of animal lust: God sees in their true
"nakedness" those who have thrown off the garment
which calls them to the heights of life's attainments.
Woe to the man and the woman whose marriage is but
"Ervah" in the eyes of God (Lev. 18)! We stand mourning at the grave of human dignity forfeited.

The Jewish woman understood this admonition.
Her marriage was henceforth to be Divine. Although
she once dimmed the light of her husband's soul, she
is henceforth resolved, as his "Ezer kenegdo," to increase
that light for him, and, united with him, to consecrate
her marriage to the fulfillment of the goals set by God.
She lights the Sabbath candles for her husband to let
him know that she is ready to build a home consecrated
to the Sabbath, to a life that will find favor in the eyes
of God. And she covers her hair, (in mourning, as it
were, because she once did succumb to sensual desires
and thus robbed her marriage of its Divine quality?)
(Pirkei de R.E. 14); she modestly hides that which
would ordinarily commend itself to the eyes and the
senses, for it is not that which is her pride. This symbol
speaks loudly. Whoever wishes to respect and esteem
her should honor in her the wife who brightens the path
of life for her husband, and the mother who guides her
children through life. Are our Sages not justified if they
suspect "Ervah" wherever a Jewish woman scorns this
symbol which commends itself to her under such lofty
prerequisites?

Jewish women, if you wish to honor yourselves,
if you wish to be recognized at first glance for what you
are — then do not reject this Jewish symbol! The history
of our people looks with pride upon its women. They
were once instrumental in saving their people; the redemption of the future, too, lies in their hands. The

Jewish woman who proudly and confidently covers her
hair upon entering the married state silently takes a
sacred vow and with profound understanding she sees the
path that is ahead of her, a path to which she was called by
Divine command.

*   *   *

You have understood me. This covering is a holy
symbol for you. You will fulfill what it demands of you.
You will now understand why the proud and happy mother
who saw high priestly honors vested in her sons, simply
replied, as follows, when she was asked which particular
merit of hers enabled her to be so successful in raising
her children, "The walls of my house did not look upon
the hair of my head" (Yoma 47). But you will also
understand how right our Sages were when they said
pensively and sadly, "Many did likewise and yet had no
such success" (ibid.). For not all women at all times
understood the meaning of this covering and its requirements — and not all those who did understand had
sufficient strength to fulfill these requirements in their
married lives. May God grant you His aid in this your
sacred endeavor.

THE WEDDING WEEK

If you are indeed prepared to dedicate yourself to a marriage in which the will of God shall find receptive recognition, then you will do your best to fulfill all the great and sacred duties which Jewish women are expected to perform. But if you should deny God this obedience, then, while your home may still bear some external signs of Jewishness, God — before whose watchful eye every thought, every emotion and even our most hidden acts lie openly revealed — will still strike your marriage from His Divine Register in which each contribution, however small, made by man, is recorded for all eternity — and Zion, which had also expected a great deal from your marriage, is now the poorer by one more measure of hope.

Do not ever forget the expectations with which Zion looks up to every newly-established Jewish home. You will do well to recall always those words of blessing uttered at the wedding of every Jewish couple, never forgetting to measure by them the extent to which you in your own life have fulfilled these expectations. We are here referring to the "Seven Berachoth" which sanctify every Jewish marriage and which, for thousands of years, have striven to win every new Jewish marriage for the noble Divine ideal.

Your thoughts are directed towards God ברוך אתה ה' to Him, to Whose service all the forces within you shall be eternally dedicated, שהכל ברא לכבודו Whose glory every living thing is ready to serve. There could hardly be another milestone in your life at which such a thought could move you more profoundly. You do not enter into marriage for the attainment of goals and ideals you have set by yourself, much less still for the satisfaction of momentary sensual desires. It is before His countenance — before which an entire world of Creation is united in service and a Universe pays homage on bended knee, — that men, and you too, find your place in life! יוצר האדם The Divine spark within you would indeed sutter were not your lips at this moment to murmur a sacred vow that you, too, are willing to dedicate your life — in the midst of all the other servants of Divine creation — to the Will of God.

But let us go further: Hear this and never forget it throughout your married life: אשר יצר את האדם בצלמו The first human being came forth from the hand of God; man's spirit and soul are Divine, but his body, too, is Divine, an instrument of God which must never be allowed to stagnate in the mire of animal lust and must never lose its likeness to God in horrible "Tumah." God expects you to carry on the work of Divine human creation; together with your husband you are to build further the בנין עדי עד to work on a "structure" that will reach far into the remotest future: your children בנים are your "building blocks"; it is your task to see to it that they do not ever do anything to violate or endanger this structure. Remember this always: יוצר האדם thus the blessing ends; today God still looks to your efforts to bring forth that type of human being that He desired from the very beginning, when man first came forth from His creative hand!

And the mother hears it — Zion, the grieving, tempest-tossed, inconsolable mother, robbed of her children, rudely deserted by them — do they hear it, too, they who are about to unite in the bond of marriage? Are they willing to return to Zion the children for whom she so painfully yearns? Jewish hope cannot conceive that this could be otherwise; it is confident that the last remnant of receptiveness to that which is sacred and eternal has not yet disappeared from among men; and thus it calls out to Zion with joyful reassurance: שוש תשיש "rejoice and be glad, thou barren one: here they stand and are willing to come to thy aid. Here is the woman whose heart goes out with longing to lead her children to you one day, O Zion!" "Thy children gather together in thy midst!"

Come, O come — thus plead the two final Berachoth: dedicate yourself to the achievement of this goal if you long for happiness — and who does not long for happiness, for gladness and life? Zion awaits you, God awaits you, and He is ready to bless you.

You love one another and wish to be happy? שמח תשמה Thou, O Lord, alone canst bestow that joy of Paradise which is true happiness. Thou gavest it to Thy first couple of human beings (יצירך) in the Garden of Eden; Thou art ready to give it also to this couple, and to all others who fervently long to attain it through Thy nearness: וְמשמח חתן וכלה!

Jewish women! You wish to make your husbands happy and God has placed your husband's happiness in your hands. משמח חתן עם הכלה — the blessing ends with these significant words: it is only jointly with you that Jewish men find their true happiness. This Berachah says that God created "happiness, gladness, bliss and joy." Build a home for your husbands where these genii dwell. "Love, brotherhood, peace and friendship" — this was the greeting used in God's own Sanctuary (Berachoth 12a) — establish that sanctuary for your husbands in your homes and you will hasten the coming of redemption for our people. From your homes the path will lead to "the cities of Judah, to the streets of Jerusalem."

Need more be said about Jewish marriage and its lofty significance than that these Berachoth are pronounced at every wedding ceremony, even that of the poorest among us?

These Berachoth are to be recited in the presence of ten men, as is stated in the Psalms (Ch. 68) "bless God in congregations from the source of Israel" (Ketub. 7). And this points to a further admonition: Whenever a Jewish marriage ceremony is performed, "congregations" are to be present. In every new marital union, Jewry sees itself once more at the source of the birth of Israel and hopes that the new marriage will serve as a new source for a rejuvenation and strengthening of the Congregation of Israel. But Israel's Congregations, as well, may rejoice in this certainty which raises their hearts above all the trials and tribulations of the present day: Out of every Jewish marriage there may come forth the fulfillment, at long last, of Jewish hopes for the future; and salvation for mankind and of the world may spring forth from such a union.

These Berachoth are to be recited not only once, but should be said over and over again during the first seven days of marriage, in order to ask the blessings contained in them upon the young couple.

Who, then, can justify the thoughtlessness of some couples, which leads them to adopt foreign, non-Jewish practices and thus deny themselves these Berachoth. Jewish law invites every young Jewish couple to שבעת ימי משתה Our Teacher Moses demands mourning during the Seven Days of the "Shiva," but he also requires us to rejoice during the Seven Days of the Wedding. (Jerus. Kethub. פ"א). Even those who are completely estranged from the spirit of Judaism will piously observe the "strenuous" week of mourning, but many a Jewish couple refuses to allow

Moses to prepare for them the week of rejoicing. Can
it be possible that men know better how to weep than to
be joyful? Do you not think that if Jewish couples
would stop for a moment and give some thought to what
these "seven Berachoth" mean to them, they would
proudly insist upon their right to a "Jewish wedding week"
and that they would not let go of that privilege even
in the most difficult times? This holds true for the Jewish
man, but even more so for the Jewish woman.

These seven Berachoth consecrate your home to
the fulfillment of Jewish hopes for the future, and they
expect the Jewish woman to provide her husband, within
the walls with which she surrounds him ("the wife surrounds the husband" Jer. 31:21), with that happiness
and satisfaction which causes him to place all the goods
with which life may have endowed him upon the human
altar of purity erected by the Jewish wife. It is only
the consecration of this altar that can lend the character
of sanctity to man's endeavors in life. As long as Jewish
men will be imbued with this understanding, the position of the Jewish woman will not have to become the
subject of lengthy debates. For the Torah says: "If someone take unto himself a new wife, he is not to enter the
armed forces, and he shall not be molested in any manner; he shall remain at liberty in his home for one year
and gladden his wife whom he hath taken unto himself."
(Deut. 24:5) Jewish men are to be aware of the fact
that the State and its demands must step aside respectfully
to give priority to that which gives meaning to the life
of woman. During that first year the Jewish husband
pays his tribute to the highest and most sacred tasks of
life which can be performed only jointly with the
Jewish woman. When the year is over, the Jewish
woman, with justifiable pride, may let her husband return to public life and service to the community.

She fully realizes that what she sows and builds in modest retirement is not only not inferior to the accomplishments of her husband, but rather gives her own life meaning and justification before the eyes of God.

Ever since our national sorrow has reduced all merry-making, this period of rejoicing has been cut down from one year to only one week. This "wedding week" during which the Jewish man belongs exclusively to his wife, and which is spent in the spirit of the "Seven Berachoth" offers symbolic significance for the future of the Jewish marriage.

ISRAEL — A CHALLENGE

A trip to Israel has become routine in our time. The amazing technological progress in the speed of air travel has helped in the enormous rise of volume of travellers bound for Israel. The Holy Land has become a focal attraction for the Diaspora. We would rather not analyze whether it is longing for the ancestral land which motivates the travellers' plan — a longing which all but consumed the heart of a Yehuda Halevy. Undoubtedly, the existence of a Jewish state in the Holy Land, recognized by a majority of the world's nations, draws many thousands into its orbit, who then return home warmed by the glow of the numerous achievements which the state has accomplished in the brief period of its existence.

As for us Torah-true Jews we must be permeated by the following thoughts:

From the beginning the Jewish people was assured possession of Eretz Yisrael only as *God's nation*. Every page of the Torah proclaims this irrevocable truth. To deny it would mean a denial of God's Torah itself. Only he who no longer recognizes the truth of the Divine creative pronouncement of "I shall take you as My people" — with which God called our people into existence — will fail to grasp the absolute interdependence between the "I shall bring you to the land" (Ex. 6) and the emergence of the Jewish people as God's nation. The disruption of the sole tie which bound this nation to its land inevitably sealed the fate of nation and land.

Similarly, the future of this land is intimately and forever tied to the future of this nation. Redemption of the Jewish people also means redemption of the Jewish land. Thus a true ingathering of our people into its land is not possible without our return to God and His life-shaping proximity. For the land, too, longs for the return of God's Shechina.

Far from the homeland, Yecheskel reconstructs the Jewish future. He witnesses the desecration of the sacred soil, its transformation into a horrible field of corpses. Yet they who are stricken with blindness refuse to recognize the tidings and reject Prophetic admonitions as empty talk. "It does not matter if you leave God — for the land, given to us as our heritage, will remain ours" (Yech. 11). Even when history delivered its shattering verdict, the Prophet continues to find the doomed men dream, in the midst of the wreckage, of independent statehood which they hope to regain by their own power. For was not "an only one Abraham, and he took possession of the land — we are still numerous enough — to us the land was given as a heritage"! And the Prophet retorts: "Thus speaks my Lord, God: you eat over blood, your eye does not flinch from your abominations — and you have hopes of possessing the land? You rely upon your sword, you commit unspeakable acts — and you have hopes of possessing the land?" (Yech. 33)

"I have prepared a homestead for My people, Israel — I have implanted it, so that it may dwell quietly on its site, never to tremble" (Sam. II, 7). A profound Divine admonition of eternal validity. At no place and at no time can our people prepare its homestead on the basis and as a result of its own strength. This ancient truth is our people's cradle song: "You bring them home and implant them" (Ex. 15) — and this is Moshe's warning pronouncement looking far into the future: ". . . and among the nations you will not find peace — there will be no resting place for the sole of your foot" (Deut. 28.)

Prophets have given this land its name — not actually, for here, as everywhere, the real source of Prophetic words is the Torah. And God had announced: "For Mine is the land, you are strangers and sojourners with Me" (Lev. 25) in whom the Divine Will keeps aflame the constant awareness of Yisrael's dependence on God. This, as we shall explain, bestows upon the land a name all its own.

Palestine . . . the land of the Philistines — a Roman term of ridicule designed to extinguish from the record of history any remembrance of the existence of a Jewish state. The Prophets went even further in their choice of a title. The land to which God brought His people in order to transform the desecrated soil into God's land is called "land of the Canaanites" (Ex. 13). When this land lost its Divine Character through Israel's guilt the Prophet (Yech. 16) branded in words of stinging rebuke the degeneration and alienation which even surpassed "the sin of the sister Sodom"; he does not hesitate to restore the label "land of Canaan" to this desecrated soil (ff.) — for at this price the Canaanites could also have remained in the land.

Admas Yisrael (Is. 14, Yech. 37) the Prophets call our land, a soil which seeks the union with Israel (as *Adomoh-Le'odom*) and tolerates the Jewish people only if it proves itself to be "Israel" — and if not it will "vomit" the people out (Lev. 18). To him who sets foot on this land the admonition of the Prophet rings even stronger: *Admas Hakodesh* (Zech. 2): "Soil of sacred destiny". This awareness must never leave us for an instant; it must motivate our deeds and sanctify our will. For wherever we tread we are met by the Divine call with which God's messenger once challenged Joshua (Josh. 5): "Remove your shoes from your feet, for the ground upon which you stand — it is soil of sacred destiny". (Ex. 5).

It is certainly true that the constant awareness of Divine rulership must never leave us — wherever we may be. For "God's is the earth and all that fills it" — and every place on earth is transformed into "God's Mountain", "God's holy site" (Ps. 24) where only devotion to the service of God entitles us to stay. But with man's estrangement from God the world's alienation from God goes hand in hand. Since then the earth smarts under the oppressive domination of man. Since then God awaits the "heritage" which is to be His "share" from *man's world* and from humanity. Israel was to be. "God's share, God's heritage" (Deut. 32), "the first of the fruit to be reaped by God" (Yer. 2) — and Eretz Yisrael was to be. "God's inheritance".

For God guided His people which His creative will awakened to life and which can exist only through Him, and implanted it "in the Mountain of His heritage, in the site of His presence on earth, in the sanctuary founded by God's hands" (Ex. 16): Through God's nation the Divinely sanctified soil was to be transformed into one singular Mount of Sanctity looming high to a humanity estranged from God as a symbol of the Divine claim of inheritance to His realm of earth and mankind. Who can then measure the. gloom of the Prophet's mourning (Yer. 2): ". . . but you came and desecrated *My* land and walked *My* heritage in abomination"! —

Have we who tread upon the soil of our homeland still an ear for this stirring plaint? Do we feel shame. for our brethren who respond with derisive laughter to this heart-rending pain;

who feel no compunction to demonstrate to a world which is familiar with the Book of the Prophets how the very descendants of this people ridicule their own leaders?

Upon reaching the site of the Holy Land we tear "Keriah" as a sign of mourning, exactly as we do at the passing of father or mother. For Eretz Yisrael does not meet us in a happy frame of mind. True, we absorb with pleasure all that is beautiful and admirable: Kibutzim which build the land in the spirit of Torah, teeming Torah centers where our sacred life-values are nourished with a fervent devotion probably unmatched anywhere else in the Jewish world — scenes which impress themselves deeply on the soul of every thinking Jew. In every other country such impressions would create a feeling of profound satisfaction. Not so in the Holy Land. Here we are confronted by the painful realization, that the Torah-true population is unfortunately a numerical minority as against large Jewish masses which cherish the illusion that God's land may be possessed by a people alienated from God's Torah!

Let us face it: the Jewish state in its present form is far from being a State of God. This realization is the basis for the desperate struggle of Torah Jewry in Israel for the salvation of Torah in Israel. — Are not the establishment of the state and the resurrection of the land from the decay of millenia Divine challenges to our people: are you ready for your ultimate redemption? — That is why every truly Jewish man or woman must tremble for the future of the state, for the future of our land.

Yet we need not tremble for the future of God's Torah. Our anxiety is directed to our people and its God-willed destiny. Despite the fateful significance of the tasks confronting Torah-true Jewry in the Holy Land it would be of even greater fateful consequence were we to underestimate the importance of strengthening Torah-true Jewry in the Golah. We applaud him who chooses to make his permanent domicile in Israel in order to support and strengthen the cause of Torah in the Holy Land. However, in view of the regrettable state of affairs, a visitor to Israel will be burdened by the experiences which may be expected in the Golah but are unbearable in the Holy Land.

OUR LONGING FOR ERETZ YISROEL

אעברה נא ואראה את הארץ הטובה אשר בעבר הירדן ההר הטוב הזה והלבנון.
"Would that I could cross over and behold the good land
beyond the Yarden, this good mountain, and the Lebanon"—
into these words Moshe Rabbenu pours his flaming desire to
reach the Land of Promise for which he had reared his people in
a lifetime of dedicated labor. The sacred leaders of our people
learned from Moshe when they lent moving expression to their
longing for Eretz Yisroel and their love for the homeland (ibid.
end of Mass. Kessuboth). This longing never left the heart of the
Jewish people; it will continue to live on in the Jewish soul so
long as the Jewish people conceives of its tasks as the Nation of
God.

The Sages formulated a searching interpretation of
Moshe's longing:

מפני מה נתאוה משה רבנו ליכנס לא"י וכי לאכל מפריה או לשבוע מטובה הוא
צריך, אלא אמר הרבה מצות נצטוו ישראל ואין מתקיימין אלא בא"י, אכנס אני
כדי שיתקיימו על ידי. (מס' סוטה י"ד.)

Why was Moshe filled with longing for Eretz Yisroel? Was
he attracted by its exquisite fruit? Did he seek material satisfaction? Far from it. Moshe realized that Israel was given many
duties which could only be fulfilled in the Land. He longed for
the fulfillment of these duties.

לאכל מפריה ולשבוע מטובה. These words are familiar to us for
they are twice repeated in our so-called "great Nach-Brocho"

138

We bless God for the "delightful, good and wide land which God gave as heritage to our ancestors in order that they may eat of its fruit and be satisfied of its goodness"; and we pray for our return ונאכל מפריה ונשבע מטובה. The talmudic source (Berachoth 44a) quotes these words at the beginning but omits them at the end of the ברכה. The Rambam leaves them out entirely, as does the טור (בשם ס' המצות) who comments, in the sense of the aforementioned quote from Mass. Sota, that these words are not being recited because "our longing for the land is not directed towards its fruit but the Mitzvoth which await us there". The רי"ף, on the other hand, quotes the end of the ברכה in the form in which we recite it.

We are convinced (comp. ב"ח) that our version is fully justified and that neither its first part שהנחלת וכו' nor certainly the conclusion ונאכל מפריה וכו' contradict in any way the talmudic quote from Mass. Sota. By its very formulation this ברכה has much to tell us in our time as it demands of us a confession which, if it is not to remain mere lip service, expresses that genuine longing for Eretz Yisroel, in the spirit of Moshe Rabbenu, whose continuous nourishment and growth form the prerequisite for our ultimate Geulah.

The Sages seem to place the real stress of the question לאכל מפריה או לשבוע מטובה הוא צריך on the words: הוא צריך (not מאוה): did Moshe *need* the enjoyment of the fruit? Did he have to prove himself through their enjoyment? Still, this is the argument advanced by the Prophet Jeremiah (Ch. 2) against his people ואביא אתכם אל ארץ הכרמל לאכל פריה וטובה "I brought you into a fruitful land to enjoy its fruit and its goodness"— for in the midst of the enjoyment of material plenty the Jewish people was to prove itself as the people of God, the people which receives all its earthly possessions from God's hand to be used and evaluated in a life of Divine service. This is the spirit of the great demand (Deut. 8) ואכלת ושבעת וברכת which expects of the Jewish

people to join with "bread satisfaction" the hunger for ברכה: not
to experience physical enjoyment without the intense desire to
take hold of these Divinely granted material gifts in order to
place them in the service of a Jewish life which is dedicated to
the blessing of God, i.e. the furtherance of the precepts of His
Divine Will. This, then, was to be the "test" of the Jewish
people at the "enjoyment of the fruit" and the "satisfaction of
the goodness".

Was it really necessary for Moshe—so the Sages ask with
justification—to prove himself? His longing for Eretz Yisroel
was indeed a longing for those Mitzvoth which could only be
fulfilled in the Holy Land.—We proclaim in our "Nach-
B'rocho" that God has given Eretz Yisroel as possession to our
ancestors לאכל מפריה ולשבוע מטובה. When, at the conclusion, we
express the hope to re-possess our land, we are actually permeated by the desire ונאכל מפריה ונשבע מטובה to which we join our
determination ונברכך עליה בקדושה ובטהרה to take hold of its material plenty in order to bless God with a life of sanctity and
purity.

Our version of the ברכה gains heightened significance by
closer inspection of its text:
רחם ה' אלקינו על ישראל עמך ועל ירושלים עירך ועל ציון משכן כבודך ועל
מזבחך ועל היכלך. ובנה ירושלים עיר הקודש במהרה בימינו והעלנו לתוכה ושמחנו
בבנינה ונאכל מפריה ונשבע מטובה ונברכך עליה בקדושה ובטהרה:
"Have mercy, God our God, on Your people Israel, on Yerusholaim Your city, and on Zion, the site of Your sanctity, on
Your altar and on Your Temple; and build Yerusholaim, the
Holy City, soon in our days, and lead us up to it and let us
rejoice in its building; we desire to eat of its fruit and to satisfy
ourselves of its goodness, and we will bless you over it in sanctity and purity".

Build Yerusholaim, the Holy City, and lead us up towards
it: ונאכל מפריה וכו' refers to Yerusholaim, the Holy City, for

whose wealth of fruit and goodness we long. This is a longing upon whose truthfulness and honesty our redemption and return depend. For it is not the longing for material plenty which makes Eretz Yisroel so precious to us but the longing for those values of life which await us only in Yerusholaim, upon "Zion's height". Jeremiah (Ch. 31) lends moving expression to this longing: his prophetic eye views the return of the lost ten tribes, the "intoxicated of Ephraim" as characterized by Isaiah (Ch. 28) in a term of painful tragedy, who were "overcome by wine", enslaved by material plenty, robbed of every ennobling Divine distinction, and fell victim to the Divinely wrought storm of time. Now they return home, "in tears they return home, with fervent prayers I lead them home; I guide them along rivers of waters, in a straight way, upon which they shall no longer stumble, for I am become again Father to Israel and Ephraim is My first-born" (Jer. ibid). "And they return home—and they rejoice upon Zion's height ונהרו אל טוב ה' and stream towards the Goodness of God, over corn and wine and oil, over sheep and the wealth of cattle (which do not attract them)—ועמי את טובי ישבעו "My people, they satisfy themselves at My Goodness": Our ברכה teaches us to long for this Goodness by letting us pronounce, "build Yerusholaim, the Holy City, and lead us up towards it; we desire to eat of its fruit and to satisfy ourselves of *its* goodness".

Let us go a step further. Our ברכה asks mercy for Israel, Yerusholaim, Zion, God's Sanctuary, and then combines them all in the request: ובנה ירושלים עיר הקדש במהרה בימינו וכו' "build Yerusholaim, the Holy City, soon in our days, and lead us up towards it, and let us rejoice at its building—". Why is it that Eretz Yisroel is apparently completely ignored in this request for mercy and re-building?

The answer seems clear. Moshe Rabbenu longs for Eretz Yisroel:

ואראה את הארץ הטובה אשר בעבר הירדן ההר הטוב הזה והלבנון "I desire to
see the good land beyond the Yarden, this good mountain and
the Lebanon". This appears to refer to his eye's longing for the
"good land" which stretches from Moriah to the northernmost
border, the Lebanon. Yet the Sages comment (ברכות מ"ח: וספרי):
ההר הטוב זה ירושלים, והלבנון אין לבנון אלא ביהמ"ק, ולמה נקרא שמו לבנון
שמלבין עונותיהם של ישראל. the good Mountain, this is Yerusholaim; the Lebanon, this is the Sanctuary which is called לבנון
(white) for it transforms the sins of Israel into snowy purity.—
The Sages teach further (ibid ברכות): משה תקן ברכה הזן בשעה
שירד להם מן Moshe gave us the first ברכה of our "Table Prayer"
when the Jewish people received for the first time the heavenly
Manna.—Would that this people remain a people which is
ready, for all time to come, to receive its "bread" as Divine
Manna from God's hand!—יהושע תקן ברכת הארץ כיון שנכנסו לארץ
Joshua gave us the second ברכה when our people entered its
land: would that our Jewish people conceive of its land, for all
time to come, in the spirit of this ברכה, never to think of its land
without תורה and ברית for whose realization alone it received the
land from God's hand!

דוד ושלמה תקנו בונה ירושלים, דוד תקן על ישראל עמך ועל ירושלים עירך,
שלמה תקן על הבית הגדול והקדוש King David and Shelomo gave us
the third ברכה which, while it assumes Galuth character in its
present form, was recited as prayers by the builders of Zion and
Yerusholaim and given by them to their people because they
were deeply convinced that the Jewish people would only then
remain a nation among nations, retain its land as state among
states, as long as Zion and Yerusholaim find their God-willed
convocation in the life of the Jewish nation without whose "rebuilding" this people would irrevocably forfeit its right to exist.

When will Zion-Yerusholaim be re-built? When the Divine
Will of Torah, as laid down in Zion, encompasses the teeming
life of Yerusholaim in sanctity and dedication; when, in this

sense, Yerusholaim, i.e. life dominated by Zion, embraces all of Eretz Yisroel within its walls; when on its "holy Mount", at this "site of the Divine Law", "Judah and all its cities dwell in unity, also the men of the fields who move after the flock" (Jer. 31)—in such an Eretz Yisroel which, as God's Land, receives Zion's blessing even on its most distant hills, Yerusholaim will find its ultimate perfection as "holy city"; such an Eretz Yisroel will be ארץ הטובה, the "good land" which Moshe Rabbenu hoped to receive for himself and for his people.

Similarly comment the Sages (ibid ברכות): ברכת המזון מן התורה, ואכלת ושבעת וברכת, זו ברכת הזן, על הארץ זו ברכת הארץ, הטובה זו בונה ירושלים; they find the three ברכות of our daily Grace embodied in the verse ואכלת וכו'; the second ברכה expresses the blessing על הארץ while על הארץ הטובה envisions the rebuilding of Yerusholaim; for only when Yerusholaim is truly "built" does Eretz Yisroel become the "good" land.

They teach further (ibid.): to the inquiry as to the source for the duty to pronounce the "Nach b'rocho" on the Torah, a Sage replied:

אינו צריך הרי הוא אומר על הארץ הטובה אשר נתן לך, ולהלן הוא אומר ואתנה לך את לוחות האבן והתורה והמצוה this duty is also implied in the verse with the words: bless God for the land "which He has given to you", for God has also "given" the Torah to His people. To receive land from God's hand and bless God for it means nothing else but to offer thanks to God for the לוחות through which He has given His Torah. Thus Eretz Yisroel is the Divinely given לוחות in the form of material life formation which receives its sanctifying dedication through God's Torah.—

However another sage comments: אינו צריך ה"ה אומר טובה הטובה, טובה זו תורה (וכן הוא אומר כי לקח טוב נתתי לכם) הטובה זו בנין ירושלים (וכן הוא אומר ההר הטוב הזה). the "Nach b'rocho" on the Torah is already implied in the words: bless God for the "good land"—for only when Torah lives in this land, only when Yerusholaim is re-built, does Eretz Yisroel become the "good land."

Moshe Rabbenu longed for such an Eretz Yisroel which is unthinkable to him in any other form. According to the profound insight of the Sages, Moshe's fervent prayer ו'אראה את הארץ הטובה ההר הטוב הזה והלבנן, "I desire to see the "good" land, culminates in the words ההר הטוב הזה והלבנן as Moshe envisions a land which receives its sanctification through the all-embracing domination of Zion and Yerusholaim ההר הטוב זו ירושלים, in which the holy Mount of Zion rises as Yerusholaim והלבנן זו בהמ"ק and where the purifying and atoning potency of the בהמ"ק reaches to the most distant snowy heights of the Lebanon!—

Our longing is directed to such an Eretz Yisroel. Our "Nach b'rocho" expresses it in moving terms: רחם ה' אלקינו על ישראל וכו' Bestow mercy oh God, upon Israel, Yerusholaim, Zion, Your Sanctuary;—if Israel, Yerusholaim, Zion, are to be living truths, then ובנה ירושלים וכו' Yerusholaim must rise as the erected "holy city" which places all of Eretz Yisroel with its entire wealth of material blessings in homage at the feet of Zion and its Divinely charted precepts of life.

The return to *such* an Eretz Yisroel is then in truth a return to Yerusholaim והעלנו לתוכה ושמחנו בבנינה for with each act of enjoyment of material benefit granted to us by Eretz Yisroel we bless God in gratitude for the precious values with which Zion-Yerusholaim elevates our lives towards the proximity of God in sanctity and dedication.

RABBINER HIRSCH IN ERETZ YISROEL

Eretz Yisroel is in the grip of a raging cultural battle ("Kulturkapmf"); a development all the more tragic as it involves our Holy Land, its State, its population and its Rabbinate. Proclaiming religious freedom the State, in its educational system and cultural program, caters fully to the way of life adopted by the religiousless Jewish masses. The reform and conservative movements are also actively preparing to establish themselves on holy soil. Still, the State hesitates to take the fateful step of depriving Torah-true Jewry and its Rabbinate of its remaining prerogatives (mainly in the area of marriage law). The Torah-true population, consisting of the so-called "old Yishuv" and immigrants from all over the world who have found a homeland in the Holy Land, faces difficult tasks. While men and women are united in their determination to rear their children as conscientious Torah-Jews, it is not surprising that they are deeply divided in their various approaches to education which culminates in the desire to maintain the educational standards and values to which they were accustomed in their countries of origin. However, these are trends which are familiar to us in the United States, especially in New York.

Conscious of the eminently timely significance of Rabbiner Hirsch's teachings for the contemporary Torah-True Jewry in America, our Kehilla considers itself as successor and bearer of

Rabbiner Hirsch's community and ideology and entrusts its
school system with its educational and cultural ideals to the
guidance of the great leader in Israel. As his program once saved
the Torah-true Jewry of Western Europe, so our Kehilla confidently expects his spiritual leadership to succeed in rearing its
youth to become upright and conscientious Jews who, surrounded by foreign cultural influences, are מקרב הגאולה with their
lives.

This way, important as it is for America, is perhaps of
greater significance for Eretz Yisroel. Rabbiner Hirsch is alive
in the Holy Land. This was impressively demonstrated by a
book which appeared there under the title רב ש. ר. הירש משנתו
ושיטתו "Rabbiner Hirsch: his teaching and his way". The
Hebrew volume, containing a number of articles by prominent
writers, is introduced by a lively Hirsch biography which is followed by excerpts from the Torah commentary; Mitzvoth and
their meaning; Halacha and the Hirsch Commentary; evaluation of the "Nineteen Letters" and "Chorev"; the Kehilla: its
structure, character and significance for the entity of our
people; Hirsch's predecessors; also memoranda and responsa.

A central place in this work is reserved for those articles
which deal with the way of education and culture proclaimed by
Rabbiner Hirsch under the motto of Torah im Derech Eretz.
One of the three pertinent treatises notes that the question of the
attitude towards the demands and implications of the Torah im
Derech Eretz precept agitates all circles of contemporary orthodoxy, especially in Eretz Yisroel. Western European Torah-true
Jewry owes its survival to its loyal adherence to this precept.
Does this teaching also bear inherent dangers? Unquestionably
so. It has cost victims in the past and will also have them in the
future. Yet the author poses this pointed question: Is not the
way of life which aims at the complete isolation of the youth
from the influences of the contemporary world of culture a far

more dangerous one? The tragic victims of the Haskala in Eastern Europe speak a moving language. Torah-true Jewry in Eretz Yisroel cannot afford to forgo the presence of Torah-true academicians, teachers, physicians, lawyers, engineers, farmers, scientists, economists. Through intensive study in the Yeshivoth, training centers of Jewish Torah living, our youth in Eretz Yisroel must draw the strength to live up to the tasks of life as upright, uncompromising and conscientious Jews.

Rabbiner Hirsch was well aware that his Torah im Derech Eretz precept would not find the wholehearted acceptance of all Torah leaders in the Jewish world. He was also well aware of the talmudical references to the occupation with מינות ואפיקורסות which are also quoted in one of the treatises in this Hirsch volume. Rabbiner Hirsch was above all a historical thinker and thus he saw his teaching of Torah im Derech Eretz imbedded in the תורת כהנים to ויקרא (18,4) which contains the following phrases so significant for the study of the Divine word:

ללכת בהם: עשם עיקר, ואל תעשם טפלה. ללכת בהם, שלא יהא משאך ומתנך אלא בהם, שלא תערב בהם דברים אחרים בעולם, שלא תאמר, למדתי חכמת ישראל, אלמד חכמת אומות העולם, תלמוד לומר, ללכת בהם, אינך רשאי ליפטר מתוכן.

This means: ללכת בהם, the goal of all your strivings must be directed at them (the laws of Torah); they must be to you the primary, absolute premise, and not the secondary, changeable by-product. All your spiritual and intellectually creative activity should be motivated exclusively by them without the added mixture of foreign substance. Thus, you may not say: I have absorbed the Jewish science, now I shall turn to the sciences of other nations. Therefore it says: ללכת בהם, you may not move outside their sphere.

"If we interpret these words correctly, the introductory remark עשם עיקר ואל תעשם טפלה opposes the contention that the ensuing sentences might imply the complete exclusion of any knowledge and science gained and applied in non-Jewish circles and not directly connected with the realm of Torah. The pre-scription of עשם עיקר ואל תעשם טפלה pre-supposses the validity of the study of other fields of human culture. What it does mean is that we must make absolutely certain that the science of Torah and the knowledge emanating from it remain the central, firm and supremely unchangeable entity. Secular cultures may be studied only as an auxiliary force and only inasmuch as they truly help to promote the study of Torah wisdom, subordinating themselves as the טפל to the עיקר. Torah and its eternal truths must be everywhere and at all times the supreme measure and judge of any knowledge flowing from other sciences. True and good be to us only that which is able to stand up before the truth of Torah. All our intellectual perception and creative thinking shall always move forward within the orbit of Torah and the course prescribed by its maxims, so that we accept and retain only that which meets the test of Torah and refuse to allow the injection into our Torah-dominated science of any foreign idea or thought emanating from different viewpoints and attitudes."

"Torah-science must never be one among many sciences in that there would exist for us a Jewish science, a Jewish truth in the same degree of importance and authority as secular sciences and secular truths. Upon absorbing the Torah-science to the best of our abilities, we must never turn in the same spirit and with similar motivation to the acquisition of secular culture, giv-ing it equal status with Torah-science and Torah truth, an atti-tude that by its very lack of uniform conviction and stand-point would surely spell spiritual and moral bankruptcy as a result of the inner conflict in knowledge and thinking."

"As true as Torah is Divinely created and all other human sciences and wisdom are but man-made products containing relative and eminently flexible deductions and conclusions of man's insight in the nature of life—so truly there is to us only one all-decisive science and truth which alone may evaluate the culture of the world in their relative importance. Thus, even while we are occupied exploring other fields of science and knowledge, we must never once leave the foundation and aims of our Torah to which all our spiritual and intellectual labor must be dedicated: אינך רשאי ליפטר מתוכן."

Rabbiner Hirsch's reply to an inquiry from Eastern Europe in regard to Torah im Derech Eretz is typical of him: he considers his educational and cultural program essential for Western Europe in view of the circumstances there; whether it is right for the countries of the East should be decided by their own Torah leaders.

The afore-mentioned treatise in the Hirsch volume is perfectly right in demanding that scientific and biological theories discussed in our schools must be evaluated in the light of Torah and its eternal truths. It maintains that the occupation with מינות ואפיקורסות, if connected with academic studies, cannot be avoided and this will be the case as long as we do not have *Jewish* universities where the spirit of Torah rules, before whose throne of majesty all scientific theories must establish their right of admission. It declares emphatically that Torah-true Jewry in Eretz Yisroel cannot afford to do without academic studies.

In a profound treatise, Rabbi Josef Weinberg, Montreux (a recognized Torah Great) shows how Rabbiner Hirsch's attitude to general cultural values is determined by the world and life view ("Weltanschauung") to which God's Torah guides its followers—and they are all those who consider themselves members of the nation of God. He concludes that Rabbiner Hirsch, as he was a hundred years ago, is and must be the spiritual leader who will once again rescue large segments of our people from threatening secularization and assimilation.

In the preface to the Hirsch volume, the editor discusses the aims which the book is intended to serve: that which Rabbiner

Hirsch meant to an era when the walls of the Ghetto fell and a new fateful epoch began for Western European Jewry, he must and can also be to our youth of today which is faced with a new epoch fraught with dangers and problems emanating from the rise of the Jewish state on holy soil.

ERETZ YISROEL
AND THE GOLAH*

I

The creation of a Jewish State in Eretz Yisroel is a world-historic event deeply affecting our people in all its parts as well as the nations of the world. What is the attitude that we, as Torah-true Yehudim, are to take in relation to this event?

We have expressed it repeatedly in all clarity and intensity: This State will have a future only if and as long as it is organized as a Jewish State, i.e. a State of God, rising on sacred soil. It will be a State of God if it proclaims the Torah as the fundamental law of its constitution and propagates its practical realization in the life of our people.

For as long as our people are imbued with the knowledge of its position as the nation of God; as long as it is an irrevocable truth that God created the Jewish people with His ולקחתי אתכם לי לעם, "I will take you for myself as a nation," (Ex. 6, 7); as long as it is true that our people owes its existence not to its land but to the Sinai which witnessed its birth as a nation היום הזה נהיית לעם, "today you became a nation," (Deut. 27, 9); as long as it remains true that our people received from God's hand the land that was promised to the forefathers, to fulfill on this God-owned soil לי הארץ, "Mine is the land," (Lev. 25, 23), in the midst of the nations, its God-willed mission on earth, we can

*This essay was written in the Spring of 1949.

conceive of a Jewish State only if it unites as the State of God, the People of God in the Land of God. Any other attitude would mean the denial of the tragic experiences of our historic past.

The world-shaking predictions of the Torah in the majestic chapters of the תוכחה have already come true twice in the course of our history. Twice the Jewish State broke apart because it failed to conform to the conditions set by God's Torah which alone would guarantee its continued existence. If after almost two thousand years there is again a Jewish state taking shape on sacred ground, the very same laws apply to it which God's Torah formulated for all eternity.

God's Torah and God's Prophets have predicted the Galuth of our people with all its tragic aspects as an inevitable result of the refusal to comply with the Divine demands. "Galuth" is a terrifying term. Derived from גלה "bare, uncovered," it describes the state of a people deprived of its most important assets, its land and state. Deprived of its state, robbed of its land, a nation, dispersed throughout the world, faces certain doom. Not so the Jewish people. For as a nation we owe nothing to the land, our national character owes nothing to the State. The creative Will of God formed us into a nation in the midst of the wilderness; God's Torah is the tie which firmly unites all parts of our nation. Torn from our native soil, catapulted into the midst of the nations (thus Golah refers to that part of the nation which lives outside of Eretz Yisroel), we have remained a nation because God's Torah guided us through Galuth. We will remain a nation as long as God's Torah remains the essence, the soul of our existence. It is the God-willed task of the Galuth to prepare and educate us through the Torah for our eventual return to the land promised to us and to our ancestors under these conditions. It is an immensely difficult task whose successful solution is constantly menaced—foremost among the dangers being the threat of assimilation with its deadly consequences. These dangers have been predicted by God's Torah and Prophets. The potent force of the Torah must prove itself by the victorious struggle against these dangers, thus solving the task of the Galuth.

Nothing can change this, even if in our time a Jewish State is again to rise on sacred ground. It only serves to give increased actuality to the task of the Golah.

"Eretz Yisroel and the Golah in the past and in the present"—by exploring this question we follow the admonition of the "Song of our fate" for our road through history זכור ימות עולם בינו שנות דור ודור (Deut. 32, 7): Consult the days of the past, retain vividly what the past teaches you, and you will understand the present, know its demands and your duties!

The Golah of our people has never ceased to long for the Geulah of our people. Intimately connected with the Geulah-longing was its intense love for Eretz Yisroel. Coupled with this longing and love was the strong determination to accelerate the Geulah of our people by means that alone can bring about redemption.

There was always among the Jewish people an elite which realized its position as God's nation and kept faith with the Torah. In our national history it has never been decisive whether this elite was numerically strong or small: אתם המעט "you are the few in number," (Deut. 7, 7). This was true for the periods of both the first and second Jewish state. During the existence of the first State this preservation of the faith was the work of the great, God-sent Prophets and their disciples. While the State lost its Jewish character as rapidly as the Galuth approached, they succeeded in salvaging a שארית, as they called it, a "nucleus" for the cause of Torah. And when Babylonia (6th century B.C.E.) destroyed the Sanctuary and wrecked the State, there were among the exiles, (Yecheskel was one of them,) חרש והמסגר "craftsmen and locksmiths" (Kings II 24, 14): These, according to the Sages, were the spiritual leaders who "hammered and built" at the future of our people in the Golah of Babel.

This Golah in the Babylonian "two-stream-land" (between Euphratus and Tigris) was destined by Divine Providence to be of immeasurable significance for the entire future of our people and its Torah.

True, our people experienced Geulah after seventy years' return to Eretz Yisroel, restoration of the second Sanctuary, rebuilding of its second State. Was this Sanctuary to be the everlasting one, would this second State last? Its future depended on whether God's Zion-Sanctuary, i.e. the Torah, was allowed to govern the entire realm of Jewish life and shape the land of God in accordance with the Divine plan. It depended on the ability of the Jewish State to prove itself as the State of God. This second State lasted over four hundred years, as long as the first Sanctuary. Yet, what are four hundred years in the history of the Jewish people? An episode of tragic proportions.

Greek and subsequently Roman influences contributed to the increasing disintegration of the second Jewish State, rapidly depriving it of its God-willed character. Rulers arose who attempted to secure the welfare and future of the State by political maneuvers and power-politics and succeeded in convincing a large part of the people that theirs was the right leadership. This sealed the fate of the State in the eyes of all to whom God's Torah was the only and eternal truth.

Our spiritual leaders made valiant attempts to save the State. At the same time they strove, with every means at their disposal, to rescue at least a "nucleus" of their people from the deadly entanglement of such a State. Theirs was an overwhelming success. Aside from the Anshe Kenesseth Hagdolah, this was primarily the work of our immortal teachers, the Tannaim.

Under the hammer blows of Roman might, Sanctuary and State broke apart (70 C.E.) and Jewish blood flowed in unending streams. Yet while Rome celebrated its supposedly final victory over Judaism and the Jewish nation, the surviving remnants of the people rose again and under the incomparable leadership of its great teachers, embarked upon a golden age of spiritual rejuvenation unequaled in the history of mankind: On the ruins of land and state the Jewish tree of life sank its roots deeply into the sacred soil. Yet all this would not have been possible if, prior to the destruction of the State, the groundwork for God's Torah and Jewish life had not been laid in the Golah, in the land between Euphrates and Tigris. Eretz Yisroel and this Golah, their houses of learning, teachers and disciples, maintained a constant mutually beneficial contact and exchange of ideas of which the Talmud is the great and eternal monument.

When the Roman fury of persecution made the existence of the Yeshivoth in Eretz Yisroel increasingly precarious (during the 2nd and 3rd centuries) and slowly undermined Jewish life in Eretz Yisroel, this Golah became the second homeland of our people for many centuries (until the year 1,000).

What would have become of Judaism, what of our people, if Divine Providence had not charted the course!

II

Wherever God's Torah and thereby Jewish life can develop freely, there is our real home. This profound truth was deeply impressed upon the soul of our Galuth-people by its great leaders who manifested its significance in various phases of the Jewish law.

חיבת הארץ, the longing for and love of our land, is very precious and dear to us. Nothing can surpass the moving and eloquent words that the Talmud—at the end of Kesuboth—finds for this emotion. Yet, the longing for and love of Torah must be even more precious, more intense: As the Rabbis once branded the exodus from Eretz Yisroel as a sinful action, so they now opposed strongly the tendency to leave Babel, the land of Torah.

During long centuries, Jewish life in Eretz Yisroel was almost extinguished. Galuth dispersed the Jews throughout distant lands. Yet wherever they settled, they were taught by their

spiritual leaders to pronounce a Tefilloh יקום פורקן, for the preservation and welfare of the Yeshivoth and their heads, not only
in Eretz Yisroel, but especially in the Golah, in Babel. The
national prayer for rain in the שמונה עשרה is recited during the
winter, a season when in a majority of the Golah-land rain is
not needed; this prayer thinks of our homeland. Yet in Eretz
Yisroel it is already interpolated on the 7th day of Cheshvan,
while the entire Golah adds it later (on the 60th day after Teku-
fath Tishri), because then the Golah, in Babel, depends on the
falling of rain.

These prayers have remained—and they shall remain—in
spite of the fact that Jewish life in the "two-river-country" has
been practically non-existent during the past 1,000 years. The
Golah of our people must remember this for all time to come:
all its love and longing must be directed toward Eretz Yisroel;
but its true homeland lies wherever God's Torah finds its resting
place!

Our people finds itself in the Galuth. It has become used to
wanderings. Yet God's Torah wanders with it into the exile.
Therein lies the secret of its preservation, the immortality of our
people.

The "two-river country" was our second homeland. Even
before we were deprived of it over 900 years ago, Divine Providence prepared various other countries as homelands for God's
Torah. Jewish life emerged and developed in North Africa,
Southern Italy, Spain, the Gallic countries and Germania.
There was constant literary and spiritual contact between these
lands and the Babylonian nerve-center of Jewish intellectual
activity, a unique phenomenon in the cultural history of mankind. When the latter gradually lost its importance, the Torah
settled in the Western countries where it opened new vistas of
learning and Jewish culture.

Proud indeed are the memories we associate with the
Spanish period, which, despite its length of 500 years, was but a
period in the extensive history of our people. It was ended by the

barbaric persecution and terror unfolded by the Church. The survivors fled to Italy, the Netherlands, Turkey and also to Eretz Yisroel. Thus God's Torah found new resting places and homelands, especially in Turkey.

Jewish life in France and Germany, equalling that of the Spanish golden age in intensity and intellectual significance, suffered pitifully under bloody persecution during these centuries. Divine Providence again intervened and provided our people and its Torah with a new homeland in the wide areas of the Polish Kingdom. The torrent of wandering flooded from West to East only to reverse the direction in the 17th and 18th centuries. The same picture recurs inevitably: God's Torah wanders with God's nation.

Throughout these long centuries, there lived in our people the longing for Geulah, the longing for the ancestral homeland. There also grew the strong and holy determination in the heart of every faithful Jew—wherever he happened to be—to bring about the final Geulah by the full devotion of his life to Torah and the realization of its demands.

III

Now, in our time, Divine Providence has plunged our people into a catastrophe of unheard of, inconceivable proportions. One full third of our people fell victim to brutal destruction. Wide lands were devastated where once Torah and Jewish life flourished. Those who succeeded in escaping from the holocaust sought new goals, a new homeland.

What role is America destined to play in the strategy of Divine Providence? There remains a mysterious yet undeniable fact: America was discovered in the same year (1492) which saw the infamous expulsion of the Jews from Spain. This great land, America, opened its gates to the unfortunates in the world, absorbed the endless flow of refugees from Eastern Europe at the close of the last century, and now has also granted us refuge.

In this time of crisis, filled to the brim with suffering and martyrdom, the eyes of our people, as never before in two thousand years, turn longingly to Eretz Yisroel. All Jewish hearts are profoundly stirred by the latest developments. The land, sacred to God, deserted and waste during long centuries, home for a few isolated Jewish settlements, this land awakens from its long sleep, resounds with new activity, absorbs great masses of our people who embark upon the formation of the Jewish State: A historic event of fateful importance and significance.

There must live in us this unshakeable conviction: This state will last only if it will rise as God's state on God-holy soil. This alone will prevent it from suffering the fate of the previous Jewish States. Will this state live up to this condition? It is still a question, a source of terrible worry. We wished it were no longer a question!

As certain as it is that this state, the mere fact of its formation, does not mean that the Geulah has arrived, as potent is its ability—as perhaps never before in our Galuth-history—to hasten the coming of the Geulah. What a tragedy if this state, either by delusion or folly, were to prolong the Galuth and provoke new and terrible catastrophies! May Hashem prevent this from happening.

Can there still be a doubt as to the tasks which await the Golah in these fateful times? It is of supreme importance that our brothers and sisters, the Yereim in the Holy Land, never forget for a moment that this state can last if it matures into a state of God; that they do their utmost to achieve this goal with combined forces. It is of supreme importance that they are supported and strengthened in this fight by all Yereim in the Golah. This support could be given most effectively by ever-increasing waves of immigration of our Torah-true brethren, especially the young element. But it is equally important that we, as part of our people in the Golah—its majority living in the United

States—realize clearly the tremendous responsibility which faces the Golah in our time.

The following thought must be emphasized again and again; What would have become of our people, what of God's Torah if, at the time of the second Jewish State, the Jewish intellectual life had been confined to Eretz Yisroel instead of finding at the same time a homeland in the "two-river country"? If in our time—and we pray that it may come true—Eretz Yisroel will become a land of Torah, if the state will become a state of Torah, then it is certain that rich blessing will emanate from Eretz Yisroel to all parts of the Golah. If this is not the case—and there is no certainty that it will be—the Golah (and this includes us) is faced with this urgent and holy duty: to strive, with all the means at our disposal towards the strengthening of the Jewish life in the Golah; to enable the Jewish tree of life, the Torah, to take ever stronger roots in our lives. This is our sacred duty. We owe it to God, to God's Torah, to our people, to Eretz Yisroel—and we owe it to our children!

CRISIS IN THE HOLY LAND*

"Will birth-pangs seize the land (but) on *one day?* Will the nation be born at once? Will Zion bear her children in the midst of her labor?"

(Is. 66)

"Labor precedes the birth," proclaims the Prophet to the mourners for Zion and Yerushalayim as he paints for them the Yerushalayim of the future in all its brilliant glory, paving the way for the ultimate Geulah of his people. His people's sufferings the Prophet interprets as the painful labor which leads to the re-birth of his nation. Zion suffers with the tribulations of his people, as does the land of God. They too, Zion and the land, achieve their final, long awaited redemption in the re-birth of our people.

The past Galuth history of our nation—almost two thousands years old—was filled with indescribable suffering. To the Prophet they were the sufferings which precede ultimate re-birth. The hour of re-birth appeared to have arrived in our time. The Jewish State, restored by Divine Providence, seemed to be the instrument of this great event. But deep and bitter disappointment filled Zion and God's land and with them all those who mourn for Zion and Yerushalayim: the hour of re-birth had not arrived.

They who mourn for Zion and Yerushalayim are deeply troubled as they follow the events in the Holy Land. It bitterly

*This essay was written in the Spring of 1959.

160

pains us to witness the desecration of the holy soil by wide segments of the population which belie and deny the Divine nobility of the Jewish name. They can never be children of God's land, children for whom Zion longs.

It is true that "Charedim"—as the Prophets calls them (Is. 66, V. 5)—to whom God's sacred Torah-Will represents the loftiest task of life, fight the heroic battle for Zion and Yerushalayim in ever increasing numbers. But we must note with profound regret that the lack of guidance by the great Torah leaders—who, thank God, abound in the Holy Land—has still prevented the "Charedim" from achieving the unity which would be so urgently required. The future of the land, however, is decided by the Jewish State whose own fate is insolvably tied with the fate of the Holy Land.

The clearer we realize that the birth-pangs of the Holy Land did not end with the founding of the State but rather continued to increase with unabated violence, the less we can fail to recognize the difficulties the government faces considering the heterogenous population of the country. Thus, we cannot hope to expect from the Jewish State and its government that which will only become reality when God's land and God's Zion will witness the real re-birth of God's nation.

However, our patience is being stretched beyond all limits when the government proceeds on a course which severely threatens the future existence of Divine Judiasm. We are referring to the incredible attempt of a Jewish government in the question of the identity card, to accord recognition as a Jew to anyone who declares himself as such (even though he may be the son of a non-Jewish mother) without having undergone the lawfully prescribed process of acceptance into Judaism. This move represents the vilest onslaught against Divine Judaism and the nation of God. It proves only too clearly to what extent this government lacks even the most elementary incentive to live up to the demands of the Divine Law. It may not even be conscious of the ridicule it heaps on—let us label it—"the Jewish religion" in the eyes of the adherents of other religions. While it is unlikely that this frivolous motion will ever become law, the very fact that such an attempt was made at all is outrageous as well as humiliating.

The Holy Land and the Jewish State are beset by serious internal crises and threatened by no less serious external dangers. "Who would not tremble—who would not hear God's warning call designed to protect our suffering people from even greater misery?—Who would not himself be like a prophet?" (Amos 3). Would there still be a need for the mouth of the Prophet when the Torah's monumental words of admonition have proven their infallible truthfulness throughout the millenia of our national history? Does this truth not chart the course of the Jewish State, the only course leading to a secure future—or to its inevitable destiny?

SH'MITTA IN ERETZ YISROEL

With every recurring seventh year God demands the "Shabbos of the land—Shabbos for God." During this year most of the activities connected with work on the field must cease. Whatever grows by itself during the year belongs as little to the owner as it does to the animals roaming the fields. As every seventh day proclaims God as master of the world, so every seventh year proclaims God as master of the land. "Mine is the land, strangers and sojournes are you with me" (Lev. 25).

Confronted with the reality of the emergence of a "new Yishuv," the great rabbinical leaders of the time tackled the various problems that arose: to determine, above all, whether Sh'mitta (independent of Yovel) during the Galuth is a divine law or a rabbinic rule; also to examine the possibilities (sale of the field to Gentiles and work done by them) to cope in the framework of the law with the heavy economic burden resulting from the observance of the Sh'mitta law. Even those rabbinical authorities (such as R. Yitzchok Elchonon Spektor) who assumed a more permissive attitude towards these problems, allowed their ruling to be interpreted only as a decision dictated by the need of the moment without influencing a subsequent final Halacha. Other rabbinical authorities (among them Rabbi S.R. Hirsch) admonished the "new Yishuv," in deeply moving terms, to fulfill its great and sacred duty; at the same time they called upon the entire Golah to assist their brethren, pioneers on holy soil, in unity of purpose to enable them to observe fully the sanctity of the Sh'mitta law.

It is certainly not a discovery of our time that it is difficult to bring the Sh'mitta law in conformity with agricultural requirements. The same Torah demanding the Divine Shabbos for the land offers but one answer to the question borne by worry and anxiety, the agricultural problem of "what shall we eat in the seventh year": "Fulfill my laws and my ordinances, keep and fulfill them, and you will live without care, borne by the land. The land will give its fruit, you will eat to satisfaction, and will live, free of care, borne by it—I shall command to you my blessings in the sixth year" (Lev. 25).

"If our people (in Eretz Yisroel) could only be convinced that ignoring the Sh'mitta law might, God forbid, entail punishment—the threat of drought and the locust plague. For we have to realize the following basic premise: as the preservation of the Jewish people is immediately dependent on God, completely independent of normal and lawful conditions—so Eretz Yisroel is set apart from all other lands, for its development and prosperity does not depend on the material prerequisites so essential for the other lands, but depends, as the object of Divine Providence, on the conscientious fulfillment of God's law." Thus wrote the Gaon of Wolozin (שו"ת משיב דבר).

Decades later, the great leader and famous Gaon and Yerushalmi-Commentator, R. Jacob David Ridbaz, who settled in the Holy Land at the end of a stormy life in order to fight for the sanctity of Eretz Yisroel, took the lead among the rabbinical authorities of his time in demanding the strictest adherence to the Sh'mitta law. With unparalleled sharpness he attacked the Torah-dissenters in the Holy Land. He maintained that the great leaders who propagated the "new Yishuv" did so only in the firm conviction that, tilling again the sacred soil and keeping Sh'mitta in accordance with the Torah-Law, the Jewish colonists would atone for the sins committed by their forefathers—thus moving a step closer to the coming Geulah. The Ridbaz called on the Golah to support with all resources the sacred work of the God-fearing colonists. Yet he was painfully aware of the hate generated by those estranged Jewish brethren of whom the Sohar says that, once Moshiach will prepare the world's redemption under mighty Gag-Magog struggles, these degenerated sons of the Jewish people would join the ranks of Gag-Magog in order to fight against Moshiach. And he adds the prophetic words: "This is what I fear, for history will bear this out"; and he closes with this moving prayer:

"I sink down on our sacred soil: my land, my land, do not turn into your children's prosecutor before our heavenly father. Behold the suffering of the learned men and of the holy people, writhing in pain and hurt, dissoved in tears at the desecration of your sacred Shabbos. O, entreat the Creator that He bestow mercy on us and redeem us soon, that His children may return from foreign soil and preserve your Shabbos in sanctity and purity—for Your will is our will!" (רידב״ז ה׳ שביעית).

A large number of rabbinical authorities spoke out in a similar vein and only isolated voices considered the economic problems in their halachic decision.

Divine Providence has caused the unbelievable to happen: the existence of a Jewish state on sacred soil has once again become reality. Will the state endure, will it pave the way for the ultimate Geulah of our people? Questions of tremendous consequence. In terrible seriousness God's Torah links the fate of Eretz Yisroel with the sanctity of the Sabbath-Year. The Torah proclaims the Galuth of the Jewish people and the devastation of the land as results of the desecrated Sabbath-Year:

"I will disperse you among the nations and pursue you with the sword—and your land will remain desolate and your cities—rubble. Then the land will find its satisfaction in its Sabbaths, as long as it is desolate and you are in the land of your enemies—then the land will keep the Sabbath and find satisfaction in its Sabbath-Years. For the duration of its desolation it will keep the Sabbath, the Sabbath which it did not keep during your Sabbath-Years when you lived in it" (Lev. 26, 33–35).

And now in our days God's land has awakened from desolation and devastation—a Jewish state rises on it. After two thousand years of Galuth-affliction God directs this inquiry to His people: are you finally ready, as God's nation, to welcome His Torah in His land and thus to fulfill the conditions under which God secures His people's renewed possession of the land? (Deut. 30).

The fight for the future of our land and for the ultimate Geulah of our people is led by our brothers and sisters in the Holy Land who are determined, despite all economic difficulties, to dedicate the holy soil to the Sabbath for the sanctification of the Divine name before all the world.

SHILOH'S DOWNFALL

The plaintive chords of mourning sound from Assaph's harp (Ps. 78). They mourn the misery of mankind's history. It is mourning without end. For there is no end to human misery. Divine nearness alone will banish it from the earth. Alas, men shun the nearness of God. That is why their lives are stricken by misery which is handed down from father to son.

Timidly, from time to time, Divine Shechina knocks at mankind's gate: Are you tired of your misery? Do you long for the Divine nearness of Paradise? These then are moments when the genius of mankind listens quietly—and sorrowfully veils his head at the sight of erring men indifferent to the cooling breeze of God's blissful nearness, allowing their lives to pass listlessly.

The desert presented mankind with its first Sanctuary. To us, henceforth, the desert is not barren. Of all places, it alone was able to bear the most precious gift. For, only when men see their lives rot into deserts are they willing and glad to give their utmost to help raise the sanctuary which will bestow permanence on their lives. Wherever the Sanctuary finds a lasting home, nature gains the glory of Paradise and bears men who are happy and safe under Divine protection.

Rest came. Israel's Congregation prepared to secure rest also for the Wandering Tent. In Shiloh וישכינו שם את אהל מועד (Josh. 18,1) the Tent of the Desert found its permanent resting place. This was the essence of Shiloh's sanctity. Its name is forever tied to the history of the first *resting Sanctuary*. The moment was sacred and great when Israel's Congregation erected a base of stone upon which the Desert Tent was to rise (Z'vachim 112), restless no longer, but awaiting the time the rough base would bear the eternal Mikdash.

Shiloh became a sacred center. From its sacred nearness each tribe received its heritage and each member of the people a share of the land (Josh. 18). The land became holy soil impregnated by Shiloh's Sanctuary which rose far and wide.

At Shiloh, the tribes which found a homeland East of the Jordan separated themselves from the rest of Israel. In Shiloh (ib. 22) they heard the farewell message of their beloved leader and received his passionate blessing. He had sworn them to keep the faith to Shiloh, never to forget it in distant lands. Then the tribes left. Before crossing the Jordan, they erected an altar in its majestic height, for all eyes to behold. News of the event reached Israel's sons. Was this already treason against Shiloh? United, as a Congregation, they assembled around Shiloh. Their battle cry: Fight for Shiloh! The world must not so soon mourn the Sanctuary, barely erected. Pinchas became their leader. His holy zeal imbued an entire nation. Holy a people in whose soul burns Pinchas-zeal. Shiloh lived its proudest morn.

Fortunately, their zeal found no target. They had thought wrongly of their brothers who had parted from Shiloh with heavy hearts. Anxiety filled the souls of the brothers that the Jordan, in the years ahead, might bar their return to Shiloh. Never, in all distant times, should their belonging to Shiloh be in doubt. Their monument, thus, rose for Shiloh, bearing witness to their life-blood's loyalty to the altar which rose in Shiloh "before God's Mishkan." Then, mightily, Shiloh's altar fire blazed afar. Could such flames ever be extinguished?

Once more, before his death, the dying leader gathered the Congregation of God to receive from his mouth the heritage he had sworn them to uphold. From Shiloh he had set out with the Ark of the Covenant and had called his people to Shechem (Josh. 24). In their minds, they were to retrace the steps taken by the site-seeking nearness of God ever since the time when for the first time it appeared in Shechem (Gen. 12, 6) to the oldest forefather and dedicated him, in the midst of a depraved and utterly miserable mankind, to become the bearer of the Divine Shechina and the redeemer of the world. In Shechem the cornerstone was once laid for the Sanctuary of mankind. Now, in Shechem, a whole nation united joyfully behind their leader with the moving premise henceforth "to serve God, our God, and to hearken to His voice." In the inspiration of this joyful oath of faith the Desert Tent in Shiloh, erected on a stony base, grew ever more into the Mikdash (Josh. 24, 26).

Four hundred years, almost, lasts Shiloh's history, the record of a sorry downfall reflected in the pages of the book of Judges. He will never understand its words who fails to glean from the hopelessness and sorrow of each line this challenging and pathetic question: where is Shiloh, where has Shiloh gone?

No bloodier pen could have inscribed the history of Shiloh's downfall. Shiloh called God's people to the return to Paradise. Yet Israel chose life in the desert, rejected the bliss of Paradise, and followed a lost mankind which stumbled past the gates of Paradise with blinded eyes. Israel's eyes were open, but only for a short time. Then they also closed and drowned in night and misery. All too soon, the warning testament with which the dying builder of the Shiloh Sanctuary entrusted his work to his people was fulfilled. Thus is placed Joshua's death in the Book of Judges (Chap. 2).

Shiloh could only prosper in pure surroundings. It could not be allowed to rise on soil plunged in Tum'oh by the perversion of its inhabitants. Shiloh had to demand their removal. Alas, this step required an unbending will for a firm decision—which never came.

God's spokesman had pleaded and fought for Shiloh. And the tears of the people flowed (Judges, Ch. 2). But what are the fruit of tears? At best, they could mourn Shiloh's downfall. Such tears may have also been shed in the years following. For it would be unnatural if Shiloh were no longer to evoke tears.

Shiloh's adherents will not die as long as there are men who long for the paradise.

Who could fail to be deeply moved by the sight of *Elkana* and his family during Shiloh's final years? The eyes of the Sages missed no detail. We follow him on his annual pilgrimage from his town to prostrate himself in Shiloh and to offer sacrifices to the God of Hosts. Traveling with wives, children and relatives, he spends the night at the market place in the city. The inhabitants question him as to the goal of his journey. What is your destination? To Shiloh—the ready answer—to our House of God, the source of Torah and Mitzvoth. And you, why do you not join us on our journey? And their eyes brim with tears and they join in the pilgrimage. The following year five families join, the next year ten, and from year to year the number grows. Elkana travels along new roads calling on new brothers to join in the march. To this achievement Elkana owes his son Shemuel (Midrash). He cannot save Shiloh but he presents the world with the child who guided his people anew on the road to the Sanctuary.

During the entire period of the Judges tears accompanied Shiloh. Never were the roads leading to Shiloh entirely deserted, even in the wildest phase of the Judges. Yet these tears failed to save Israel, as a people, from world-historic suffering. This is the real cause for Shiloh's downfall. Thus, when Assaph read the pages of the Book of Judges, he complained bitterly of his people "which, like the ancestors, broke the faith with God, angered Him with their altar heights, interfered in His rights with their idols, and so aroused Divine fury and disgust that God left the dwelling at Shiloh, left the tent which He had dedicated as the Site of His Presence in the midst of mankind"—(Ps. 78, 57–60).

Small wonder that the Book of Judges omits express mention of Shiloh even at a time when it must have heard the song of praise and Divine homage by a people saved from danger and distress. No mention is made of Shiloh even at the recurring brief phases of elevation and return to God and His law when the roads leading to Shiloh came alive and the hearts of God's nation longed for its proximity. Or is it conceivable that Deborah's victory song, the song of the "mother of Israel," the song of "God's nation" marching out of the gates, failed to penetrate Shiloh's chambers?

But why describe Shiloh's glory at a time when the song of God had become a mere whisper and the pen of the Divine chronicler, trembling with pain, had to record the shameful fact that "the land had but forty years of peace and that then Israel's sons committed anew evil in God's eyes" (Judges 5,6). By writing the book of Judges, he also records the account of Shiloh's downfall.

What was *Gideon's* fight against the Baal altar other than a desperate attempt to delay the downfall of Shiloh? This very action of offering sacred and pure sacrifices to God on an altar outside of Shiloh—contrary to the Divine directive of establishing Shiloh as a firm, permanent sanctuary and thus prohibiting, as later in Zion, sacrificial service outside of its walls (Megilla Perek I, Mishna 11; see also Yerushalmi)—demonstrated the gradual weakening of the firm base on which Shiloh rose in Joshua's days. More and more, Shiloh turns into a wandering tent only to disappear eventually in the wild confusion of war.

Shimshon's giant strength also failed to give firmness to Shiloh's base. It is often easier to remove city gates from their hinges than to open for a misguided mankind the gates to Paradise.

Fleetingly, here and there, the Book of Judges refers to Shiloh. Whoever is not satisfied with the reasons for this treatment may turn to the final chapters with which the Book of Judges closes. At the end of the Book, the chapters dealing with the "Pessel Michah" (site of idolatory with Michah as Priest— Ch. 17–18) and "Pilegesh Begiv'a" (crime committed on a woman in Gibeah Ch. 19–20) have found their place. Chronologically, these events do not at all belong here. But he who wishes to understand the Book of Judges will take his leave under the impact these chapters exert on the thinking reader.

No need to wonder how "Pessel Michah" was possible. If there had not been at all times the opportunity to erect a "Sanctuary" outside of the soil set aside by God for that purpose, mankind would have never forfeited the God-willed Paradise, world-historic misery would have spared mankind and Israel. As it happened, Israel had taken "Pessel Michah" already from Egypt and even brought it safely through the Red Sea (Sanh. 103). "Pessel Michah" destroyed our Sanctuary, it lengthens our Galuth—and this "Pessel Michah" and its sanctuary stood "during all the days when God's House rose on Shiloh" (Ch. 18, 31). The reader who senses the full scope of this sentence will no longer inquire why Shiloh's Sanctuary finds but fleeting mention in the Book of Judges. The book describes the catastrophe caused by "Pessel Michah." It need never have been written if Shiloh had succeeded in conquering "Pessel Michah."

In direct sequence, the Book of Judges immortalizes the drama of "Pilegesh Begiv'a." This phase is also not in its chronological place but it also belongs in the pages of "Shoftim," in the account of Shiloh's downfall. "Pessel Michah" must never cause Israel's shame to be mentioned without recalling Israel's glory. Are there not moments which remind of Joshua's power and his farewell? Israel is "assembled as a Congregation, like one man" (Ch. 20, 1), "like one man, intimately bound together" (ib. 11), "as the Congregation of the People of God" (ib. 2)—in its heart flames the Divine fire, on its lips live the sacred words of the ancestors fighting against "evil deeds in Israel" (ib. 6). The sword defends the desecrated Sanctuary, the symbol of frivolous attack, and the blood of an entire tribe flows for the sanctity of Jewish morality.

The Sanctuary of marriage is preserved—and our eyes seek the other Sanctuary: Shiloh. Is it an accident that the Divine Ark of the Covenant does not rest in Shiloh? (20, 27) From the deserted chambers of Shiloh comes God's angry complaint: why does not the power which fought so heroically for Israel's moral purity succeed in the fight against "Pessel Michah." (Pirke R.E.) A bitter thought: Why is it that the triumphant day of "Pilegesh Begiv'a" does not coincide with the building of Shiloh as the eternal Sanctuary?—

Seek Shiloh in the days of Jewish triumph—the chapter of "Pilegesh Begiv'a" shows the way: Shiloh lies "north of Bethel, east of the road which leads from Bethel to Shechem," to the south of Lebanon!" (21, 19) Do you not perceive the ironical reproach: in the days of "Pilegesh Begiv'a" Shiloh is forgotten and its location must be discovered—geographically.

Thus sketches the Divine pen of the chronicler in unmatched and deeply moving strokes . . .

Our Jewish women apparently understood Shiloh's Sanctuary. The Deborah-spirit which was enflamed by its Menorah found wide and lasting response. In the chambers of the Sanctuary, Hannah became the mother of prayer finding in its proximity immortal words of gratitude and prophetic vision.

When the inevitable became sad reality and Shiloh sank down in ashes, it remained for a *Jewish mother* to bid life's moving farewell to Shiloh's Sanctuary.

In order to make certain of victory, Eli's sons had brought the Ark of the covenant to the warriors' Camp (Samuel I, 4). Did they not realize that the Philistine sword would have never been raised in enmity against Israel's land if Shiloh had remained the true Sanctuary of God, the life Sanctuary of the Jewish people? Had Shiloh lived up to its destiny, Israel, after cleansing the Holy Land from the depravity of the nations, could have laid aside the sword forever. With the doom of Shiloh's Sanctuary a certainty, how could victory be achieved through the Divine Ark of the Covenant!—

With trembling anxiety the aged Priest awaits the fate of the Ark. News arrives. The death of his sons fails to shock him; they had long been estranged from him. But his heart breaks at the tragic news of the loss of God's holy Ark.—

A pathetic mother approaches her "miserable" confinement (ibid, v. 19 הרה ללת). Having lost her husband and father-in-law in one blow, she is stunned by the news that "God's Ark was gone, gone her father-in-law, gone her husband." The pain of suffering overwhelms her; she slumps in agony and, dying, she brings a child into life. As death beclouds her gaze, her attendants attempt to comfort the unfortunate woman. She no longer responds, her mind is far away (20); but she still summons the strength to give a name to her child: אי כבוד "gone is Israel's honor," apparently referring to "the Ark, the father-in-law, the husband, all gone . . ." (21). Her dying words "gone is Israel's honor, far removed is the Ark of God" (22), her last sigh mourns, not the father, not the husband, but the broken Sanctuary in Shiloh.

Thus dies a great strong Jewish mother who perceived the significance of Shiloh's Sanctuary. And Assaph turns to the lute and immortalizes this death scene in a mourning song: "God exposed its (the Ark's) invincibility to imprisonment, its glory to the fury of its foes; its priests fell by the sword, its widows cry not" (Ps. 78). The tears of the widow were not meant for the man—כי נלקח ארון אלקים the downfall of her life's Sanctuary was her final and greatest hurt. — Yet she does not exclaim וארון אלקים נלקחה (V. 17, feminine), the wording received by Eli, but כי נלקח ארון אלקים (V. 22, male) she did not fear for the fate of the Ark, for even in the hands of the enemy, ויתן לשבי עוזו (Ps. 78, 61) it proved its invincibility.

Her final sigh mourned the Ark's preferred presence with Shiloh's enemy for even in Israel's midst it would have been surrounded by adversaries. — Israel had failed to understand Shiloh's significance. The Ark of the Covenant resumed its travels awaiting the hour when Israel would be stirred once again by the longing for its lost paradise.

Who would not feel the pain raking Yirmiyahu's breast when he witnessed the similar downfall of Yerushalayim's Sanctuary which had been destined to be the lasting successor of the Sanctuary of Shiloh! During his entire life he had borne in his heart the vision of the fallen Shiloh Sanctuary (Yer. 7, 12). But his people had forgotten Shiloh. That is why they had to mourn on the ruins of Zion.

KRISTALL-NACHT*

In silent reflection, we commemorate the annual recurrence of the day which heralded the greatest catastrophe world Jewry ever had to endure. We can only sense the full impact of this world-shaking event in the Divine act of Providence which caused the Prophet Yecheskel (Ch. 24, 17) "to moan in silence" as God's Sanctuary was reduced to ashes.

On the 16th day of Marcheshvan we witnessed the destruction of our Houses of God which our fathers and mothers had erected with their life-blood and which were lovingly maintained by their descendants. Every stone bore witness to the tender care and joyful spirit of sacrifice which enabled generation after generation to perpetuate their way of life which found its tangible and symbolic representation in their towering, and often modest, Sanctuaries.

Wherever truly Jewish life throbbed and pulsed, these Sanctuaries—far from rising as cold structures of wood and stone—served as visible expressions of the mysterious inspiration which bestows the mark of immortality upon our people. They served as the powerful source from which flowed the life-giving currents of dedication and inner strength, of purity and sanctification of life which elevated the men and women who, as integral parts of the Kehilla, viewed these Sanctuaries as the central bastion of their existence.

We were deeply attached to our Houses of God because they

*This essay was written at the first anniversary of Kristall-Nacht, November 1939.

176

were Sanctuaries of the Torah, the soul of our existence, without which our lives would wither and fade in the darkness of nocturnal suffering.

Our Sanctuaries were the precious objects of our fierce loyalty for they guided us through life, stood at our side, admonishing, always ready to assist us when we were in danger of succumbing to the economic pressures amidst the ugliness and profanity which engulf us in our daily struggles for survival. In the midst of turmoil our Sanctuaries infused our daily labors with the radiance of Sabbath peace and holiness.

We longed for the proximity of our Sanctuaries, for we visualized the poverty and emptiness of our existence if we were deprived of their rich blessing for our lives, their healing nourishment for our souls. From them we receive the joyous awareness of God's blissful proximity in our existence.

Together with our Sanctuaries, sacred Torah scrolls became victims of fire, victims of destruction. With Yeshayahu (Ch. 64:7,10) we lamented: "O, God, You are our Father; we are the clay, You form us, we all are the work of Your Hands—do not, O God, pour out all Your wrath"—"our sacred site which was our glory and where our forefathers sang Your praise—it is consumed by fire and all our treasures have been laid waste."

And yet—this dark day was only the beginning. It was followed by suffering of an extent unmatched in the painful history of our martyred people. The devastating fire storm raced across national boundaries, and from country to country the tattered remnants of our persecuted people fled the smoking and shattered ruins of their homes to escape the fate of the millions who fell victim to the merciless brutality and murderous orgy of the sworn enemies of their people.

Is this the time for the mournful plaint when "I despair over the breakdown of my people—blackness envelops me—the specter of terror has taken hold of me" (Yirmiyahu, Ch. 8:21).

Bitter mourning over destroyed sanctuaries, burned Torah

scrolls, the cruel slaughter of innocent men, women, and children—it is entirely justified, necessary, natural; but the urgency of the hour poses an even greater challenge.

We and our children have been saved from the holocaust through Divine grace which permitted us to find refuge and homestead in a free land. We must show ourselves worthy of this merciful gift.

Sanctuaries may be reduced to ashes, Torah scrolls may be burned, but the Divine light of the Torah may never be extinguished. Over ruins and graves God's Torah seeks new bearers. As his Torah is eternal, as immortal is the Kehilla which received God's Torah from Moshe Rabbenu as its everlasting heritage. God's Torah guides God's Kehilla to new life whereever the remnants of our people find haven and home.

It is to this new life that we must devote all our strength. Permeated by the lofty awareness of our responsibility, we must put shoulder to shoulder in order to build stone upon stone so that our Sanctuaries may rise again, which alone guarantee the survival of our Kehilloth, the survival of our people.

This great work counts on our determination to join together and to sacrifice with joyful devotion. No one may and will passively and selfishly stand aside. How else could he face the accusation raised against him by the world-shaking events of the recent past?

The desolate ruins of our old Kehilloth pose the serious question to everyone of us: what do you do, what are you ready to do to infuse these ruins, object of your and your forebears' tender love, with renewed life and vigor?

The torn Torah scrolls exhort all of us in the name of God: will you stand aside when your fellow Jews join together to prepare a new home for God's Torah?

From the graves of the numberless victims sounds the reproachful plaint: God has allowed you and your children to live—and you would hesitate even for one moment to do all in your power to be deserving of life?

Many of us will commemorate the 16th day of Marcheshvan as a fast day—not a memorial day, for we do not need to be reminded of our pain when every day and every hour bring home to us the incomprehensible extent of our loss.

This fast day is not a day which exhausts itself in bitter tears—moans and tears are sad products of faint weakness if they do not lead to awareness and understanding of what God expects of our Jewish lives.

With this 16th day of Marcheshvan we vow to be conscious of our duties ever anew if we desire to stand erect before our God, our forebears, our children.

Let us not reduce this day to a day of reckoning, of reproach, of disappointment. Let it rather be a day of reflection and of re-dedication towards the goal of establishing true homes for Torah in our houses and Kehilloth. Where the will is strong and the determination unbending, God lends miraculous assistance. May this Divine help inspire us to continue our sacred work of reconstruction.

AUSCHWITZ — THIRTY YEARS AFTER

Thirty years ago, a world power, maddened by insatiable lust for conquest and obsessed with the utopia of a thousand-year dominion, succumbed in total collapse to the victors. Again the prediction was fulfilled which God, through the mouth of His Prophet, proclaimed for the history of a mankind estranged from God. "Though you were to rise as high as the eagle, and though you set your nest among the stars,thence I will bring you down —Divine proclamation" (Obadiah). And again the Prophet could intone his "mashal" which is true and valid for all time to come: "How you have fallen from heaven, brilliant morning star, how you are hewn down to the ground, oppressor of nations! You had said in your heart, to the heaven I will ascend, high above the stars of God I will erect my throne . . . I will be equal to the most high . . . but you crashed down into the grave . . . those who see you will say, reflectingly: is this the man who caused the earth to tremble, who made kingdoms totter . . ." (Isaiah 14).

Thirty years ago we dreamed a dream that after such catastrophic events the history of mankind would enter upon a new road, the only possible road which could lead to the long-elusive permanent peace. It is with bitter disappointment that we leaf through the pages of the history of these thirty years. The picture that emerges is well-nigh incredible: a mankind torn to the very roots of its being trembles in the face of its threatening destruction. It is a state of complete bankruptcy, an utter abandonment of hope to secure not only the peace but the barest self-preservation. Should this not lead to the long overdue realization that only the full recognition of the Divine rulership, of God as the Creator and Master, may lead His mankind on the road which the Prophets tirelessly proclaim as the goal of the history of mankind? May God give that this will come true in our time.

Thirty years ago—the memory of the most dreadful catastrophe which ever befell our people remains deeply etched in our minds. Six million of our people—"like sheep dragged to the slaughter" (Isaiah 53) by a madman and his despicable satellites, victims of bestial brutality. We ask not why Divine love and justice demanded such sacrifices. The mysteries of Divine intervention in the life of mankind are no less puzzling than the mysteries with which the realm of nature, from the minute to the gigantic, confronts us. Vainly, human intellect searches for the answer to the question: Why?

Let us not ask why the martyrs had to give up their lives; let us ask why God permitted us to survive?

We shall never forget these victims, never forget the sacrifice. We shall preserve their memory for our children and children's children. We shall not cease to pronounce for them the moving *kel moley rachamim* in our prayers. In their memory we kindle an eternal light in our Synagogues. These are symbols of pious and loving remembrance which touch our deepest emotions.

But this alone will not do justice to the martyrs of our people. On the positive side, we must imbue ourselves with this thought; if these unfortunate victims would have been promised their lives on condition that they henceforth would live up conscientiously to their Jewish life duties, they would not have hesitated for a moment to swear joyful allegiance to their Jewish life duties. We— who were privileged to save ourselves and our children—how can we stand up before the martyrs, how can we preserve their memory without feeling infinite shame at their reproachful question: Did you deserve to live?

Not merely thirty years—not mere memories—but forever shall these, martyrs live on in our people. This will be true if we are determined to live for those ideals for which they endured painful death: "The righteous live on after their passing" (Berachoth 18).

OUR PRAYER FOR PEACE

Our daily prayers climax in the ever-recurring plea for Divine help in securing peace in our lives. This applies to the Shemone Essre as well as to the Kaddish which terminates all of our prayers. For peace is the greatest award attainable in life. God's Torah promises it to our people chosen by God to bring peace to the world. It is for this reason that the Prophets never tire to exhort our people to gain this peace. Again and again the Prophetic writings chart the course which alone leads to peace in our lives. Peace is not and must never become a nebulous phantom idea. In the reality of truth mankind must regain the peace it had lost. For peace introduces the history of man, the peace of paradise in which God had placed His first man: for Gan Eden means—Peace.

God, as "King of Peace", called the world and men into being in order to promote peace. There is no peace without God. Only the will of the Divine Ruler is capable of conquering human egotism and unbounded lust for power. Yet, ever since men elected to destroy the throne of Divine Dominion and erect in its place their own throne of human rulership, man's God-given earth world has been transformed into a brutal battleground the horror of which forms the background of the history of men. The Prophets painted this tragic picture in all its terrible aspects and, alas, it became the sad burden of our people to witness and experience this incredible tragedy.

The end of the second great war in our century had come.
A suffering humanity heaved a sigh of relief: peace on earth.
But anxious, fateful questions dampened the joy of victory. Was
this to be a lasting peace? Or was it again a brief interval before
the sinister terror of lurking world conflict would provide the
nations with new weapons, unlocked from the secrets of nature
by the irresistible progress of science and capable of destroying
all of mankind? In vain all the uncounted sacrifices?—

Peace on earth. Human conceit and human folly have banished peace from the world. Peace has become the ward of the
"All-High", the "King of Peace", who is ready to restore peace to
mankind at a time when men "open the gates" to receive God in
their midst. The Prophets, however, proclaimed the ultimate fulfillment of this longing as an absolute certainty guaranteed for us
by the truth of Torah itself. Yerushalayim "beholds the peace"
which God keeps in readiness for mankind. For Yerushalayim
rises at the feet of Zion and its teeming life must be dominated
by the Divine Will centered in Zion. The Divine Zion-Sanctuary
rises wherever Jewish souls offer allegiance to the Jewish truth of
life. Only there true peace may be found with which God, in the
midst of a strife-torn world, initially "blessed His people".

Significantly, at the threshold of each new Jewish year, our
prayers conclude with the reference to God as the "Creator of
Peace", who, as the Universal Judge, is the Father of Mercy,
waiting to guide erring mankind on the road to the true peace.

In the weeks of Yamim Noraim our fervent prayers center
on the one great theme: peace in the world. "Oh God, bestow
your awe upon all your creations, upon all your creatures, that
they may give themselves to you in worshipful homage and join
together in one union—to fulfill Your Will with all their
hearts . . ."

HIGH HOLIDAYS

Whoever coined this title for Rosh Hashono and Yom Kippur has, intentionally or not, falsified Jewish truth and strangled Jewish life. If this title should be applied at all, it is God's Shabbos which deserves it. God has established His Shabbos as an exalted, eternally sacred monument in the midst of His nation. Whoever denies its truth destroys the bond between God and His people; those who remain loyal to the Shabbos and realize its demands in their lives, are looked upon by God as His very own, welcomed as "co-workers" in the Divine work of creation. Their lives are blessed and sanctified as they receive the inexhaustible wealth of values and inspirations flowing from the Shabbos, the timeless source of all life.

Rosh Hashono is preceded by the Elul Shofar which, together with the Rosh Hashono Shofar, is God's annual Sinai-call to His nation. It admonishes us to examine ourselves during the ten days of self-reflection and penitence, honestly and earnestly, whether God is in truth our God and whether we are ready to bar all idolatry from our lives and to erect the throne of rulership for the Shabbos.

"You are our King,"—a shameless lie on our lips if God seeks the Shabbos in our lives and fails to find it.

"Remember us,"—a justified plea if we are willing to remember God in our lives. Whoever denies God's Shabbos bans God from his life.

"Remember us for life," you cannot expect God to help you attain a life which is worthless before His eyes. God desires that you live; only God's Shabbos helps you to live. You desire to live—then pray for Divine assistance, that He may help you to realize the Shabbos in your lives dedicated to His service.

This Divine assistance is forever guaranteed. Yom Kippur proclaims it year after year. Therein lies its sanctity and greatness. Its merciful gift is the restored Shabbos and the fresh vigor and joyous determination to secure the Shabbos as life's most precious ingredient.

"High Holidays!" The Sukkoth week found little favor with the creator of this term. We can hardly blame him. For, if Rosh Hashono and Yom Kippur are but tools in the achievement of sad self-delusion, it is only too obvious that the Divine Sukkoth message is ignored as it is deemed quite superfluous.

And yet, it is strange: Men pine for peace and long for life's joyfulness. It is the Sukkoth week which calls for peace and joyfulness, a peace to be secured amid strife and dissent, a joyfulness to be attained in the face of life's torments and terrors. Yom Kippur, truly experienced, offers us these priceless values of life. The Sukkoth message reads: Keep the Shabbos, adhere to the Divine will with utmost loyalty and leave to God in childlike trust the future of your fate.

Week after week, God's Shabbos invites you into the "abode of peace" which the nearness of God prepares for you. In it there live the peace and the never-ending joyfulness flowing from the knowledge of faithful fulfillment of the Divine demands. With each Shabbos you pronounce your gratitude to God, as expressed in the prayers of Friday evening, "that He has made you to become His nation," possessing "the satisfaction of joyfulness," despite the incredible hardships; and you utter but one fervent prayer: "Sanctify us by Your commandments; let us partake in Your Torah; satisfy us with Your good and make us joyful with Your help . . ."

This, to us, is God's Shabbos. This is what the Shabbos should mean to us. Surely, the long-awaited hour of redemption would come for our suffering people if God's Shabbos were to be proclaimed and kept as His "High Holiday" throughout its ranks.

ובכן תן פחדך

Throughout the history of mankind the fear of a threatening universal destruction has played a role which cannot be underestimated. The common origin of the human race—more and more acknowledged by science—explains the phenomenon that the memory of the Torah-recorded Noachidic flood continues to live on in Noach's descendants, albeit in a frequently distorted form. According to a profound comment by our Sages, the nagging fear of a possible recurrence of a like world-catastrophe was the cause for mankind's single-minded determination to meet this danger with joint force by mounting the heaven-conquering attack against God (the Tower of Babel). The goal: to "unseat" God and erect, in His place, the throne of human might.

God will not be "unseated". God employs the very forces deeply imbedded in human nature—egotism and greed—which stand in the way of unity, resulting in an ever widening split within mankind. The egotistical tendencies still cause the wars and sufferings which fill the history of mankind. The incredible scientific and technological achievements of our generation provide mankind with the horrible weapons which make the threatening danger of world destruction a distinct possibility. But it is not God Who awakens in modern man the fear of such world catastrophe. It is the terror of the atomic age which shakes our generation to its very foundation.

The Jewish concept of world and life is prepared—and prepares—for these fears and anxieties. It views the Universe as God's Creation whose continued existence depends on God's Creative Will. It is His Will which decides its future—as our daily אדון עולם teaches us to pronounce. The world's existence is conditioned on God's Shabbos finding bearers within mankind. Without them, the world would sink back into the deluge of תהו ובהו. It is not the atom bomb which threatens the world's existence; it would be the absence of men who are overwhelmed by the revelation of God's creative omnipotence as evidenced in the terrible mystery of the Laws of Creation working in every tiny atom.

Man's conceit and illusion may threaten the world's existence: "let us break His chains, throw off His ties"—and still: "He Who is enthroned in heaven smiles, God makes a mockery of them—yet He speaks to them in His anger and in His fury exposes them to confusion" (Ps. 11).

After all of history's catastrophes mankind appears to approach the age of confusion. Are these the times predicted by the Prophet in which "the eyes of conceit", man's aspiring pride find their deserved humiliation; in which men, drunk with the power which they worship as their God, become painfully aware of their own sad impotence, "hiding in rocky caverns and dusty caves (fear of the atom bomb?) in terror of God and the Majesty of His Omnipotence as He rises to master the earth" (Isaiah II)?

God's Shabbos will always find bearers in mankind. For this purpose God placed His people in the history of mankind. Its mission serves God's Shabbos. The millenia of historical development will find in the world's Shabbos their ultimate crowning and fulfillment. Not world destruction—world rebirth is the goal of Divine guidance of history.

Must universal suffering reach proportions when, as

viewed by the Prophet, two thirds of mankind will have to perish before the surviving third, purified in the flames of Divine fire, "rises as nation of God" (Zech. XIII)? This will have to be borne out by the events of the coming atomic age.

Our daily Tefilloth pray for this world-rebirth (Kaddish and Olenu). In our Rosh Hashono Tefilloth, this longing finds deeply moving expression. But not merely to awaken this long-ing—to arouse our will and determination to serve mankind's future is the purpose of God's Sinai-Shofar on Rosh Hashono. "Today a world approaches its Rebirth" (היום הרת עולם). It is we who must help the world to be re-born. For God counts with our lives. It gives our fleeting existence its immortal meaning. "For, as the new heavens and the new earth, on which I labor, stand before Me, says God, thus your name will exist forever" (Isaiah 66).

ובכן תן פחדך, "Give, oh God, Your fear upon all Your cre-ations—that they may worship You, and unite in one bond in order to fulfill Your Will with all their hearts"—

Since millenia our people prays for this gift to mankind and its preservation. Nothing else can save it from total destruction. *This* fear will redeem mankind from the great fear which all political efforts of men are unable to banish from the earth.

TASHLICH

The understanding for Jewish customs goes hand in hand with the understanding which the entire institution of Judaism receives from its adherents. They share its destiny. The more complete the acceptance of the divine truths which shape the lives of those whose longing for knowledge as to the purpose of life brings them closer to God, the more receptive the ground will be for the understanding of all areas of Jewish customs. These customs are, after all, only the ripe precipitate of an atmosphere saturated with Jewish concepts. It would therefore be a wasted effort to attempt to gain from strangers something more than just a polite nod of the head for such "practices." Besides, our customs do not require such approval. It would be sad if they would have to struggle against a lack of understanding in our midst.

First, we must be permeated by that yearning for the guiding Arm of God which bids us to take the revealed Word from the Hand of our God. We need this Word, if we are not to despair of our lives. It leads us through the shadowy paths of our existence. It is the sun that illuminates the night of seemingly insoluble enigmas. We could not for a moment exist without its guidance.

Only he to whom Judaism is an ever renewed experience bears within himself the prerequisite for understanding his Judaism. Only he who has planted within himself the Jewish tree of life with its roots and has himself grown along with its growth—he needs only to listen to the inner voice in his breast and to feel the pulsations of his own heart in order to become familiar with all phenomena of Judaism.

We must breathe Jewishly, think Jewishly, and feel Jewishly, if we want to understand Judaism. The Shofar on Rosh Hashono reaches only the Jewish ear. Only the Jewish heart can feel the bliss of Yom Kippur, and only Jewish joy finds its ever-lasting source in the Succah.

It does not take much effort to participate in the Jewish custom of reciting the prophetic words of Micah while standing at the bank of the river on the afternoon of Rosh Hashono towards sundown. But we would do well, and we owe it to our self-respect, not to learn about the "Song of the Spirits upon the Waters" only from the lips of non-Jews. In our opinion, much less emphatic understanding of nature is needed for inclining one's ear to the thunder of the majestic waterfalls, learning the language of the foaming mountain spring, meditating dreamily on the waves of the river which roll on unflaggingly, or immers-ing one's eyes soulfully in the quiet, mirror-like lake, than is required for looking up with every sip of water to the One "through Whose Word everything came into being." But the dying leader called unto us, "Hear O Israel, you are this day passing through the Jordan," and all at once our Sages realized שמע ישראל וכו' הלכה אדם מישראל ששותה מים לצמאו אומר ברוך שהכל נהיה בדברו why it is a lawful precept in Israel to recall, with each sip of water, the miraculous omnipotence of God which rules the world by its creating Word.

"Behold all the miracles that God did unto Israel, they were all performed by virtue of water." Do not drink even one drop of water without crossing the Jordan in spirit. Each day we cross the Jordan anew. Then the most common natural occurrence becomes an incredible miracle in our eyes. The loving care God lavishes on man represents a far greater miracle than the parting of the sea. The voice of God is upon the Waters.

We passed through the sea, we crossed the Jordan, and the waves of the sea parted for us and the rising flood of the Jordan receded before us. This the others did not experience. That is why we are so much more familiar with seas and rivers, and we do not fear their depths. Even if "the waters had surrounded us within an inch of our lives," "if the earth had forever slipped the bolt before us," the "shadowy depths of the sea" would still cast us up and return us to life" (Jonah 2).

The sea heard our songs and they have remained on our lips ever since. Thus Moses willed it. That is why he sang his song to the future (אז ישיר). Our Prophets walk before us, singing. "For if you wander through the water, I shall be with you, and if you pass through streams of water, they shall not carry you away" (Isaiah 43). Wherever the despotism of nations brandishes the Pharaonic whip over us, the Prophets show us the Divine staff which "is stretched upon the waters" (ibid. 10) for all eternity. This staff paves a path through the seas for those redeemed by Him (ibid. 51) and therefore ועבר ביום צרת, our historic misery passes through the sea (Zech. 10). This gives us the strength to sing the song of the sea to God each day.

On Rosh Hashono afternoon we stand by the river and we exclaim מי אל כמוך "Who is like unto You, O Almighty, Who overlooks guilt, Who passes over the crime of the remnant of His inheritance; He keeps not His wrath forever, for He rejoices in love." He mercifully turns to us and drowns our sins: ותשליך במצולות ים — "You cast all their errors into the depths of the sea." The "redemption" which the people of God experienced at the sea, "when its pursuers, like unto stone, sank into the depths of the sea," finds its eternal repetition in the aid that is assured anyone who yearns for redemption in his fight with the foe that dwells in his own breast. Ours is, of course, the decisive step forward; we have to summon the courage and the firm determination which does not fear struggle and enable us to tame the opposing waves within us. Then God's waves mercifully close over our "pursuer," God's כפרה drowns the "pursuer" in the depths of the sea and in the rising dawn there appears before us the path of pure accomplishment in the service of God.

This is the word of the "Akeidah" to the height of which the Shofar calls us on Rosh Hashono. The "mighty stream" had also crossed the path of Abraham when he was on his way to the "Akeidah." He cut through the waves for he had cut the wood for the "Akeidah." This was the hour in which God consecrated Abraham's descendants as the People of the Song of the Sea.

This is why the Jewish mind lingers pensively at the banks of the river when, in the afternoon of Rosh Hoshano, the waves of the Shofar tones still reverberate over the water. Purity, eternal youth beckon to us. טהרה במים-The Song of the Sea of redemption lingers on our lips. Once we are prepared for the "Akeidah" of our lives, our adversaries sink into the depths of the waters.

For many, the pilgrimage to the water has become a mechanical rite. Jewish custom does not concern itself with this. For how many of us in the daily "song of the sea," the "miracle Berachah" before a drink of water, more than just empty words? Jewish life must awaken our Jewish curiosity.

For others, the pilgrimage to the water has become a gesture of superstition. We have to be careful to remain free of delusion (ניחוש) and to keep ourselves pure in our undivided adherence (תמים) to God and His Law.

Adorning our lives with symbols should not frighten us סימנא מלתא היא (כריתות ו'). They should permeate our beings with inspiring thoughts without worrying that they might proliferate into poisonous growths in the morass of stagnating sentiments (see הוריות י"ב — מהרש"א).

Thus Jewish duty prescribes that Israel's kings be anointed at a spring of water (כריתות ה').

As the Sage said to his disciples: "When you study, study at the banks of the water" (ibid.).

The water murmurs in a mysterious language whose meaning has been interpreted for us by the Word of God and by the teachings of the Prophets.

KOL NIDRE

The evening shadows descend. The night before the great day approaches. Wherever Jewish souls breathe on earth, a mood of deep and solemn reflection seizes hearts and minds. The Kehilloth are assembled in dedicated devotion. Garments denoting festivity and dying alike are worn by the men to remind them of death and yet arouse them to life. For our lives would be empty without Yom Kippur with its welcome message of Divine mercy gladdening our hearts in the blissful knowledge of promise and forgiveness. Purity is within reach even where sin has left its threatening traces; Divine favor and heavenly atonement are ever ready to remove any obstacle blocking the path to a new and pure life.

He who still nourishes in his heart a longing for such life will lend fervent and grateful expression to his feelings. Which poetic inspiration could interpret the wealth of emotions with which Jewish hearts tremble towards the Great Day? Did it remain for the overwhelming rhythm of a Yehuda Halevi, the tenderness of a Kalir, the poetic fluency of a Rabbi Shimeon, to stir the sacred silence with the harmony of their song and the winged impact of their thought-provoking word. . . ?

On soft waves of whispering awe the messengers approach to herald the coming of the Ruler. Their melody's melting passion and swelling intensity draw tears of remorse and restore courage in man's breast. For to his heart comes the call, ever louder and more confident, that God is near to ban despair and awaken hope, to strengthen those who believe in Him and bestow blessing on those who put their trust in Him.

Aroused by the impact of these sounds, countless lost sons of the Jewish tribe have regained the road to the father's heart—countless erring men, failing the strength to tie anew torn threads, have regained the longing for a home, a homeland, long lost, long gone . . .

Is it the stormy pathos of a passionate longing, awakened by this melody? Is it the fiery rhetorical outburst of poetic emotions endowed with magic power by the music of the sounds? No poet speaks. But we perceive the speech of the lofty Jewish soul and listen to the words of the most moving Yom Kippur sermon.—כל נדרי "All vows by which we have bound our will . . . vows which we may take between this Yom Kippur and the one to come upon us to good . . . we regret them . . . let them be dissolved, renounced, annulled . . . without firmness or validity . . . our vows are no vows, neither are oaths our oaths . . ."

Is it conceivable that the Jewish people inaugurates its Great Day of the year by killing that which ought to be sacred among men, by erasing the truth which was once proclaimed to it by the revealed Word of God amidst the trembling of the whole world? How can such motives be suspected of this people without depriving its Great Day, pride of the people, of its shining glory and dragging it through mud and filth? It should not surprise us that envy and evil dare to desecrate the most sacred possession of our people in a bold attempt to rob from it the pride of its consciousness. For it remains eternally true: *the Jewish people has taught the world the sanctity of the spoken word. Its very existence is built on the sanctity of the word.*

The living word founded the Jewish people's history—the נעשה ונשמע was no lie. The people owes its immortality to its word and it is the word which rears its future generations. The sanctity of its word guarantees the truth of its traditions—the people of the תורה שבעל פה does not break with the truth! Its word founds the cornerstone of its marriages, sacred, God-willed, Divinely endowed, and בעון נדרים בנים מתים מחים מתה אשה של אדם exclaims the Talmud (Sabbath 32): he who violates the sanctity of the word is unworthy of having children for he is unable to rear them for God; he is unworthy of the wife whom he bound to himself by the vow of the sanctifying word ... And this people, proud of the majesty of its word, should be suspected of violating and desecrating the sanctity of the word?

The word is sacred to the Jew, his whole personality is founded in it. This guarantees the fulfillment of the word. Only the thoughtlessly, carelessly pronounced word, obligating one's own person, is subject to examination. Once understood and classified as thoughtless, התרת נדרים—it may be, not dissolved, but recognized as invalid from the beginning (comp. Hirsch Comm., Numb. 30,3).

What is the purpose of our כל נדרי declaration? Does it concern נדרים of the past (supported by the wording of the introduction)? R. Tam (Nedarim 23b) doubts that such vows could be annulled by this type of formulation. And: מיום הכפורים זה עד יוה"כ הבא עלינו לטובה, thus directing our minds to vows which might unknowingly be pronounced in the course of the coming year only to be forgotten or disregarded. On the other hand, vows which are pronounced with full intention and purposefulness would retain their validity.— Three times, with rising intensity, Kol Nidre intones the a priori annullment of the thoughtlessly pronounced word with its possible consequences. It is as if this pronouncement were never made.

What is it that motivates the Jewish people to make this proclamation at the very moment when the evening of Yom Kippur descends?

Israel's communities tremble fearfully at the thought that they may be deprived of their only weapon. They come near before God: when our forefathers sinned they were able to approach You with sacrifices and express through them their hearts' real motives. We—עניים אנו אין לנו להביא קרבנות—we stand before You in all our poverty. And God replies: "The word of your lips have been preserved for you." Even if Israel, worm-like, would cringe under the heels of the nations, the word of God calls reassuringly אל תירא תולעת יעקב (Is. 31, 14): as the worm with its steadily drilling weapon is able to fell even the strongest cedar tree כך אין להם לישראל אלא תפלה Israel, in its תפלה, commands a weapon which enables it to conquer the most powerful foe (Mechilta 14, 10). Its תפלה brings him ultimate victory, for it is the תפלה which vows ever new our eternal loyalty to God.

What if Israel, by frivolous misuse, should also lose this weapon? Does not every תפלה represent a solemn oath renewing the Sinai promise and recalling its demands with each recital? Woe if תפלה were to remain mere lip service! For תפלה receives its true value only when "the will is placed in the hand" (Taanis 8) משים נפשו בכפו i.e. when from the outset the will is directed towards the deed as its main purpose (שני נשא לבבנו אל כפים). But what is the תפלה on the lips of a man to whom the absolute validity of the word means nothing? *Every unfulfilled vow disables the mouth and prevents if from further raising the prayer to God.* Every vow, vainly waiting for its fulfillment, henceforth robs prayer of its potency and deprives it of its special function of dedicating the human deed to God.

Should not Israel's communities tremble with anxiety at the thought that they might have dealt frivolously with the word, their most sacred trust and that their prayer, their families, their most precious possessions, might be at stake?

Thus it is the spirit of uncompromising conscientiousness

which emanates from the Kol Nidre declaration of the Jewish people. It is inconceivable what lack of understanding and ill will dared to read into its text. A Jewish community, an individual congregant should employ this declaration as a means of shirking obligations towards others, thus—one hardly dares to say it—"legalizing" falsehood and perjury?—Sacred solemnity, the pure Divine breath of moral dignity permeates the moment when, throughout the world, a nation dedicates itself to the realization of the sanctity of the word in the awareness of the inviolable validity of its oral pronouncements. Only thoughtlessness and evil intention could attempt to desecrate the sacred silence in which mankind, stirred to reverence and admiration, should perceive this lofty declaration which flows from a spirit of profound conscientiousness and purest nobility of soul.

In all its poverty and weakness Israel stands before its God unable to dedicate any possession to Him save *one*: לקח טוב (Hos. 14,3). Would that one offering should remain unstained . . .

Oh, God, trust our word! Leave unspoken that which is pronounced unknowingly or in error.

While the Halacha doubtfully weighs the legal implications of our Kol Nidre and its ability to meet the requirements of a formal התרת נדרים, we come before God even before we begin our prayers and express our serious determination to live up to all pronouncements of our lips. The words may be dry and halting with which the Kol Nidre formulation (alluding in the first part to the past and then to the future), in ever rising intensity, directs the rousing message of the sanctity of the word to the trembling heart of the Jewish people. But the impact of these simple words cannot fail to draw hot tears from the listener who stands in reverence before the loftiness of the Jewish spirit.

Kol Nidre, with its dry, halting words, is תפלה in the most sublime sense of the term. Surely, our centuries-old tradition could have presented no more stirring sermon, no more moving text to the Jewish people that they may sing of Yom Kippurim's sanctity and solemnity in an ever-swelling melody of deep longing and mournful intensity.

ונסלח, ברוך The knowledge of the profound importance of the human word and the realization מות וחיים ביד לשון (Mishle 18) of the word's power to cause death and life alike flow from the fervent prayer, expressed in Kol Nidre, that God may graciously overlook any accidental or unknowing misuse of our pronouncements.

Did not God also promise His mighty סליחה in the event that the thoughtless word would cause death? Even if the decision of the leaders (of the Sanhedrin) would have jeopardized the very foundation of the Divine Law וכי תשגו וכו' "you could fall prey to the false assumption that you need no longer live up to the full scope of the Law" (Numb. 15, 22 ff.), and the Congregation would have permitted the deed to follow this error. ונסלח לכל עדת בני ישראל וכו' כי לכל העם בשגגה "God forgives the whole Congregation, He condones all, for it occurred to the people in careless error." ונסלח Rather than endangering Israel's whole future and development through the consequences of a careless word, Divine סליחה extends to every erring man!

Victoriously, the ונסלח לכל עדת בני ישראל is proclaimed over the Congregation and its message fills all hearts with quiet joyfulness and infinite strength. While on the other festive moments we lift the cup of joy, filled with wine, in worshipful welcome to the approaching יום טוב, at this great moment our cup of life also fills with the most precious possession of Divine mercy—and from our lips should not pour the ברכה joyful and solemn, blissful and proud? שהחיינו וקימנו והגיענו לזמן הזה.

Thus gather Israel's communities as the evening shadows of Kol Nidre descend . . .

יום כפור MORNING

ברוך אתה ה׳ אלוקינו מלך העולם הפותח לנו שערי רחמים ומאיר עיני
המחכים לסליחתו. יוצר אור ובורא חושך עשה שלום ובורא את הכל:

"Blessed be You, God our God, King of the Universe,
Who opens for us the doors of mercy and Who fills with light
the eyes of those who await His forgiveness; Who forms the
light and creates the darkness; Who provides peace and creates
the All."

אור עולם באוצר חיים אורות מאפל הוא אמר ויהי:

"Eternal light reposes in his treasury of life. Light from the
darkness; He spoke , and it was".

סלח לגוי קדוש. ביום קדוש. מרום וקדוש:

"Forgive the holy nation on this sacred say, highly exalted
and holy are You".

ברוך: To ברכה calls the rising morn of יום הכפורים Israel's
communities. The blessing conceives of every young day which
emerges with the first ray of the sun from the receding night as
revelation of the eternally rejuvenating creative omnipotence of
God. In its service light and darkness rise in peaceful harmony.
The blessing directs our gaze towards the opening gates through
which the morning enters upon God's command. On כפור יום
morning these gates become the morning doors of infinite joyfulness and hope. God's merciful, fatherly right hand opens
them for His children who long for His nearness. The light of

200

Divine help softly spreads over the night which threatened to engulf man in his weakness and guilt. In the lives of men God also plants the peace, causing light and darkness to find their place in His plan of Creation.

אור: and thus, God preserves eternal, life-giving light in His treasure in order to bestow it upon men who long for the Divine light from the confines of their nocturnal existence. With the light of Creation the Divine creative "it shall be" (ויהי) assured the world of man of a light without which their lives would be conceived in night, fading away in the darkness of doom.

סלח: as members of a nation which is permeated by the consciousness of its sacred Divine destiny—to the renewed realization of which the קדושה of יום כפור calls—we may stand before God, "exalted and Holy", clinging to Him in the awareness of our frailty, that His proximity may bring our re-formation and rejuvenation.

ברוך שם כבוד מלכותו:

"Blessed be the Name of the Glory of His Kingdom".

מלכותו בקהל עדתי. וכבודו היא אמונתי. אליו בקשתי. לכפר עון חטאתי. וביום צום כפור סליחתי. יענה ויאמר סלחתי:

"His Kingdom—in the assembly of My Congregation. His Glory—it is my devotion. I beseech Him that He may atone the deceit of my frivolity; and on the fast day of יום הכפורים, bringing me forgiveness, He speaks to me in gracious consent: "I have forgiven".

המאיר וכו': Creation has awakened. Majestic streams of light flood through it. They stimulate hidden potencies which pledge, with the young day, renewed fulfillment of the God-willed plan of Creation. Throughout nature penetrates the קדושה of God-serving creatures finding like-minded response in the breast permeated by יום כפור solemnity. Jewish thought meets this response with ברוך שם כבד מלכותו which refers to the two names of God whose recognition signifies God's rulership in God's world. The attribute אלקים describes God as the source of all lawful manifestations as evidenced in overwhelming testimony in the forces of nature: nature's קדושה pays homage to the proclamation of God's Kingdom in which אלקים is revealed.

God's Kingdom is not confined to nature. As ה' God shapes every phase in the lives of men. Human delusion deprives ה' of the קדושה of devoted obedience. Yet God seeks the Glory of His Kingdom—i.e. the ultimate completion of His Creation in which the God-serving free human deed proclaims God's Glory—in the free devotion to mankind's homage to God (in contrast to nature's lawful limitation). שם מלכותו, the name which bears witness to the Kingdom of God in which God's Glory is above all revealed is thus the attribute: ה'.

ברוך ה' לעולם ועד: This name of God will also find its future recognition ברוך: Israel's Congregations join in nature's קדושה with ברוך שם כבד מלכותו vowing the blissful furtherance of the Divine Will upon whose realization the קדושה of God in the lives of men depends.

מלכותו forms the commentary to ברוך שם וכו'. This מלכות deals with the Kingdom of God which rises in Israel's *communities*. In *this* מלכות God finds His Glory, for its fulfillment depends on the אמונה, the free devotion of God-serving men. And God, Whose Will longs for כבד מלכותו in the lives of men should not be ready, through סליחה, to grant His men—having found the way to Him from a guilt-ridden past—the possibility to lead an existence which lives up to the demands of the Divine Will? With ברוך שם כבד מלכותו on our lips, permeated by the firm determination to dedicate our lives to the attainment of this goal, we pray for the gift of Divine סליחה.

MUSSAPH ON יום כפור

Our thoughts—as in every תפלת מוסף—turn towards the homeland and before our eyes rise the Sanctuary and its sacred service which bestowed upon the festive day a character all its own. As we live our Jewish lives far removed from homeland and Sanctuary, our souls are permeated by unspeakable melancholy,—ומפני חטאינו גלינו מארצנו ואין אנו יכולים לעשות וכו'. The fervent longing for ingathering and reconstruction יהי רצון שתשוב ותרחם וכו' touchingly expresses the yearning for the return of a Yom Kippur as it could only be experienced on the soil of the homeland by the people of God united by the Sanctuary of God.

What can we do to hasten the return of the incomparably great day as it passed in sacred structures before the eyes of the Jewish nation?

What can we do?

The שליח צבור calls his congregants to עלינו לשבח in order that they may fully appreciate the glory of Jewish live-convocation and determine to dedicate all their strivings towards the realization of the Divine demands upon life in the midst of a world estranged from God. Overwhelmed by powerful emotion, the Congregation kneels—to rise again with the firm vow on all lips: הוא אלקינו אין אחר shall become אמת, shall become lofty truth in our lives!—

To us—whose hearts are filled with the burning hope for
the return of the Divine values of the Sanctuary—Rabbenu
Meshulam presents the עבודה of Yom Kippur: in artistic syntax
the directives of the Mishna find their pregnant expression;
every line consists of five words the initials of which repeat the
letters of the alphabet four, eight, twelve, twenty-four times,
respectively.

The עבודה is preceded by an introduction whose comments
seem strange at first sight: before our eyes a creation appears
from the void, awaiting man;—the developing course of mankind in its widening estrangement from God is sketched in brief
almost laconic outline, as we know it from the pages of the
Torah, until the moment when from mankind emerged Avrohom and the ensuing circle of men who proceeded on their
Divinely guided individual paths through history. Then, almost
abruptly, we stand before the עבודה of יום כפור. We are quite certain that it was the Paiton's purpose to sketch the world-histori-
cal background before the impressive presentation of the עבודה
של יו״כ.

In the שני שעירים, the two goats which assume a central position in the עבודה-procedure, the grave alternative finds expression with which God confronts the life of every Jew. "They are
both exactly alike; both invite in equal measure and with equal
opportunity to the decision לה׳ or to the decision לעזאזל. God has
bestowed שעיר-strength on us, the will-power of endurance, and
perseverance. We may place it in the service of God, subordinate ourselves (through שחיטה) to the Divine Will of God and
thus enter the Sanctuary for the eternal union with the Divine.
We are also free to offer opposition to the demands of the
Divine Will in stiff-necked egotism. We are free to turn our
backs to the Sanctuary while still cherishing the hope that we
will be able to preserve ourselves חי in "living self-existence".
Alas we will be sadly mistaken: such עז, such stiffneckedness אזל

fades inevitably in the forlorn wastes of the desert (comp. Comm. Lev. 16, 10).

Thus we understand how the שני שעירים symbolize the fateful choice of decision with which Yom Kippur confronts every Jewish life; how it puts into clear focus the world-historic contrast in which the ways of mankind and those of the Jewish people separate towards opposite goals. Let everyone of us perceive the language of the עבודה של יו״כ against the clear perspective of historical truth.—

אשרי—true to life, as a great blissful experience, Yom Kippur on sacred site rises before the spiritual eye of the Paiton—as in a dream he sees its glory. The dream ends, his eye views reality, his ear hears words which cannot convey the incomparable—and unbearable pain assails the wildly pulsating soul.

ובעת—it is the time of מוסף on Yom Kippur which brings to the Jewish soul the tragic realization of the loss of all that was once ours . . .

ומעת— . . . and a poor, hunted Galuth-people relieves amidst hot tears its soul's unbearable burden.

ומרוב— . . . and to admit that its own guilt has caused the unending misery. Who can measure how often bitter disappointment cruelly undermined the perseverance and confidence of our nation so sorely tried . . .

ואתה—and yet . . . is He not alive? Has He not guaranteed, for all eternity, that His children will never have to knock in vain at the gate of the Father's House, however pronounced their estrangement, however blind their thoughtless refusal of the fatherly right hand, as long as their hearts are filled with genuine yearning for the return to God?

ומרוב—this suffering people sheds hot tears of bitter remorse at God's fatherly breast; —as Yom Kippur supplies new strength and pure hope to the life of the *individual,* so it is the prayer of this Galuth nation that Yom Kippur may pave the way for the realization of its *national* aspirations.

אוא׳. תתן—as this people pours out its longing before God—neither state nor land, but the *Beth Hamikdosh* is the primary object of its prayer! Oh, that the Prophet's אחרית-vision (והיה באחרית הימים וכו׳) Is. 2) may come true "Firmly founded on the Mount of God's House on the summit of the mountains." (ff.).—For only when this Zion-Mount will have become the "summit of mountains" will there be the certainty of fulfillment for the national future of the Jewish people; only then will the "shattered horn" be restored (Echa 2, 3). God prepares for the redemption of His banished people, for the Galuth has transformed His people into a nation of God. This people harbors but *one yearning*: to be recognized before all the world as *God's nation.* This gives it the right to look to Divine assistance in attaining this lofty status (comp. Deut. 26, 17).

אל— . . . and such a nation should be fearful of threatening disaster, should never again be restored to "strength", should be paralyzed and "chained by a hopeless yearning"? (Zech. 9, 12).

תוכחה—in all phases of suffering this people sees but Divine acts of admonition.

תקרב. תאמר—what is it that this people expects from its Moshiach? That he may erect its Beth Hamikdosh which will find favor in the eyes of God. However, the gathering of the dispersed segments of our people is God's work, and the state built by God rises in intimate union with God (like a "belt", Jer. 13, 11), as it is dedicated solely to the mighty realization of the precepts of the Divine Will!

אורך—praying for the light to illuminate its darkness, the great thought elevates the soul of this people: what a mighty demonstration of the world-shaping, all-powerful Divine Will before the consciousness of a great mankind will be the historical reality of a nation, despised and ridiculed through millenia of universal rejection, ultimately attaining all that it has ever dreamed about!

אופל. אלקינו—all these hopes which painfully fill the breast find their moving expression in this final prayer: in climactic unity it embraces the lofty ideas of Zion, Yerusholayim, Jewish nation, Jewish state, and the elevation of mankind.

אלמנה—Zion-Yerusholayim, shunned, isolated (Echa 1, 1; Is. 49, 21). ותשוב—bring the morn unto Zion that it may send forth the rays of the young dawn of nations . . .

חבר—the Beth Hamikdosh, the sacred site of the nuptial union between God and His people . . .

טנף—Yerusholayim, cleansed from the merest trace of טומאה (Is. 52, 1) will rise as the sum total of all "beauty" (Ps. 48, 3) on "precious soil" (Is. 28, 16) provided by Zion. Then, even material wealth (כדכוד, Is. 53, 12) will not be able to deprive Yerusholayim, the Jewish state of the future, of its pure, Divinely orientated character.

לאורה—"nations walk in Your light" (Is. 60, 2); Zion-Israel rises as the eternal "monument" of Divine life-dedication on sacred soil (Zech. 9, 16); שבע—and finds "joyful satisfaction before the Countenance of God" (Ps. 16, 11) where Divine Shechina proximity bestows highest attainment on human ambition.—Yerusholayim, whose corner-towers rise in God-given glory, harbors a population of צנועים, "humbly walking before God" (Micha 6, 8) from whose midst all rebels will have vanished, for they will not be borne by sacred soil (Lev.18, 28).

One sacred idea, *one* great goal unites all segments of God's nation on the שלש רגלים as they ascend "the House of God in restless impatience" (Ps. 55, 15). Israel, once split apart, dispersed, bereft of the major part of its tribes, receives the Divine Tekia-call which also proclaims the return of the ten tribes, the "forgotten", to God's sacred Mount, to the homeland.—

Zion—"House of Prayer for all nations" (Is. 56,

7)—towards this singularly great goal of humanity there issues in the Mussaph-Tefilla on Yom Kippur the fervently longing cry for Selicha directed to God the א׳ מלך יושב על כסא רחמים.

NEILAH

As the great, holy day nears its climax, the setting sun casts ist dying rays over the "summit of the trees". The sacred hour of Neilah commences. While formerly each תענית צבור concluded with Neilah (Taanith Ch. 4), Yom Kippur alone must never be deprived of this Neilah-Tefilla. The moment nears when the "Gates of the Sanctuary" close (נעילת שערי היכל, Yerush. Berachoth Ch. 4) but the "Gates of Heaven" are still open and will not close until the day merges into the night (נעילת שערי שמים comp.)—and God waits for that last erring Jewish soul to plead, with childlike longing, for admission at the "Gates of Mercy." He holds out His hand to the sinners and His right hand is stretched out to receive those that return", for God "has no pleasure at the death of the lawless—rather let him return and live"—"return, oh return, why do you want to die?"—

Is there a Jewish soul—unless it were bereft of even a trace of pure Divine emotion—which could fail to be stirred by the indescribable sanctity of this parting hour when תפלת נעילה, in a final appeal of repeated insistence, formulates the great demands as well as the blissful promises of Yom Kippur?

אב—As the "Redeemer" God waits for His children. As Avrohom once pleaded for Sodom's rescue, so does His eye search at the time of Neilah for one of his erring children who longingly desire God's proximity. If these children gather around Avrohom; if they are determined to accept for themselves their ancestor's way of life—then the Divine Gates of Mercy open wide for them at the hour of Neilah.—

Neilah calls for the Kedusha-dedication of our lives. Desiring to partake of its wealth of blessing, overwhelmed by the holiness of the moment, who could fail to choose a life to which the "open gates" of the Neilah lead a people which has forever perceived the Kedusha-demand of its Jewish existence?

There are but a few fleeting minutes left—not enough to permit Selichoth to lend expression to the feelings which the יעלה ויבא-prayer evokes in us in all תפלות—but in passionate, stormy outbursts of intense longing the Jewish soul presses for admission at the Divine Gates of Mercy.

In these final moments we relive the entire emotional realm in which every Jewish soul moved during these Selichoth weeks having concluded with the Yom Kippur that is now also passing. At this moment the שליח צבור calls his Congregation to join in "Pismonim" the majority of which is gleaned from the Selichoth of the past week.

המבדיל. When the Neilah coincides with the end of the Sabbath, this Pismon brings home the two-fold admonition with which the Shabbos and Yom Kippur release us into daily living: One of the main sources of our misdeeds lies in the tragic misconception of the division between קדש and חול which surely was not intended by God to result in the "holy" Sabbath remaining dedicated to God while the "business-like" week would be allowed to fall prey to desecration. These two concepts have received their "separate" positions by God for the sole purpose that from each Sabbath should emanate the spirit of sanctity and consecration and infuse the entire "business" of the whole week. Having spent the Shabbos and Yom Kippur in truth before God, we forever renounce these "misdeeds" as we are determined to elevate even the "non-sanctified" to God. At the

same time, we need not shy away from asking God for "the
increase of our possessions and of our children": as every child
that we receive from God's hand is a sacred possession, so every
particle of our belongings, acquired before the Divine eye, is
evaluated in the service of God—sacred possessions, dedicated
to God.

זכור. As there is no erring child that knocks in vain in the
Neilah hour at the Divine Gate of Mercy, so for many centuries
no Yom Kippur has come to a close without Rabbenu Gershom
dedicating to the dispersed Galuth communities of his people
this deeply moving prayer that we may use its stirring words to
bemoan with tearful sobs our unending misery and to direct the
anxious inquiry to God whether we have not suffered enough,
whether the Galuth has not accomplished its work of purifica-
tion and whether God was not willing to lead homeward the
"prisoners of Jacob's tents".

Does Yom Kippur find us also members of a Divine nation
which at Neilah is justified in directing such inquiry to God?

Meanwhile night has fallen, the night of the coming week-
day—Israel's Congregations extend the final farewell to the
passing of Yom Kippur—the quiet, great lofty moment permeates every Jewish soul.

Breathlessly listening it hears the sacred farewell message of
the great day: Are you ready?

With שמע ישראל and the seven-fold ה' הוא האלקים Israel
presents its Yom Kippur with its life's oath of loyalty.

As the sounds fade away, there penetrates the call of
Tekiah.

Is it the signal for the conclusion of the holy day? (Sabbath
114 b, Tossaf. ff.)

Is the Tekia, as on Sinai, directed to the parting Shechina?
(סלוק שכינה).

Does it evoke the memory of the call for freedom with

which once Yom Kippur's Yovel aroused the Jewish people?—
To bring it back must be the lofty goal to which Jewish life,
rejuvenated by Yom Kippur, must be rededicated.

SEDER NIGHT

An evening full of restless activity precedes the Seder Night. We owe this restlessness to the mothers of our people. For they taught us how one removes Chometz from the Jewish houses, how one erases Chometz from the Jewish hearts. If we are to partake fully of the Seder Nights with its delights and bliss, then we must remove before the eye of God every trace of independence, every trace of arrogant pride and strength. Only then is there room for the divine gift of mercy which the Seder Night offers to us.

By the light of the flickering candle illuminate the darkest corners of your homes and remove from your hearts every last trace of Chometz. For he whose hand holds the Chometz has no room for the Matzo. He who possesses Chometz is not hungry for the Matzo. Be active yourself in searching for the last trace of Chometz and do not wait until God has to step in your midst in order to release the Chometz pride from your hearts.

Do you see the mysterious light which illuminates the nocturnal night? God is מבער חמץ.

It is horrible when God "has to search Jerusalem with light" (Zeph. 1:12) לבער משם ע״א ולעקור משם יצר הרע With the flames of His anger he smashes the God-denying monuments of their pride and breaks the frivolous conceit of their hearts which are permeated by passionate illusion. God is מבער חמץ.

This refers to men who are satisfied and do not long for the Matzo—who feel that "from God comes neither bad nor good".

Woe to the man, הגוי לא נכסף who no longer experiences longing, ואשר לא בקשו את דבר ה' ולא דרשו who is indifferent to the divine gift of life. A time will come when he will long for the Matzo with burning desire for "their wealth has been blundered, their houses are destroyed".

How can we preserve for our children and for ourselves the blissfulness of the Seder Night? Then go and search yourself for the Chometz and wherever you find even the most minute trace remove it before the Seder Night approaches.

Children's shining eyes. Children's questioning mouths. If your aging eyes no longer reflect the glory of the Seder Nights; if on your fading lips the searching, meditating question no longer lives, then do not be surprised if the day comes when your children chew on the matzo with yawning indifference, when they will reject the bitter herbs and tolerate in ill-concealed boredom the sacred round of the divinely presented cups of wine.

מה זאת? Is this the question of the immature and undeveloped infantile mind? Oh, if this question would only emanate from the hearts of our so-called mature adults whose shameful thoughtlessness and sated indifference threaten to extinguish any trace of true life.

Even for them the time comes for the question of מה זאת. When the horror of war and death floods mankind and millions of our people succumb under the overpowering catastrophe of our time—then the question of מה זאת forces itself onto our trembling lips.

Must we wait that long?

The hungry may come and be satisfied. Millions suffer

from hunger and only a few are satisified. Or are there too many who are satiated in this world? Must the misery and suffering be evermore intensified until they finally feel the first pangs of hunger?

God calls upon His men to crying and mourning—but in man's world there is rejoicing and happiness; there one slaughters cattle and sheep and eats meat and drinks wine— "Only eat and drink for tomorrow we will die" (Isaiah 22)

Pass the crowded tables, flee in disgust their nearness. For there lurks death. Their tables are filled with excrements. There is no pure spot.

Then you know why the Redeemer has not yet come. For there are too many of us who have no need of him. The Redeemer will come, he must come when men will have learned to swallow their bite of bread, for their throat tightens with pain; when men will have awakened and will ask each other if it is true that their life's content be no other than the acquisition of material goods; no other than to fill their stomachs and to earn the piece of bread in order to satisfy the tyranny of hunger. How long will men join in the mad dance from early youth to late age, work and labor so that the stomach may be satisfied in order to sink into the grave exhausted and disappointed? How long will men continue to bear generation upon generation in senseless continuation so that they should labor through life in similar senseless activity? Are we to wait until our children approach us with this question on their lips: Who has given you the right to give us life? What have you to offer us in true values which will mean life to us? And should there be a foolish father who will answer, my dear boy, I have built up my business for you, I have piled up thousands of gold pieces and it is now your turn to begin to labor and to acquire all the knowledge and efficiency which is necessary in order to continue my business and to pile up the money more and more—the thinking son will have but a derisive, mad laughter and the father will shudder before such laughter. Parents will search for the bread, for the bread of life, before they dare henceforth to give life to children.

This, then, is Israel's immortal convocation. While the whole world looks proudly to the "strength of their horses" and rejoices at the sight of the "thighs of man", Israel is un-impressed by such boasting, for the word of the Psalmist lives on its lips which show him how God cloaks the sky in clouds and prepares the rain for the earth which provides the grass for the fields and the bread for the animal. Nature receives effort-lessly that which God provides—why must men labor to achieve the same gift with the strength of their horses and the thighs of their men? *That* should be life?

Israel rises in the jubilant knowledge that it has grasped the meaning of life.

And the night of the 14th of Nissan approaches and Israel prepares the table and calls the hungry that they may come and be satisfied—and Israel waits.

And when they come, those that long to be satisfied, Israel presents to them from the table of its life the Matzo and smiles in bliss and joyfulness. The time will come when the world and those of our people who are estranged will understand. Oh, if we, too, would fully understand what blessing, what life we grasp with the Matzo in our hands.

Bread from *His* hands, bread from *God's* hand. Bread of the slaves? Yes, it is *God's* bread which is presented to men who consider themselves *God's* slaves. Life, free and joyful life, per-meates the man who knows how to break such Matzo.

Give such Matzo to your children and they will henceforth know why they have received life from you. Give them this Matzo so that they may know that it represents the most pre-cious achievement of life and that you, impoverished and desperate of life, would have never found the courage to give them existence had it not been for the Matzo in your hands which enabled you to give life to children to whom the service of God is life's loftiest goal.

ליל שמורים.—Songs; midnight songs of a sacred, blissful night. This is not a night like any other night. The light from the stars above us illuminates the poor hunted soul of our people. We who are bereft, persecuted and enslaved rise up and blissfully view the light which shines to us from the nocturnal night. ליל שמורים pronounce our trembling lips. Who dares harbor any doubt?

This night calls to us and to a great world: He is awake above me who causes our night to be illuminated. Since I know that it is He who brings me this night, I can live through it peacefully and calmly and await Him.

His word causes the evening to approach. It is *His* insight which changes the seasons and orders the stars as guards in the nocturnal sky. Every night is truly a ליל שמורים. That is why He causes the darkness to recede before the light. He is ה' צבאות— *my* God, for I need but view Him as my God and every night becomes ליל שמורים. He is my redeemer, He is intimately close to me, as He bears me through the night. Thus my life does not end in the grave.

The message of redemption penetrates my ear and refreshing dew of freshly blooming life falls in the awakening morn.

Thus, according to ancient wisdom, the Seder Night equals the Kol Nidre in sacred dedication.

לחם עוני

The bread of affliction was the first bread of freedom which our ancestors ate when God assumed the leadership of His people. It was produced by the suspenseful moment of the hasty flight into freedom. This bread was poor compared to the bread which adorns the table of the rich. Yet for our forefathers it was the most precious nourishment for it was prepared in the security of God's protective proximity. This bread of affliction was to elevate our people to become the most affluent nation on earth. For with it God presented to His people paradisian nourishment from the eternal homeland of man.

For men have abandoned God's table. Their materialistic greed demands use of their products rather than those given to them by God. And God regretfully withdraws from their midst. Without the Divine presence misery and despair enter their lives. The earth turns into a chaotic battleground of unleashed passions and insatiable hunger. The angel of death passes through history. Under his wing man chews his bread in the sweat of his brow. Is it worth all the sweat? He calls it the bread of culture. Can it hide the bestial nakedness which is the price of its acquisition?

Ever since this sad hour of separation bearers of the Divine message of redemption move quietly forward, far away from the crowded highways of war. They were dispatched to earth by a

God who remains close to His men even from the distance and who has sworn a solemn oath never to deprive them of His messengers who are to proclaim the eternal possibilities of redemption of an erring mankind, and who, as Divine Cherubim, will chart the ultimate course toward Gan Eden for a mankind saturated by suffering.

In Noach and his descendants mankind survived the shameful downfall of degraded generations. In the narrow circle of Avrohom's family mankind received the noble herolds in a world drowning in egotism and self-deification. It was in the great night of redemption when Avrohom's children were to prepare themselves, with the bread of affliction in their hands, to chart the path of redemption for a pathetic mankind.

The bread of affliction was the bread of immeasurable wealth which they received from God's hand; it was the bread of freedom which was forever cleansed from the furies of jealousy and greed, of hatred and enmity.

This bread guided them through deserts; it transformed the deserts into a Gan Eden. For God's bread was their nourishment. It was ennobled by God's Shabbos which placed it as precious Manna on their table where it protected them from Gehinnom tortures under which an erring mankind must fight for its bread of culture. It is this bread of affliction to which we address the prayerful blessing which is the daily food for the Jewish soul and with which Jewish parents nourish the souls of their children from earliest childhood:

הזן את העולם כלו בטובו בחן בחסד וברחמים, הוא נותן לחם לכל בשר כי
לעולם חסדו. ובטובו הגדול תמיד לא חסר לנו ואל יחסר לנו מזון לעולם ועד.

Is it the rich, the sated who pronounces this blessing after the opulent meal? And if he is of the chosen few who are able to say that "they never lacked anything"—what gives him the right to this claim, almost frivolous in its calm assurance, that "he will never lack food for all time to come"?

Does the sated not have any regard for his impoverished and hungry fellow-men when he dares to proclaim: "For He feeds and sustains all and does good to all and prepares nourishment for all His creatures"?

And what of the starving who get up hungry from the table and whose heart is torn by the hungry look in their children's eyes? Do they not also proclaim this blessing; do they not also teach it to their children? Is it not one great lie on their lips? Is it not life's great lie to which they educate their children?

Thus only he can speak who has never drunk from the cup of Jewish affluence of life; who has never met his ancestors with the bread of affliction in their hands and the Hallel of gratitude on their lips; who passes thoughtlessly by the Seder table which God sets annually for the poor and the rich of His people; who has never understood why God's Will demands that Jewish fathers present their children on this night with the bread of affliction from God's hand in order to prepare their young souls for the Divine message of redemption for their whole life ahead.

King David, driven into the night as a homeless beggar (Psalm 34: לדוד בשנותו את טעמו), has taught us the significance of this blessing confession of our daily existence as he pronounced it with overflowing intensity and experienced it in its moving truthfulness.

מי האיש החפץ חיים . . . לראות טוב You "demand life" want to "see only good". כפירים רשו ורעבו. Then turn away from those who profess to be mighty "as the lion" in their futile dream of building their lives on their own strength. Let them persist in their insistence to erect their own life edifice; let them sink their support deep in the soil of their own colossal conceit—the supports will break down and their life structure will collapse. Then, the "poverty" which they dreaded all their lives comes over them, the gnawing hunger will draw their emaciated bodies into the grave to which they had long since sold their souls.

דרשי ה' לא "No lack for those who fear Him" אין מחסור ליראיו
יחסרו כל טוב "they who fear God will never lack the good"—
You have sought God for you could not live without God.
You have found God and achieved Divine proximity by unconditional acceptance of His Divine Will. God has become to you
the "all-knowing God" to whom "all acts of men are counted"
(Samuel 1, 2). Now none of the mounting enigmas of life may
frighten you any longer: they all find their only possible answer
in the nearness of God.

The creative, world-shaping Divine Will which also calls
human life towards joyous participation in His world-order—it
alone knows why "the sated of yesterday must fight for their
bare bread while the famished ceases to hunger"; why "the
childless bears seven children while she who was blessed with
children buries them in the grave" (Samuel 1, 2).

Where life which was lived away from God, רשעים בחשך ידמו
"silenced in the darkness" (ib.), succumbs under the terrifying
pressure of an inconceivable fate which seems the fruit of utter
senselessness—life which is lived close to God finds the right
and the strength, in the midst of hunger and suffering and death,
to sing of the "eternal good" bestowed on an existence which is
joyously dedicated to serve as a willing tool of Divine Providence. For it is "God who kills and revives, who brings poverty
or affluence" (ib.). A life can never "be empty" (יאשמו) which
receives from God the cup of rich fulfillment; שמר כל עצמותיו.
"the bones never break" (Ps. ib.) of those whom God has burdened with suffering.

Should not God turn in the pride of fatherly joy towards a
people (Berachoth 20b) which requires but a poor piece of bread
in order to proclaim in prayerful blessing that it gained rich
satisfaction of life before God?—

נער הייתי גם זקנתי ולא ראיתי צדיק נעזב וזרעו מבקש לחם "I have been
young, have also become old and I have yet to see a righteous

man forsaken whose children begged for their bread" (Ps. 37). In a profound interpretation our Sages taught us to understand this confession: even if the righteous were burdened with the heavy lot of seeing his children yearning for the morsel of bread, he would still never feel forsaken and he would never cease to proclaim daily before God that "he never lacked in anything and that he will never lack nourishment . . ."

"This is the bread of affliction" which our ancestors ate as pharaonic enslavement embittered their lives with Gehinnom tortures.

"This is the bread of affliction" which our ancestors ate when they exchanged Pharao's servitude with the service of God—this bread was destined to prepare Gan Eden for their lives.

"May all who are hungry come" and reach for this bread.

Has the poverty of our existence still failed to produce the yearning for the kind of affluence which only the "bread of affliction" is able to provide? Such wealth may be obtained only from God's table.

On the Divine table of the sanctuary rested the "bread of affliction" of the Jewish people. It was renewed from Shabbos to Shabbos. The priests of the sanctuary greeted each other with the sacred greeting of Shabbos to which they were inspired by the breath of paradise which ennobled this bread of Jewish affluence:

מי ששכן שמו בבית הזה הוא ישכין ביניכם אהבה ואחוה ושלום וריעות

"He whose name rests upon this House, may he cause to prevail among you love and brotherhood, peace and friendship" (Berachoth 12a).

This then let us recount to our children when in the Seder night their eyes turn questioningly towards the "bread of affliction"; so that they may experience true affluence and satisfaction for all their days and that they may never lack the good even when their life's table is bereft of materialistic values.

צפון
(HIDDEN)

Three מצות repose on the Seder plate. The ones on top and bottom remain unbroken for they serve as לחם משנה and must remain whole to be eligible for the subsequent ברכת המוציא. However the ברכה על אכילת מצה requires a broken piece between the two whole מצות, for the מצה is the "bread of affliction" and the poor must be contented even with a piece of bread. For this reason the middle מצה is broken; we break it in two uneven pieces: the smaller half is being placed between the two whole מצות, the larger part is covered with a cloth and later eaten as Afikomen before ברכת המזון.

The eating of this מצה bears the connotation צפון, the hidden, and serves to commemorate the eating of the קרבן פסח.

This act, as so many others during the Seder night, is marked by a simple yet profound symbolism. At the outset of the Seder, this מצה had been placed, "hidden", in a cloth. For, at the exodus from Egypt our forefathers covered their baking troughs containing the unleavened dough with their clothing, placed them on their shoulders and departed hastily on their journey (Ex. 12, 34): in the very hour of their redemption they were still the old slaves who could do nothing to achieve their own liberation, who were so "driven" into freedom that the dough on their shoulders had no time to leaven. God alone had liberated His people. God elevated this unleavened bread to

serve as a sacred symbol for all time to come. Its consumption is
to express the recognition that God liberated his people so that
it may henceforth dedicate itself to the Divine Service and forever receive its bread from God's hand. Thus, the eating of the
מצה in the Seder night is imbedded in the הלל which sings of
Israel's selection by God and which calls on all parts of our
people to dedicate to God the jubilant song of their lives as
"Servants of God".

Hidden in the מצה, which was borne out "hidden" on the
shoulders of our forefathers, lay Jewish fate, lay Jewish future,
lay all happiness and all suffering—our fathers carried their fate
and future on their shoulders and they still rest on our shoulders
unto this day.

This מצה, when we consume it in melancholy commemora-
tion of קרבן פסח, bears for us the message of hidden hope for the
future, of hidden certainty of the events to come.

Hidden, as the מצה, is all that fills us with fear and anxiety,
and all that is subject to our fervent longing: redemption of our
people; the downfall of the Edomite rule on earth; life and death
with all their suffering; the tribulations of פרנסה; the infinity of
emotional processes; the understanding of Divine justice (פסחים
נ"ד).

Let us reiterate this thought: as long as we accept our life-
bread as מצה from the hand of God, we may calmly entrust to
Divine Providence all that is "hidden", all that lies unknown in
the future, enigmatic, incomprehensible. Our human eye may
never be able to penetrate the impenetrable—we are satisfied
that God watches: "He will act for those who look to Him" (Is.
64, 3). In the knowledge of Divine Providence and Divine Guidance we may confidently look to the good which God preserves,
for those who fear Him, in hidden trust (Ps. 31, 20).

AT MIDNIGHT

חצות לילה אקום להודות לך על משפט צדקך, "At midnight I rise to give thanks unto You for the manifestation of Your righteousness born of Your love" (Ps. 119). According to the Sages, this is King David's confession at the Seder night: at midnight I rise ושמרתי מצות קרבן פסח שנוהג עד חצות. I have met the demand of the Pesach offering which had to be consumed before midnight; therefore, I am able to offer thanks unto You for the manifestations of Your righteousness born of your love: זה דין מרור, these manifestations are the bitter experiences, the phrases of suffering with which life burdens us. To me, proclaims King David, these are the manifestations of Your righteousness—more: I possess the evidence of Your love, זה מצה for I receive the Matzoh from Your hand. It is because I brought the Pesach offering to God that I may receive His Matzoh—and with it the Moror—from His hand. Therefore, I rise at midnight to give thanks unto You, oh God.

This is the great proclamation brought to us by the Seder night which our people celebrates as ליל שמורים since that distant night of redemption and through the millenia of its history until our own days: offer the קרבן פסח to God; pay homage to Him as the Shepherd of your lives to Whose guidance you entrust an existence which—without it—would be incomprehensible. Secure God's guiding *proximity* and you may receive from *His*

hand the Matzoh of your life's nourishment borne to you by the
Divine love. Yet from *His* hand you also receive the מרור, all that
is bitter and painful, given to you to endure by the manifestations of Divine righteousness.

Woe to him who denies God the homage due Him through
the Pesach offering; who falls victim to the illusion that it is possible to master life without Divine guidance; who deprives his
bread of the Matzoh-character and is driven by the ambition to
gain the bread of independence—to him all the inconceivable
suffering is reduced to a senseless game of a blind fate capable of
destroying ruthlessly even modest happiness from one moment
to the other, smashing life's vigor by the sheer force of senseless
brutality.

It is this great Jewish truth of life which permeates the
hearts and souls of the fathers and mothers of our people and of
the martyrs of our own tragedy-filled era. This truth gave them
the heroic strength to celebrate their wretched Seder nights in
upright strength, despite the terror of nocturnal death agony.

And we? After all the indescribable and incomprehensible
suffering which we have endured and witnessed—are we
approaching a better morn? Is there the promise of a dawn in
the life of mankind? Are not our hearts wracked by the pangs of
anxiety? From where do we draw the strength, the joyfulness,
the rest in the midst of all restlessness, the peace in the face of
the absence of peace on earth?

Let us remember: we may be bereft of the tangible קרבן
פסח—but the great truth which it proclaims must continue to
inspire and permeate us in all its actuality: You, oh God, be the
Master over our lives עמו וצאן מרעיתו (Ps. 100)—we, Your people,
wholly dedicated to Your Divine guidance הוא עשנו ולו אנחנו . . .

To You we entrust our fate that You may shape it in
accordance with Your truth; from *Your* hand we receive the מצה

as our life-nourishment; with it we also receive the מרור presented to us by the Will of God.

Then—neither bitterness nor pain nor the fear of an incomprehensible fate can deprive our lives of the peace and joyfulness. "At midnight I rise to give thanks unto You for the manifestations of Your righteousness born of Your love."

תפלת טל

I.

Sacred custom of our forefathers prescribes the recital of the "Prayer for Dew" in the Mussaph of the first day of Pessach. On this day, according to the Halacha, we cease to add the prayer for rain in our Shemona Essre. Throughout the winter this prayer forms an integral part of our daily Tefilloth.

At a time when the winter season begins to spread a cloak of snow and ice over our hemisphere, the Holy Land expectantly looks forward to its rainy season. Dispersed in all corners of the globe our most fervent feelings well up for our homeland and thus the scattered remnants of our people are gathered around their spiritual center of unity. (Significantly, the date on which this prayer is added was set with Babylonia in mind, the erstwhile land of the Torah, our second homeland).

Give rain to Your earth, give rain to Your land! מזכירין גבורת גשמים בתחית המתים. "Where the resurrection of the dead is mentioned (in the Shemona Essre), reference to the power of the Divine gift of rain is in place" (Berachoth 33). Let science interpret the formulation of rain as a natural atmospheric process of nature—*we* are forever admonished by the Word of the Prophet (Zech. 10): ה'—שאלו מה' מטר bestows rain in accordance with the educational needs of His humans and forever retains the "key of rain". As at the onset of creation the rain awaited the coming of man, so rain continues to fall for men through ה׳ (Cf. Comm. Gen. 1).

Wonder of all wonders to the Jewish mind is the raindrop falling on the earth. It symbolizes the joyful certainty of ultimate resurrection: do you not see the dying soil restored to life under the wondrous impact of the falling rain? שקולה כתחיית המתים: to such view man's rise from the dead is in no way a greater miracle!

As you thoughtfully gaze upon the falling rain, you follow the traces of daily renewed Divine omnipotence of creation: "how great is the day on which rain falls; it resembles the day when heaven and earth came into existence" (Taanith 7).

Rain falls on the earth only because men still live on it who offer undivided loyalty to God (בשביל בעלי אמונה Taanith 8). For them God deems worthy the continued existence of His creation, for the world of creation depends at all times on the pronouncements of the Divine Will of creation.

As the Day of Sinai once bestowed renewed future on a decaying mankind (Sabbat 88), so every day of rain promises joyful certainty to Jewish hopes: the oath of Sinai finds eternal allegiance—else God would not quench the thirst of His earth—"for every day of rain is as significant as the day on which the Torah was given" (Cf. 7).

When the earth is being deprived of rain, it is time for Jewish thinking to lament the neglect of Torah, to mourn man's loss of humbleness and modesty, and to record sadly man's ignorance of his duties towards his fellow-men (Cf.) Jewish thinking rejoices when the longed-for rain begins to fall again: God forgives the transgressions of His people Israel (Cf)—this is the heavenly message brought by the falling raindrops. These drops revive the hopes of blessing which are the object of our longing (Cf). Every rainy morning magically recreates before our souls the day when God gathers the dispersed of His people (Cf 8), when the sun's rays are refracted a thousandfold.

Thoughtless superficiality refers to the "melancholy of rainy weather";—it could learn and derive enrichment from the poetry of Jewish thought.

And Israel should not ask for its rain in fervent prayer?

Sharpened is the eye of the Jewish people in observing the processes within nature. It is *God*—Who grants rain, and Who withholds it. This singular statement embodies the wealth of our world view.

The Jewish eye penetrates even deeper.

II.

During quiet summer nights the dew descends softly upon the meadow. Even where rain does not fall—dew is always there. Are we also to pray for—dew?

The Sages have not made the prayer for dew obligatory טל אינו יורד בזכות בריה, dew comes also when it is not deserved; it grants life even when rain ceases to fall. While the prayer for rain during the winter is preceded by the prayer for dew, ותן טל ומטר לברכה, the latter need not be uttered during the summer when the dew descends. For dew falls regardless of our prayer. Even in Elijah's days, who swore to withhold rain from his depraved generation, dew did not cease to fall. Did he not announce אם יהיה השנים האלה טל ומטר (Kings I. 17) only to promise subsequently, in the name of God, the renewed gift of rain for the soil of men ואתנה מטר על פני האדמה (Cf. 18)? Dew did fall—but it was not טל של ברכה (Taanith 3), the dew of blessing to which Elijah referred when he mentioned it in his oath. This dew was never missed by his generation—hou could he announce its return? "Did dew not fall all the time?" the fools would have exclaimed. "Dew falls and it should not be לברכה?" Thus thought the fools of that time, and thus they still think unto our own days.

Israel knows better—its eye penetrates deeper. *Its* dew does not cease, it may not cease, for it is the dew which Avrohom's children need and which God promised to the ancestor (ירושלמי ברכות פ״ה) that it may forever bestow life upon his descendants.

לך טל ילדותך (Ps. 110). *Yours is* the dew of youth which receives the eternal gift of life from Your hands—God has sworn it unto Avrohom.

לך טל ילדותך (cf. Hirsch Comm.): the Davidic gift of dew brings lasting morning freshness to a youth which nourishes its energies from its spirit.

When Yitzchok conveyed Abrahamitic blessing to Yaakov's children with ויתן לך מטל השמים, his words bespoke the certainty of his conviction: מטל השמים, זו תורה, זו ציון that his descendants shall always be aware that the dew will fall לברכה, for a blessing, only if they learn to secure for themselves, for all eternity, the heavenly dew which emanates from Zion alone in a mighty flow through the whole world שם צוה ה׳ את הברכה (Ps. 133). For in Zion God "stores" the "dew of blessing".

The dying leader, Moshe, has pronounced it, for all time to come: אף שמיו יערפו טל (Comm. Deut. 33, 28):if the dew is to become a blessing for Israel, it must descend from *its* heaven. Thus, when we pray for rain at the onset of the rainy season, the prayer for dew precedes the prayer for rain ותן טל ומטר לברכה—we pray for *that* dew which alone is worthy of the rain. If rain is to fall in our land, the quest for טל של ברכה must come first; while ordinary dew never ceases, we must learn to long for the dew of blessing without which our land, even when bathed in ordinary dew and rain, would revert to utter desolation.

This heavenly dew will never cease to descend for us—God has sworn it unto our forefathers. Abrahamitic spirit, Davidic melodies, will forever inspire our people with Divine dew.

It is *this* dew which provides our people with an indestructible strength of living. Its soul longs for it during the night; it is the object of its hymns when the morn dawns. Our people witnesses the defeat of its enemies whose strength ebbs away (Is. 26, 14) for they are not aware of the dew which alone grants life.

III.

When Spring draws near and in the glitter of dew awakens nature to renewed life, Pesach lets us also celebrate *our* Spring. We need not pray for nature's dew: it will come. But he whose soul is filled with the longing for life; who requires the spiritual dew which *we* need, which our *land* needs and which does not descend unless *we* will it—let him follow the admonitions of the fathers and perceive from poetic lips heart-warming and simple melodies:

Give us dew, *our* dew; let us, our land with us, arise to life!

טל תן—Give dew; we long for life. Like nature, we also long for rejuvenation. Give us *Your* dew which alone secures the God-willed lasting prosperity of our land; Give us *Your* dew which alone accelerates the upbuilding of Zion-Yerusholayim.

לברכה ולא לקללה—Give us *this* dew, so that nature's dew which bathes the earth may be a blessing to us and not a curse.

לשבע ולא לרזון—Give us *this* dew which alone sustains us and saves us from decay.

לחיים ולא למות—Give us *this* dew which alone helps us attain true life.

Our souls, as nature, breathe rejuvenation: in the service of God, to which Pessach calls us, we find our miraculous, ever-recurring rebirth.

Ancient heritage significantly added the sacred ימים נוראים mood to our prayer for טל. Will our hearts be equally receptive to such depth of feeling?

OUR PROPHETS SPEAK TO US

Note:

The following essay on the role of the study of our Nevi'im appears warranted in view of the incredible neglect of this vital study area by most of our higher Yeshiva institutions. This is a phenomenon which probably has its roots in our recent history. At the time when the so-called "Haskala," spreading its vicious propaganda, tried to expel the Talmud study from the educational program and to replace it with the study of Tanach and Hebrew language, a negative attitude of the Yeshivoth towards the role of Tanach study was understandable. In our time there is no reason for this attitude. The present trend towards almost exclusive occupation with the Talmud leaves the study of Tanach to the individual Talmid on whose private interest it depends whether he wishes to broaden his knowledge and understanding of Tanach beyond that which he acquired in grade school. The study of Tanach, no less than the study of Talmud, requires the mature guidance of those who are able to provide it for our mature youth.

It is the purpose of this essay to demonstrate in brief strokes the approach to the Books of our Prophets and the vital significance of this research.

I

Our Prophets must be read in a spirit of sanctity, for they meet us as Divinely inspired leaders, commissioned by God to assist us in comprehending the enigma of life.

233

Our Prophets are alive in our midst; they must never be relegated to the relics of the past. As eternally alive and direct the Divine Word of the Torah addresses us, "which I command you this day", as alive and timelessly pertinent are the words of our Prophets, inseparable from the Words of the Torah, never to be evaluated as "historically and culturally significant" documents, voices from a past long gone. Their message is timeless, eternal (Megilla 14a).

Our Prophets "serve man's earth", "a man that serves the earth am I" (Zech. 13, 5): their loftiest task is the liberation of the earth from the cursed chains in which it is imprisoned by a mankind estranged from God. "As man and for man he has summoned me" (into His service) (ibid.) towards the re-education of such men for their erstwhile, pure, Divine destiny.

Initially, the Prophets address our people. They are our teachers: "God gave me a language for disciples, to address the fatigued at the right time." (Is. 50, 4). Prophets expect us to look up to them as disciples. They shake us out of our lethargy, to reflect, to perceive . . . From the millenia their words reach us in majestic timeliness.

Life, secular, estranged from God, overwhelms us with its demands. Let us find refuge with our Prophets so that they may stand at our side when we threaten to succumb; when clarity and self-judgment threaten to fade. Let our Prophets become for us *the* source of spiritual fortitude and strength.

Our Prophets lay open the lies and deceit with which ignorance, indifference and weakness attempt to deprive us of our most precious possession of life by falsifying it beyond recognition. Let us read their books from beginning to end: their incomparably heroic energy is wholly dedicated to this great task. For they were fighters who lived and suffered and fought for their people, for mankind, unto their last breath.

When nature and history threaten to engulf us in nocturnal darkness; when they no longer speak to us as divine creations; when we no longer perceive in them the traces of eternal Divine Providence, then — onwards to the Prophets, that they may clear our gaze from the cobwebs of illusion; that they may remove the veil which beclouds our free outlook and our pure judgment; that we, through them, may rectify our "errors" *Al Shigyonos* (Hab. 3, 1), fight our way through life's enigma to the brilliant light, and intone with Yirmiyah (16, 19) our life's "song of victory."

For Prophets lead us, pave the way for us, "Behold, I send My messenger, and he shall clear the way before Me." (Mal. 3, 1) leading to our salvation; they remove the stones and rubble which obstruct our ascent to the proximity of God: "lead upwards, upwards, pave the way, remove the stumbling block from the path of my people" (Is. 57, 14).

Our Prophets heal the treacherous and unholy breach which separates "children from fathers, fathers from children" (Mal. 3, 24). Thus their eternal admonition *Zichru Toras Moshe Avdi* (ibid. 23). This means: Return to Torah.

A seemingly inexhaustible theme. A few basic thoughts will illuminate it further.

II

Prophets stand before us with the Torah in their hands — this must not be forgotten or ignored at even a single line of prophetic literature.

The lofty ideals which Torah aims at and to which it obligates us — we learn them from the Prophets. For they present to us the Torah as the concrete evidence of Divine love (Mal. 1, 2). Our twice-daily proclamation in prayer — Torah, the life-giving source and confluence of Divine love — this recognition, this consciousness we gain through our Prophets.

They are at our side, as they gaze upon those who are unnerved and poisoned, senselessly drunk in their greed for wealth and enjoyment as they adorn themselves with their fading wreath, proudly boasting of achievements which only contribute to their own fearful degradation. Prophets stand at our side as they gaze upon those whose table no longer has space for the pure and holy, who have but shrill scorn for Torah whose spirit is foreign to them, and who consider total emancipation from the Law the prerequisite for life's happiness (Is. 28).

Our Prophets are well aware that there is a stage of estrangement when every word is in vain and when only harsh experience and bitter disappointment bring belated and painful awakening (Is. 50, 11). Our Prophets hurry to our side to protect us from such shipwreck of life.

They spell out the curse which inevitably afflicts a life without Torah (Zech. 5). Tremble, before you forfeit forever the most precious possession of your life in frivolous superficiality. Remember, always, what you possess in your Torah. By helping us to attain the genuine, pure knowledge and recognition of Torah, our Prophets prove to be its most forceful interpreters.

III

Torah never tires of compressing its entire contents into pregnant formulations: "this Commandment," (Deut. 30, 11); God places us at our post which we must fill with our lives in accordance with God's Will; "nothing, but to fear", (Deut. 10, 12): only through the most minute fulfillment of the precepts of the Divine Will shall we be able to attain that true fear of God which does not permit the presence of God to fade from our consciousness even during one moment of our lives; "Complete shall you be with God" (Deut. 18, 13): undivided devotion to the Will of God and thereby the most intimate union with God; "the way of God" (Gen. 18, 19): strict adherence to the divinely charted path which alone enables man to practice *Tzedakah Umishpat,* love and righteousness — the all-exhaustive contents of man's mission on earth. All this calls for the total fulfillment of the Divine Law.

In the same way, our Prophets view Torah in all its unabridged entity (Makoth 42a) by interpreting in many places *Tzedakah* and *Mishpat* as the sum-total of Torah (Is. 56, 1-2), Torah being our great guide towards "good" (Micah 6, 8), towards "total dedication", *Emunah* (Hab. 2, 4), towards the "search for God" (Amos 5, 4).

Let us read our Prophets if we wish to be saved from shameful compromise and from misinterpreting our own relationship to God and His sacred Will.

Let us read our Prophets if we wish to comprehend ourselves as *Jews,* with all the obligations which this noble title entails for us. Let us learn with the Prophets and through the Prophets what it means to be bearers of Torah knowing that this our Torah counts on us to ease the burden of its "fate" (Zech. 9-14) placed upon it by its timeless course through the storms of time. Yet this Torah depends on our "hunger" and "thirst," that we may not rest until the full realization comes upon us that true happiness and satisfaction — even in the midst of abundance — derives solely from the possession of this truly "good" (Is. 55; Jer. 31). Are we of those who are "impoverished and needy," who "search vainly for water and do not find it" (Is. 47, 17)? For us the Divine well runs full, and daily there still falls the bread of life for our satisfaction.

Let us obtain clarity from our Prophets regarding that which fully characterizes the *Jewish national concept*: *Am*

Hashem, a people rooted with all fibres of its being in God and His Word. Every page of prophetic literature recalls the Divine "to Me as a nation; I, your God," the proclamation which founded Israel's nationhood. Unless we dedicate our whole lives towards the perpetuation of this eternal destiny, we have no claim on membership in this nation. Let us never forget: "You are bearers of the Divine design" (Is. 52, 11).

IV

Our Prophets never tire of defining and outlining the role of *Eretz Yisrael,* so that we may be able to distinguish it from the other lands in the world.

None have recognized so clearly — as they have — the Tum'oh effects on the whole Jewish national body which threatens from this soil, ideal site of Israel's pure, God-willed existence. The Prophets suffered from these effects which transformed their lives into a martyrdom without compare. In the firm confidence of Divine assistance and of the future of Israel, and with heroic strength, they tore their people from a soil which spelled certain death, in order to train and prepare it for the true Eretz Yisrael of the future. (This is the central theme of the Book of Yecheskel).

In the eyes of the Prophets, Eretz Yisrael is inviolably bound to Zion and Yerushalayim. They view Eretz Yisrael as the site of a national life which centers around Zion as the most sacred monument of the majestic Law which shapes Divinely inspired living. At the feet of Zion they see Yerushalayim as the beacon, the exemplary national center dedicated to the worshipful devotion of an entire national existence to the precepts of the Divine Will. On the fortresses of this Yerushalayim they stand, its faithful guardians, tirelessly laboring to admonish and educate their people towards its task as "holy nation", "redeemed through God," ultimately to shake off the Galuth dust of millenia (Is. 62).

Let us read our Prophets if we are to perceive the meaning of *Galuth,* experience *Ge'ulah* and fulfill the conditions which lead to Ge'ulah as the certain goal of Divine promise. For Ge'ulah is no mere belief — it is a necessity for Israel and for mankind ,as true as a God lives who shapes history and human progress towards His God-willed goals (Zech. 9). Israel's Galuth is nothing but a renewed "march through the desert" (Yech. 20, 35), the only possible path upon which a purified Israel will ultimately return to its homeland.

Prophets teach us to understand Israel's historic position always in the context of the great *world historic* events and developments. Thus they are, also in this realm, merely interpreters of the guidelines to history and mankind's growth as laid down in the early pages of the Divine Book. Together with our Prophets we must read these pages if we wish to appreciate their profound significance: the aims of Creation for mankind, as revealed therein; their connection with a paradisic life of proximity to God; the contrasting tragic estrangement from God; vile inhumanity; the illusion of humans fighting against God, silhouetted against the brilliantly emerging eminence of an Abraham — such phases we must learn to pursue further in the mosaic of world-historic events.

Invariably, the Prophets guide our gaze from the blinding illusion of man's existence to the tragic "temporariness" to which the achievements of God-denying aspirations are condemned. (Is. 66, 24, Hab. 2, 13). They point to the "debris" which covers the history of mankind (Mal. 1.); to the scarred victims incessantly demanded by the "flames of the coiling sword;" and to the "nocturnal night" (Zech. 1) in which human deceit turns to utter despair. In the face of the shattering testimony of human folly, the Prophets raise God's eternal demands and proclaim God's eternal readiness to restore to an erring mankind renewed paradisic joyfulness in order to end forever the misery of its suicidal existence.

Thus our Prophets reveal history before our eyes, that we may behold Him in the ceaseless labor of completing the work of Creation. The idea of "war against Yerushalayim" runs like a red thread through history (Zech. 12). The victorious recognition of the way of life as demanded by Yerushalayim means Ge'ulah for mankind, Sabbath-peace for the world (Is. 2).

Such Weltanschauung derived from our Prophets-literature brings with it the most profound appreciation of the nature of the *Jewish mission*. In its national life, Israel must realize the precepts of the Divine Will in selfless devotion, must erect the throne of rulership for the Will of God and await then confidently the time when, as bearer of the "light" and as herald of the "peace" (Is. 42), cherubim-like, it will chart the course towards the eternal homeland for a mankind thirsty for redemption.

Need it be added that only from such Weltanschauung flows the true *Jewish consciousness* as outlined by Isaiah (40 ff.) and Zecharia (9) in brilliant strokes? To be permeated by such consciousness means to reject categorically un-Jewish weakness and compromise; shame in the face of even a faint trace of defeatism (Is. 54); it means to experience invincible strength in the possession of the incomparable weapon which rests forever in our hands (Zech. 4). With unshakeable courage, and with the Divine song of victory on our lips (Is. 12, Jer. 16, 19), we will live even through the darkest of Galuth nights.

V

All this we glean from the words of our Prophets — it is *Torah* which we read with them. This thought cannot be stressed enough: not a single word, not a single thought, not a single concept that our Prophets have not derived from our Torah. Any attempt to read the Prophets in a different way collapses in its own miserable, frivolously falsifying untruthfulness.

He who reads Prophets as they should be read receives eternally sacred messages from their mouths: This is how we, the Prophets, experienced Torah — this is what Torah means to us; what does it mean to you?

The Books of our Prophets are the immortal sources from which flow Jewish consciousness and Jewish strength in an inexhaustible stream.

THE EXPERIENCE OF REVELATION

"I am ready to uphold the Torah as the Book of my life if I can be convinced that it represents the Divine Word of Revelation." We have achieved much if youth approaches us with such an attitude. For it expresses its yearning for Revelation.

How many are there who have never felt the urge to glean from the leaves of a book a solution to the riddle of life.

We have achieved much if we encounter the earnest desire to place life under the dictate of a Law. For in most cases men no longer are capable of pronouncing: "I am ready." They have long since been conquered by forces to whom they remain forever enslaved. These men will never proclaim: "We are ready."

Divine Word of Revelation. Its meaning: God must show us the course we must chart for ourselves. This presupposes the recognition that our human mind is limited. Revelation begins where the mind recognizes its limitations. While counting on the workings of the human mind, Revelation also counts on—resignation!

Revelation appeals to the intellect. Take me when you need me—that is its language.

Revelation does not appeal to belief—it does not beg to be admitted.

Belief is unsteady, changeable. Possession of Revelation as

an invaluable gift and requirement of life must never depend on the many moods of belief.

Your forefathers lived and died for the conviction that in the Torah—which they upheld even if it meant sacrificing their lives—they left you their most valuable heirloom. Is it possible that you, with inconceivable frivolity and without investigation, would refuse to accept a heritage which may bring you the most precious possession?

Are you one of those who constantly talk of the lack of "religious feeling?" Rather promote the need for more education and less brutality! How can you fail to see the old flags whose tattered shreds once heralded victory and glory for our ancestors in bloody battles of yesteryear?

Woe to him who desecrates our flag.

Has it ever occurred to you that there is not one word of your Torah, not one precept of its teaching which, hallowed by the blood of your ancestors of centuries and even millenia ago, has not guided them to victory and life?

Would you trample on this Torah with your feet? Why do you not admit it and label that as brutality and lack of education which the superficial idiom likes to call "irreligiosity?"

Who would wish to be accused of brutality and a lack of education?

You have no desire to be brutal and are unwilling to be called "uneducated." Then consider: You are not the first to pose the question whether the Book of Torah is the Book of Divine Revelation.

This Book places such great demands and such unique stamp on life that there has not been a thinking man before you who has taken this Book without asking himself whether he is obligated to recognize it as the Book of God.

You cannot but admit: You have been preceded by men whose intellectual capacity you have deeply admired; men possessed of the courage of conviction who have grasped the meaning of life in all its depth—and were fully aware of the significance of the Torah's impact. What else has caused them to turn to Torah but to accept it as their lives' Divine Message?

These men found the proof of the Torah's Divine character in the uninterrupted tradition of an entire people (Deut. V, 19; X, 5). Beyond this, the Torah bears its Divinity in its own pages: It is the pen of God, Creator and Ruler of His people, Master of its history, which has predicted the fate of our nation beyond the millenia, as formulated in the staggeringly realistic pronouncements of the "Tochacha" and in the monumental "Song of Fate." which Moshe Rabbenu placed on the lips of his people.

Only he who renounces his people and denies its history can dare to refuse to admit the Torah's Divine character.

While Torah is the embodiment of God's Plan of Life for His people and of its God-willed mission, Revelation becomes of paramount importance for men's Divinely set duties of life. Present from the onset of Creation, Revelation represents the lofty goal which will once be regained by an erring mankind.

What is the basis upon which Revelation may become a necessity of man's existence?

You must find God, experience Him. A thousand fold the rays must divert to guide your perceiving gaze towards God. You must find Him who speaks to us out of a Universe full of wondrous Laws.

Why do men fail to find God? Because they have no desire to find Him; because their greedy pursuit of enjoyment beclouds their vision and their lust for power blinds their eyes.

For this is the great question: Should man be his own God, or should God be the God of men! Little wonder that the usurper is most reluctant to relinquish his throne!

Thus it may well happen that men stagger through life, rush through life: enjoyment intoxicates them, hunger for power lures them; their eye is blind and deaf is their ear. They have no eyes for the wonders of God, no ears for the poetry of His Creation.

Leave behind you the emptiness and thoughtlessness which must arouse your disgust. Then you will awaken from the illusion and observe sadly: where is, where do I find the meaning of life? You behold the wealth of your material possessions, yet you see yourself for the first time in all your poverty and misery. Who would not be shaken to the very depth of his being when his life's pillars begin to crumble and he is confronted by the mystery: what does it all mean?

Stop the pleasure seekers in their path and ask them why they live! You will be shattered by the superficiality of which men are capable.

Stop the thoughtlessly living man and ask him why he lives on this earth and you will be shaken by the shameful fact: he has never thought of it!

If there were no God would you not be forced to say, "my life is senseless, not worth living, for I do not grasp its meaning."

"My life is my own! Who can prevent me from discarding it!" "Father, I do not want life." What will you tell your child?

Duty!

To whom? For what?

Live for the community?

You can hardly suppress a smile. Does the wave have duties towards the sea? The foam of life, born in chance, inevitably

~ ſ ʊ

drifting to chance, elevated by the wave of eternity—only to plunge back into darkness and void—and duty?

Without a meaning of life there is no duty!

"Provide the youth with ideals for which it may live and that it may live?" Fools! They do not grasp the meaning of life and they talk of the goals of life ! . . .

But you are seized by sacred awe for the rays of Divinity penetrate your beclouded gaze.

For God's is the earth and all that fills it. Sacred soil upon which treads your foot (Ps. 24).

Yet a desperate cry rings from your breast: What am I to do on earth? How can I exist on His holy Mount? (ibid.)

"Find your own way." They dare to tell you this? Is it possible? You have come into existence because God willed it. You live because He wills it. You do not grasp the meaning of life as He perceives it. And yet you should be able to chart your own course, to set your own goal, to give yourself tasks, duties?

As true as God lives—He must give me Revelation.

Why do you not let your children lose themselves in the whirl of the streets, cross the yawning abyss or even go astray in the wilderness? Why do you offer your hand to your children and then resent their frivolous show of independence? When they rush away from you—and trip, do you not exclaim: what lack of sense, how foolish! Truly, is it not easier for the little ones to find the way to parental home than it is for the grown-ups to find their way through life?

Does God not have paternal rights? God sees the unwillingness of His children to accept His word, to chart His course. "Their way I see, I will heal them," they will yet come—pronounces God in never-ending kindness, and He waits (Is. 57, 18).

As the parched throat of the poor longs for water and finds it not—so will they yearn for Revelation (Is. 41, 17).

As the tree stretches its roots towards the water springs to draw from them life and strength—so men cannot live without the wellspring of Divine Life—Revelation (Yer. 17, 8). ,

For men are created to find root on earth, unlike the chaff which is scattered by the storm in all winds (Ps. 1).

The spring overflows and calls to life. Yet men shy away from it.

Will not the heat then sear their leaves and stifle their fruit —and consume man himself? (ibid.)

As the breath of life, so you need God's Torah to guide you through life.

Teach me how to live without air and I will learn how to live without—Revelation.

Do you believe in the necessity of breathing? You hear the question and smile.

Do you believe in the Divine character of Revelation? I know that I must breathe in order to live.

And I should not yearn for God's Torah which my people handed down to me from Sinai?

ORGANIZATIONS OF
RABBIS AND CONGREGATIONS
IN THE UNITED STATES

It need not be especially emphasized that it is important for Rabbis and also for Congregations to form organizations as a framework for the joint solution of tasks which confront the Rabbinical leaders and their communities. In this country we witness a virtual mushrooming of such organizations which, alas, frequently and peacefully unite orthodox, conservative and reform rabbis as well as Congregations of similarly diversified character. This regrettable phenomenon can only be ascribed to a total lack of Jewish consciousness.

Several years ago eleven Rabbinical leaders of authoritative renown, leaders of the great national Yeshivoth, announced a halachic decision prohibiting membership in the New York Board of Rabbis, encompassing orthodox, conservative and reform rabbis, as well as membership in the Synagogue Council of America, encompassing orthodox, conservative and reform Congregations.

Following is the text of the rabbinical decree:

"Whereas we have been queried by many rabbis in various parts of the country and by numerous graduates and ordained Yeshiva students if it is permissible to join and participate in the New York Board of Rabbis, and likewise in similar organizations in other cities that are constituted together with "rabbis" of the reform and conservative movement;

Therefore in assembled session to define and clarify the issue, our unanimous decision prohibits, according to the dictates of the Law of our Holy Torah, to be a member and to participate in such or similar organizations.

Whereas we have been likewise queried on the permissibility to join and participate in the Synagogue Council of America which is similarly constituted with the participation of reform and conservative movements;

Therefore our unanimous decision is that it is prohibited, according to the dictates of the Law of our Holy Torah, to join with them whether it be in an individual capacity or as an organized community group.

In witness whereof we affix our hand and seal the fifth day of the week, 18 Adar 5716 in New York City."

This announcement follows closely the halachic decision for which Rav Hirsch, his successor and like-minded rabbinical leaders in Germany, fought tirelessly in speech and writings. The same halachic decision was made by the great Chasam Sofer (חלק ו': פ"ט) and followed by hundreds of Rabbonim, among them leaders of world renown.

The name of Samson Raphael Hirsch has become synonymous with the precept of Torah im Derech Eretz which has suffered more misinterpretation than any other epoch-making ideology of recent Jewish history. The Hirschian meaning is clearly defined in the Commentary to Vayikro 18, 4 which culminates in the great demand that God's Torah must rule supreme over the spiritual and material life of the Yehudi:

"Torah and the teachings it embodies must always and everywhere remain for us the absolute and unconditional truth; they must form the yardstick by which we measure all the results obtained by other spheres of learning. Only that which is in accordance with the truths of the Torah bears for us the imprint of truth. Torah must not be for us just another branch of all other knowledge so that we might possess a Jewish science, a Jewish truth, on the same basis and with the same importance and authority as non-Jewish knowledge and non-Jewish truth . . ."

Is it not ironical, even dangerous that certain institutions of higher learning claim Rav Hirsch as their spiritual guide which are not at all ready to live up to the elementary demands of his ideology?

Little has changed regarding the membership of "orthodox" rabbis and "orthodox" congregations in the aforementioned mixed organizations. This is all the more regrettable as no attempt was ever made to dispute the validity of the above halachic decision. At a meeting of a rabbinical group, attended by a number of rabbis who, with their congregations, belong to "mixed" organizations, tribute was paid to Rav Hirsch as the great representative of the Torah im Derech Eretz principle (the inference, of course, being that Hirsch would have joyfully welcomed the existence of "mixed" organizations). None of these rabbis have the right to claim the name of S.R. Hirsch for their own. Anyone who accepts and lives Torah im Derech Eretz as interpreted and proclaimed by S.R. Hirsch, will consider the following thought of self-understood condition: only he deserves the title of a genuine rabbinical leader in Israel who recognizes the absolute supremacy of the Divine Torah (i.e. our Divine Judaism) over our entire existence and who works ceaselessly for the realization of this demand. The true Jewish Kehilla is the one whose fundamental statutes strive towards the uncompromising adherence of all members to the demands of Divine Judaism. Could such thinking permit membership in an organization which equally and in mutual recognition joins together orthodox, conservative and reform rabbis and congregations (even though their avowed aim professes to be the furtherance of mutual interests)?

During long years Rav Hirsch fought passionately against the coercive rule then prevalent in Prussia which allowed but one local Jewish Kehilla and prohibited the withdrawal of the orthodox community, desiring to form independent Kehilloth, from Congregations which had assumed a conservative or even reformistic character. As everyone knows, Rav Hirsch succeeded spectacularly in liberating his followers from this unnatural coercion.

In America, land of liberty, there is no law governing congregational character and membership. If there are still "orthodox" rabbis, "orthodox" congregations which voluntarily join organizational ranks with the conservatives and reformers—why go back to halachic sources for clarification! Just go and question the Protestants and Catholics as to their willingness to join forces for the solution of common problems! And yet the gulf between these two religions (as repeatedly stressed by Rav Hirsch) is by far not as deep as that which separates the prevailing "trends within the framework of Judaism!" "Trends?" For Rav Hirsch (and who could fail to agree with him) there existed no "trends" within Judaism, but the one Divine Judaism of Torah governing life in all its manifold phases. All else he rejected as non-Judaism, the recognition of which in the form of an equal "trend"—and that is joint membership in "mixed" organizations—he viewed as a treasonous act against the eternal truth of Divine Judaism.

In this connection, we refer to the detailed halachic discussion in the 4th volume of Hirsch's "Collected Writings" from which we quote two select passages:

> "None of the various denominations within the Christian Church are separated by a gulf as deep as that which separates reform Judaism from Orthodox Torah-Judaism" (Page 243).
> ". . . even regarding the Karaites the need was felt for a complete separation in force unto this day, although the gulf between them and the Rabbanites and the desertion of Torah-Judaism by the Karaites was by far not as deep and decisive as the gulf that separates contemporary reform from Torah-Judaism."
> "The Karaites denied the oral teachings; but they submitted wholly to the eternally ruling power of the Divine laws without

opposing a single of its tenets. Present-day reform, on the other hand, lodges a total denial of any permanent obligation to the Divine laws; in its liturgical censorship it has abandoned truths which, founded and expounded by the Divine word in Bible and Prophets, form an integral part of the basic truth of Jewish convictions" (Page 323).

No motive whatever can justify such an uncalled for, illogical banding together. Its supporters point to the joint representation in dealings with the government. An example usually cited is the fight against the attempts to enforce a "humanization" of the Shechita-process by governmental decree. It seems to us that the colleagues of the reform movement would be rather ineffective defenders of an institution which they consistently label as "antiquated" and which, in their view, is devoid of any Divine character. Or should the orthodox rabbi, in his campaign for the lawful separation of the sexes through the Mechitza, look for support of the conservative or reform camps to combat the reformistic aspiration in his own Synagogue? By joining forces with his opponents, does not the orthodox rabbi lay himself wide open to the argument that the difference between orthodox, conservative and reform Judaism cannot be so basic, after all, for how else could the three "trends" be peacefully united in one organization; and therefore the orthodox rabbi has no right to upset the peace in his congregation by insisting upon an institution (Mechitza) which is declared "unimportant" by two "trends" in Judaism.

All those who lay claim to Rav Hirsch as the champion of Torah im Derech Eretz, should also adopt the motto with which he frequently climaxed his polemical writings on behalf of the truth of our Divine Judaism: קושטא קאי שקרא לא קאי truth prevails—falsehood fails.

בטחון

From Sinai Israel brought down a magic word which has dried its tears and stilled its grief ever since. It is the source of its courage and helped it raise its head erect and proud. It is a term which is often used thoughtlessly, and still more often it is ridiculed. However, when its true meaning is recognized and understood, it represents the proudest achievement to be attained in life: בטחן.

"We must have בטחן", says the businessman when he finds himself unable to foresee all eventualities. Does he have a right to speak of בטחן?

"Have בטחן", says the friend to his brother who suffers. With these words, too, the wife attempts to cheer up her husband when despair threatens to overwhelm him. Do they have a right to speak of בטחן?

"They must be fatalists", thinks the "enlightened" son who is unable to share his parents' point of view—without, of course, even suspecting in his half-baked sophistication that בטחן has nothing in common with fatalism, with a desolate belief in an inexorable fate against which no fear can fight and no hope can persist. Cease hoping and cease fearing, says the fatalist. What must be will come to pass, just the same. Dull indifference marks the pattern of his life. Where there is fatalism, joy disappears together with fear; hope departs, and with it the will to strive forward. And this should be בטחן?

בטחן—when gloom surrounds us and the feeling of powerless abandonment grips us and fear trembles within our heart?

בטחן—when the thought of death fills us with dread and we
shrink back before the sinister question mark which death
paints before our soul?

No! And no again! Like every other Jewish truth, בטחן
must be deserved. He who always speaks of it and thinks he has
a special claim upon it must consider carefully whether he really
has a right to quaff these drops of balm from the cup of salvation.

בטחן must never be a last resort out of difficulty, a last,
despairing sigh by means of which the frightened soul makes a
convulsive effort to gain peace and comfort.

Earn בטחן during the day, so that you may also gain it during the night. Earn the right to בטחן in life, so that you may also
gain it in death. And, truly, we must have בטחן in life; we can
have it—we may have it!

We must have it! Do we understand life? Do not refer to
the enigma of the "Beyond"; it is the enigma of the Here and
Now, of our life on earth, that confronts us.

Woe to him who places his trust in himself אשר יבטח באדם
(Jer. 17)—he relies on the strength of his muscles to guide him
through life. The penetrating view of prophecy has bestowed a
curse on such a life, for it sees such existence end in desolation
and misery.

To have בטחן means to be like a tree whose roots reach
deep into the soil in order to draw life-giving moisture and to
gain a firmness which will defy all storms (ibid).

בטחן means the conviction that we cannot, even for one
moment, exist without God's guiding arm. בטחן requires אמונה,
complete devotion to the Divine Will and to the fulfillment of its
precepts.

בטחן means embracing God's Law with fervent ardor that

it may be our guide and strength throughout life. God is משען
ומבטח לצדיקים.

בטחון means answering the לך לך of our God throughout our
days on earth. In such a life בטחון triumphs. It orients itself on
the example set by Avrohom; it dares to wander in the darkness
where no light beckons, because trust in God, the support
granted by God, does not fail even here (Is. 50).

בטחון means heeding the שבת-call of God, in the realization
that it is He who makes us cease our labors; else we would be
reduced to the most pitiable slaves of our own greed and lust for
power; else we would succumb, panting, to the scourge of our
own restlessly rushing brain—if not for Him.

We shall not succumb! We shall strive toward the summit
from which we may look down compassionately upon the daily
grind of the restless whose eyelids know no slumber and whose
bread is salted with tears—but this summit will be attainable
only when we will have attained בטחון for ourselves (Ps. 125).

בטחון means: God must build our house. His Will must
build it; each stone must be dedicated to the fulfillment of this
Will. With the birth of each child received from His bounty,
would we not then feel His blissful nearness which is certain as
long as our houses remain dedicated unto him? (Ps. 127).

Come, have בטחון!—the Jewish singer calls unto us. This
means: Be among those ירֵאי ה' who fear God and who walk in
His paths. There alone the אשרי beckons to you, only there will
you find שלום.

בטחון is אשרי, the essence of all imaginable progress towards
salvation. It is earned in a hard way, marked by bitter struggles.
First there must be אשרי יושבי ביתך (Ps. 84)—you must be able to
number yourselves among those who dwell in His House, who
do not for one moment remove themselves from His presence.
אשרי אדם עוז לו בך. God must become for you the sole source of
power whence flows eternal strength and rejuvenating courage,

ילכו מחיל אל חיל, in order to gain with each act of duty an ever closer approach to the ideal of Zion which rises in your lives, יראה אל אלק׳ בציון,—only then אשרי אדם בוטח בך, will you have earned the right to בטחון.

שבת bestows upon you the right to בטחון. Its farewell sings into your hearts: הנה א׳ ישועתי אבטח ולא אפחד. With the Shabbos you have won God for your lives; your lives have been won for God, and wherever God lives in truth, בטחון permits "saturation with joy" בוטח על ה׳ ידשן (Mishle 28). The Shabbos transforms you into a "people saturated with joy", עם מדושני עונג, because it harbors בטחון.

Wherever the spirit of the שלש רגלים is realized, there also dwells the right to בטחון. When God has become to you the Creator and Preserver of your personality; when you have accepted from His Hand the law of your life; when you have rid yourself of the delusion that barn and vineyard and bountiful earth alone guarantee your security and future—when you have thus heeded the call of the שלש רגלים to come into the Presence of God—then you also have a right to leave your boundaries behind you, unguarded.

This is the spirit of the prayer which we recite before going to sleep at night, the prayer which ends the Jewish day of the תורה. Have בטחון by day so that you may also have בטחון at night.

Have בטחון by day: this means שויתי ה׳ לנגדי תמיד (Ps. 16). Find God and set Him before you always, so that He may become your right hand from which you shall not waver. Should not then your heart rejoice in the knowledge that you, too, will one day safely rest, that He will not abandon your soul to the grave and will not turn over to ruin in death those who were devoted to Him in love during their lifetime?

תודיעני אורח חיים, let Him show us the way of life—and בטחון is ours in life and in death.

MOSHIACH

Worlds have collapsed before our very eyes. Even the most fleeting glimpse into a bright future has been denied to us. The call to reflection, to clarity of life, sounds forth with increasing urgency. Only frivolous man seeks satisfaction in intoxication and giddiness; perhaps he only seeks to forget. Let him who does not want to perish in desolation and despair fight for inner clarity and firmness, and let him be conscious of what has remained to him of the eternal values of life, and to what eternal tasks he must dedicate his entire strength, his entire life, more than ever before. And the sound of God's Shofar penetrates his ear.

In the midst of a world lying in ruins, in darkness and desolation, we must discover the ground on which we must stand, and find the path on which we must walk in order to reach life.

Let us rid ourselves of the deceptive phrase, the blinding glare, and we shall see before us the great eternally splendid task: God is waiting for us to build His world for Him! Long ago, in the midst of Egypt's night, God chose us to be His People, to be bearers of His will. His world, willed into being by Him, leads towards perfection, despite all misery, degeneration and estrangement. God guarantees us this success. He is אהי״ה. He is מהוה עולמות. He leads worlds towards their fulfillment. We are called to His service.

Behold, His truth spoke unto us, as follows: זה שמי לעולם. Entrust yourselves to its guidance, put your strength in its service. Be בני עולם הבא, sons of this world to come, a world order which shall become reality in accordance with God's will.

It is the goal for which the divine word of Torah comes to earth: a world of the sovereignty of God, of God's might, of God's peace.

As we long for Moshiach, so the world is awaiting its redeemer as well. Moshiach will redeem us. He will free a world from misery. That world which Moshiach will one day bring about is that עולם הבא to which you should devote your strength, your very lives.

You, yourselves, shall bring about Moshiach; each and every one of you shall give Moshiach to the world! Life asks no less from you. Let your eye look steadfastly upon the goal. The Torah has sharpened your view, and all the words of the prophets have revealed this world to you. אין בין עולם הזה לימות המשיח אלא שיעבוד מלכיות בלבד. Human sovereignty disappears and God's sovereignty will come true. All the bliss and all the joy of Paradise is given to us by virtue of this one fact.

You shall and you can have a share in this Olom Habbo כל ישראל יש להם חלק לעה״ב; and the earth which will then emerge from the chaos is your earth. You have created it. You have raised it from the watery grave of death. For "they who strive towards God—they shall inherit the earth, and their heritage shall be the world to come" (Ps. 37).

Dedicate your strength to the Sabbath, prepare a place for it, and the world of Divine sovereignty must come about. God carries you safely over all earthly frailty and over all the pain of a desolate present; satisfies you with length of days and permits you to behold His salvation (Ps. 91)

Humanity groans, tortured by woes and shaken by nightmares. Deserted ruins look down on impassable streets. But for you, light radiates in the midst of darkness. God leads you, satiating your soul with delight and strengthening your bodies. For, it is you who are rebuilding the seemingly eternal ruins. You have laid the foundation for future generations. You have rebuilt what had been razed. You have shown paths to a peace-

ful sojourn on earth. You have planted Olom Habbo on earth
(Is. 58).

He who heeds the call of the Shofar knows to what goal he
must henceforth consecrate his life, in order to raise it from
fleeting frailty to a state of eternal duration. He will plant and
build in the service of the world order willed by God, and he will
tremble at the thought that his life might become forfeited to
extinction in the sight of God. He will listen longingly in order
to learn the paths he must take if he is to achieve true life. He
will tear himself away from giddy thoughtlessness and sensuous indolence. Those who dance drunkenly at the abyss of their
lives and basely scorn the one value in life which could lend content to their existence, will then be revealed in all their true
wretchedness.

For his ear has heard God's call and horror grips him when
he sees the fearful words in God's Scripture: כרת to him who
scorns Milah, mocks the Sabbath, ignores Yom Kippur; כרת to
him who bars from his married life the law willed by God; כרת to
him who does not sanctify the enjoyment of his life and who
wickedly sins against God's sanctuary.

Should he scorn the divine warning call which comes to him
from the mouth of the prophet (Mal.2) and dissipate his
strength, which was sanctified by God, in extra-marital desecration, by sacrificing the divine spark within him to mere sensuality and to the satisfaction of a base lust—and thus become
subject to כרת? "Uprooted" from God's hand means to be torn
away from His creative hand and expelled from life as a useless,
worthless being; to forfeit this life and the life that is to come, to
have no future here or in the hereafter; not to live on in one's
children and not to have a share in the life which awaits us after
the end of our fleeting days on earth!

The true Jew heeds the call of God whom he has chosen as
the Shepherd of his life. Henceforth God leads him through life
beside the still waters and is near him in the valley of the shadow

of death. He does not fear evil, because His rod and His staff comfort him; and because God leads him, everything that happens to him in life is good and merciful. He will go home to God, and the House of the Lord will open wide for him לאורך ימים forever (Ps.23).

Life stretches endlessly before him. Death lies nowhere in wait for him. God merely calls him away from the station in which He had placed him, in order to live in His presence and, removed from earthly suffering, to take part in the "saturation of joys" (Ps.16). God's Shofar accompanies him through life. His Shofar opens for him the gates of *Olom Habbo*.

Deeply hidden, still another *Olom Habbo* lives as a blissful certainty in our Jewish consciousness. This life does not end with the days on earth. Death only dissolves the bond which joined the divine soul in temporary union with the earthly body. It is this body which you return to the earth when the soul departs.

Behold, Jewish custom refers even to the place of burial as the "house of life." For the separation is only temporary. We keep a sacred legacy in our consciousness—the dead shall one day rise again, מתים יחיה אל.

Is it a miracle? Yes, indeed, but no greater than any other miracle which no longer elicits amazement merely because experience has shown it to be a daily phenomenon. Behold the seed in the ground where it rots and spoils until all at once it moves and breaks its shackles and stirs upward in youthful beauty. You may shake your head in a doubting gesture: A miracle—impossible! (ref. Tifereth Israel, Or Hachayim).

But, the prophet Job sees it (Chap. 14), and a delightful certainty flows through him: There is still hope for the tree, even if the roots have aged in the soil; even if the trunk would die in the dust, it still will sprout new blossoms through the fragrance of the water—and man should die and never rise again, never awaken from his sleep?

From the very beginning God did not want death. God sent

death to earth only for man to overcome it. God's Shofar fights against death and helps man defeat it. You did not know death in your lives; "God kills death forever" for you (Is. 25).

Follow the call of God through life and plant Olom Habbo on earth. Then your soul may quietly part from your body to answer the call of God to Olom Habbo. The sound of God's Shofar penetrates the depths of the earth. Once Olom Habbo will have prepared the throne for God's sovereignty on earth, the moment will draw near when the reveille of the Shofar will break open the graves and the departed, who sleep in the dust, will awaken and rejoice at the light which they had sown with their lives and which will now banish the shadows from the earth.

"NACHTLEINEN"

Parents always worry over the future of their children. We want to do all in our power to make certain that their way through life will be a secure and successful one. We are frightened by the manifold dangers which may threaten our children as they grow up. For we know that none of us is immune to the variegated influences of the outside world.

The greatest danger to our adolescent youth threatens from their leisure time. For it is not the work but the free time which causes many a person to weaken morally. Once we have made certain that the leisure time of our youth is properly filled and spent, we will have secured the future of our children and we will have been successful in the great task of education.

"Having nothing to do", "wasting time"—this is perhaps the most dangerous evil of all. For idleness is identical with boredom. Since the healthy youth cannot bear to be bored, he is forced into the street which beckons to him with the lures of companionship, entertainment, sensual pleasure. The street demands its victims. For he whom it clutches in its embrace will find it more and more difficult to escape its magnetic force. It pulls him from one climax to the next and rests not until it extinguishes the last flickering flames which burn in each human breast and cause him to long for higher goals of life. In the place of a normal desire for spiritual and ethical strength and potency there is but left empty frivolity and ice-cold indifference.

Who can help parents to ban the dangers inherent in idleness and boredom? Let us be honest with ourselves: Our own
example, our own evaluation of leisure time and the way it
should be properly spent are the decisive factors in the upbringing of our children and in determining their future attitude and
power of discrimination regarding moral values in general and
our Torah ideals in particular. It all depends on our own attitude to the value and meaning of life itself. He to whom life is
not a sacred Divine gift will have no qualms at all to waste his
time in busy boredom. If it is true, however, that our lives are
God's possession, then it is also God's right to demand of us an
accounting of every one of our living moments. For it is the
perpetuation of the Divine will which is to be served by every
heartbeat, every breath, every particle of our physical and spiritual being. As every material and intellectual striving finds its
justification and significance in God and in the recognition and
realization of His Divine Will, so our earthly enjoyments and
sensual pleasures receive their ethical evaluation and justification only before His Countenance. Only the acceptance of the
demands of the Divine Will can lead to the possibility of a life
dedicated to God.

It is the loftiest goal of every Jew who raises his claim to a
truly Jewish life to recognize and penetrate ever more the precepts of the Divine Will. And when his back is bent under the
burden of his daily labor, וירא מנוחה כי טוב (Gen. 49) he longs for
the rest, for the time of leisure in order to dedicate himself to
that which forms his life's highest and most precious values.
Leisure time, spent thus, is a necessity without which the day
would amount to no more than a meaningless succession of
minutes and hours.

We must permeate our whole being with this realization. If
parents want their children to learn to adhere to this life view,

they must take care not to turn their own lives into a mockery of this truth. For this view of life cannot be taught; it must be *lived*, lived in the example of parents who then transmit it to their children as a self-understood obligation.

According to our Sages (Eruvin 65) the night was created to afford time to study the word of God: this profound thought points to the immense significance of our dedicated devotion to the research and study of the Divine science. Every house in which the Word of God is not heard at night (i.e. evenings) will be consumed by the flames (Sanhedrin 92): Our Sages knew these hungry flames which threaten the nocturnal existence of Israel's homes. Whoever wishes to escape them is well advised to turn his home into a homestead of Torah. God's Shechina-proximity rests with you if you do not let an evening pass without studying His words (Tamid 32). If you long for God's love during the day make certain that His song lives on your lips during the night (Chagiga 12).

From earliest childhood you are used to end your day with the Nachtleinen, המות פן עיני והאר, "illuminate my eyes lest I slumber the sleep of death"—"for the darkness of the eyelid you fill with light . . ." המאיר לעולם: The light emanates from You for an entire world.

Is it the fear of physical death which causes us to look up trembling to God when the night descends upon us and our weary body longs for sleep? Are we afraid that we shall not awaken in the morning and is the Nachtleinen but a prayer to God to re-awaken us when the morning dawns, for we want to live and not yet die?

Well may it be so. If our Nachtleinen were to succeed to make us conscious that every re-awakening is a renewed Divine gift of mercy and that every sleep may also be the beginning of the eternal sleep, the hour of sleep would become the moment of truth for the thoughtless, the time of self-examination for the frivolous.

But you . . . the hour of sleep in which the tool of labor falls from the tired hand and the never-resting brain seeks its rest in exhaustion finds you as *Jews,* as members of a nation which does not fear physical decay; to whom the most terrible death is death within life which they must conquer with all their might; who shake off weariness with ease in the knowledge of their strength as the people of God; who fear not the night, for the brilliant light of Divine Providence and Guidance illuminates the nocturnal suffering of the Galuth fate.

והאר עיני פן אישן המות, "illuminate my eyes lest I slumber the sleep of death": this is the cry of longing from the hopelessness of our Galuth misery which rings in the darkest night of despair towards the Divine ray of light which promises the eternal strength of rejuvenation and the certain knowledge that Divine assistance will help us to endure and outlive the night (Ps. 13).

This longing you must implant in your children if their souls should be so conditioned that the Nachtleinen becomes a vital necessity of life to them.

We long for the Divine ray of light for we abhor death. שמע ישראל—Let us hearken to the Divine demands and let us dedicate to His Word our hearts and strength and lives. Let us hearken to the prayer of the immortal leader which he uttered when the dawn broke over his people: ויהי נועם he prayed that his people should find happiness in God's Law and experience pride in its selection as God's Nation. And he accompanies his people on its road through history and he sees it safe and protected, guided and borne by its God, passing over terror and death, leaving far behind dull despair and hopelessness, invincible through God's proximity whose blissful call for reawakening leads it toward eternal life.

We hear this call and we perceive that which God means to us. And when His messenger comes, the messenger of light and life, His Shabbos—we do not refuse it; we receive it as one receives the loved one whose nearness spells bliss and happiness. To the Shabbos we sing our song and the joyfulnes never leaves our hearts. For the Shabbos teaches us to perceive God's work in all that He has created; it elevates us from human narrow-mindedness and limitation; it plants us deep in the Mount of God from whose summit we glimpse the brilliant promise of the Divine victory and whose soil provides the roots and nourishment for our eternally rejuvenated vigor.

Possessing the Shabbos our eyes are alight and the night frightens us not. Realizing the significance of the Shabbos for our lives we perceive the tragedy of our nation which lost everything from the moment when the Shabbos was banned from its midst. Israel's wisdom and might is the Shabbos. For "God's eye is turned to those who fear Him, to save their souls from death" (Ps. 33). Shabbos saves Israel from decay for it secures for it the Divine eye. Only with the Shabbos can and will Israel return to its homeland.

We have cried out in the thick of the night (ה' מה רבו וכו') and found peace in the *one* word ואתה ה'—the Shabbos alone is responsible for this miracle. For we have learned to bless God even at the height of darkness, secure of ultimate victory in childlike trust in His truth (יראו עינינו). For God sweeps away the suffering of death, helps us overcome all obstacle and saves us from the anxieties of the night. Because God does not sleep we may sleep, secure in the knowledge of His Shechina-proximity. For our lives are permeated and elevated by the שיר המעלות which sings of the happiness and blessing of our human existence when the fulfillment of Zion's Divine goals form the contents of our lives.

Who would not—and were he stooped in sin and frivolity—long for such sleep, such awakening?

Let us spend our evenings in a way which does not belie the Nachtleinen. Then we may be certain that our children will follow in our footsteps.

THE OBLIGATION OF מעשר

The majestic צדקה chapter in the Torah (Deut. 15) calls on us in the most solemn terms to live up to this God-willed obligation to the best of our abilities. The Shulchan Arukh (J.D. 248) formulates this legally binding rule as follows: "Everyone is obligated to give צדקה. Even the poor must give צדקה of that which they receive themselves as צדקה. He who contributes less than what he actually could may be forced by the Beth Din to part with an amount estimated as his approximate obligation." For the Torah admonishes us: "Do not permit your heart to be unresponsive, do not tighten your hand"—he who evades the צדקה duty is branded by the Torah as a "worthless one" (בליעל), a terminology usually applied to the idol worshipper (ibid. 247);—for his money is his God who enslaves his entire existence.

"Mine is the land" (III, 25) proclaims the Divine Will over the land which God's nation receives from God's hand, a call claiming for God's land the Shabbos which pays homage to the Divine rule. From the hand of God the Jewish farmer receives the blessing of his harvest which must be dedicated to the God-willed tasks. To him the מעשר laws signify the justification of this blessing if it becomes in his hands a source of true blessings for others. צדקה emanates from the same מעשר-spirit. What מעשר requires of the produce of the land, צדקה demands from possession and income.

What amount of צדקה must one give? One tenth is the minimum, for less than that would demonstrate a spirit of greed and
egotism. He must deal with the annual income from the capital,
as well as with any other form of profit (ibid, 249). If his business dealings show alternate profits and losses, the exact evaluation of the מעשר is measured from the time when he usually
takes annual stock of his finances. Inheritances are similarly
subject to the מעשר rules (ibid פ"ח). The same law applies to the
so-called "restitution funds."

Primarily, מעשר funds are to be used for צדקה purposes.
Relatives should be considered first. If the circumstances warrant the support and Jewish education of older children, מעשר
funds may be tapped (251). However, for obvious reasons of
parental honor, the financial support of parents may not emanate from מעשר funds unless there are no other resources (ibid.
ש"ך). Congregational dues (such as membership and seat fees)
may not be paid from מעשר monies. Mitzvoth for Keriath
haTorah may be acquired with מעשר funds provided this had
been the original intent (ט"ז 249). The same holds true for the
customary pledges at the occasion of "aufrufen" and for other
forms of donations (באר הגולה ibid.).

It need certainly not be stressed that the furtherance of
Torah and the support of Torah institutions count on our generous spirit of sacrifice. For the solemn proclamation which
accompanied our nation's entrance into the land of God concludes with words which must stir the conscience of every thinking Jew: "Curse on him who fails to uphold the words of the
Torah and bring them to fulfillment" (V, 27), referring to him
who refuses to do all in his power to translate the Divine Law
into daily action. Blessing awaits us only if קיום התורה, the full
realization of Torah, becomes the most sacred duty of our lives.
This is accentuated by the view (ibid. 349) that the work for
Jewish education takes preference over the duties of צדקה and
בית הכנסת.

Is the מעשר-duty on capital and income a law demanded by Torah? Tossafoth (Taanith 9a) refers to the ספרי who finds this duty embodied in the lawful status of עשר תעשר את כל תבואת זרעך (V, 14) which extends the מעשר obligation in a broader sense (כל) beyond the circumstance of harvesting (comp. 331 ט"ז). As to the implications, comp. שו"ת ח"ס סי' רל"א, שבט סופר סי' פ"ד and others).

The basic thought is obvious: The מעשר-*spirit* and the resulting מעשר-*readiness* are intimately tied to the great message of the Shabbos as it recurs week after week. If it is true that God is Creator and Master, Owner of heaven and earth, and that my life finds its ultimate destiny in His service, then it is equally true that all my possessions and wealth must be dedicated to God-willed purposes. Egotism and selfishness transform the Shabbos proclamation into an abominable lie: the lives of our ancestors were permeated by the מעשר-spirit because their whole existence was a continuous service of God. "From all that You grant me I will give a tenth", to be dedicated to God—thus vowed father Yaakov (I. 28).

In characterization of the מעשר-spirit and מעשר readiness King David has found these immortal formulations: "Joyfully, with all their hearts" his people poured out the means to erect God's Sanctuary. Filled with high joy, the King pronounces words of blessing to God: "Yours, oh God, is the greatness, the power—Yours all that which is in heaven and earth—Yours the rulership—wealth and honor emanates from You and You rule over all—for the source of all is in You and (that which we have given) from *Your* hand have we returned it to *You*";—and he prays to God, the God of Avrohom, Yitzchok and Yisroel, our forefathers, that this spirit may permeate the hearts of his people and may guide its thoughts and deeds—(Chronicles 1, 29).

Daily we pronounce these words in תפלת שחרית (ויברך דוד),

thus reiterating again the theme of our daily שמע proclamation: "and you should love God, i.e. you should give yourself fully to Him, with all your heart, with all your soul, and with your *entire resources*".

Would not these words, this proclamation be a shameless lie on our lips; could we call ourselves Yehudim in the spirit of Torah, in the spirit of our forefathers, if we were but to hesitate to dedicate all that we own to God by the minimum requirement of the מעשר-share from our capital and annual income?

OUR LONGING FOR THE MOON

Since the beginning of our nationhood the Divine Will has appointed the moon to serve as the most faithful companion for our world-historic mission. The silvery light of its celestial sphere, emerging from nocturnal darkness, represents to us the Divine challenge to search for that light which shines only in God's proximity and which alone is capable of illuminating our way through life. To those of our people who might have become estranged from the Divine light of Torah, the moon serves as a constant reminder never to permit the night to engulf and overpower us. Like the moon—as we proclaim in blessing at its appearance—we must ever strive to elevate ourselves from darkness to light. Similar to the infinite number of worlds which greet us from the starry sky, the moon, in the eternal regularity of its changing phases, is to us the lofty representative of the lawfulness of the universe which is bound to God's creative Will. At the same time the presence of the moon is an admonition to us—on whom God has bestowed the privilege of free choice (בחירה)—to strive towards the great goal of freedom within the Divine Law and thus secure for ourselves the peace and joyfulness which derive solely from faithful observance of the word of God ששים ושמחים לעשות רצון קונם. By causing us to look up to God in worshipful blessing, the moon, in the profound interpretation of our Sages, helps us to "come close to the Shechina."

Inestimable is the wealth of blessing as the Tishri new moon, more than any of the other monthly lunar renewals and accompanied by the authoritative and yet tender call of the Divine Sinai Shofar, brings us from nocturnal estrangement onto the path which leads to life renewal through Yom Kippur atonement. Then, and only then, may we look forward to a life of inner peace and never-ending joyfulness of living.

Even in regard to our Divinely affirmed future as a nation, the moon is to us a "faithful witness from the heights of the clouds" (Ps. 89, 38). What can surpass the greatness of the dynamic and indestructible strength of our national consciousness as we reflect on the dispersed parts of our Galuth nation which, in all the long and painful nocturnal centuries, looked up in worshipful blessing of God to the moonlight shining through the night as a re-affirmation of the certain conviction of the Divinely promised ultimate redemption of our people! What can surpass the lofty thought of King David, ancestor of the Redeemer, alive for all time to come, as we welcome each other at the nocturnal hour with the greeting of peace which will once become a reality for all mankind!

And we should not long for the moon, long for it with all that it could and should signify for us?

Our longing is not a longing in the physical sense. Our forefathers never dreamed of the possibility of actually reaching the moon. What would be the use? Its Divine task is to be near to everyone of us with its admonishing, comforting, joyful message.

In our time mankind is following a dramatic spectacle with breathless excitement: that which was thought to be utterly impossible became reality in our days borne on the incredible advances in science and technical progress. When they reached the heretofore unattainable, the conquerors plunged into an orgy of victory unprecedented in the history of mankind.

Triumph of human culture?

Or a culture debacle of world-shaking proportions?

Have not the very scientific and technical achievements which have unlocked untold mysterious forces in God's creation placed threatening weapons in the hands of power-hungry world conquerors who are fanatically dedicated to the shameful and inhuman concept of erecting their mighty throne on the pitiful debris of a fallen humanity?

We reached the moon. What of it! In sublime majesty it scornfully rebuffs the conquerors who are ignorant of the beauty and quiet satisfaction that flow from faithful fulfillment of the Divine creative Will. For it alone guarantees the right of existence for all creations—men among them—bringing with it peace and joyfulness of living.

In these sacred days we yearn in our prayers with intense longing for the dawn of the Divinely promised future when human conceit and delusion will have vanished from the earth; when all men will join in the unity of their Divine purpose and dedicate their lives wholeheartedly to their Creator.

YAHRZEIT

Jewish custom, elevated into law, has transformed the institution of Yahrzeit into a solemn day of remembrance. Its purpose is self-reflection, admonition and, thereby, inner enrichment.

During the first twelve months, a thousand ties bind us to
the memory of the departed (Berachot 58). While the initial
impact of shock may have taken the form of quiet resignation,
the living presence of the dead arouses ever anew the painful
awareness of his loss. But then life itself demands its rights. Even
the most acutely felt loss must never be permitted to reduce or
limit the joyful acceptance of life. For the true joy of life —
emanating from our devotion to the precepts of the Divine Will
— remains untouched by whatever fate has in store for us. Only
he who builds his life on fleeting values is exposed to the danger
of breaking down under the heavy burden of an unexpected and
painful loss. On the other hand, the knowledge of God's absolute rulership over every phase of our lives which we are to
dedicate to the unconditional fulfillment of the Divine Will becomes a source of lasting comfort to him who anchors his total
conception of life in God and who is fully ready to be led
through life at the direction of Divine guidance. Thus he will
learn not only to bear the burden of a pain which he is unable
to comprehend but also to acknowledge it as an outgrowth of
Divine wisdom. God expects of man to "shift the burden of their

way towards Him" (Ps. 37, 5). God helps us bear our burden. Even the most modestly lived life, once it is dedicated to

the service of God, is forever inscribed in God's Book of Providence. Every good deed performed during his life time bears eternal fruit. "God Who knows the days of men who strive for moral perfection" sees to it that "their heritage is being preserved for all eternity" (Ps. 37). Their contribution to the elevation of mankind towards its God-willed destiny secures for them their lasting and inviolable right to life. "The righteous inherit the earth and rest forever on it" (Ps. 37). In the remembrance of the living "the righteous remain a lasting memory" (Ps. 112).

God desires that the thoughts of the living should be freed from all that could influence negatively the strong, joyous devotion to the Divine duties of life. He does not wish the heart to react with pangs of pain to the mere mention of the memory of the departed. It is for that purpose that God created the beneficial institution of forgetting (Pessachim 54).

The memory of the dead should serve life. itself; it is designed to awaken the joyful-serious determination to continue that which the departed had begun with his life and to complete that which he left unfinished during his presence on earth. Thus "the memory of the righteous becomes a blessing" (Mishle 10, 7).

The institution of Yahrzeit invites to serious self-reflection. Ancient tradition dating back to talmudic times (comp. Sabbath 20) prescribed fasting for the day. Torah study is an equally appropriate. way of commemorating the day. For the memory of the departed is not honored by fasting but by the intensified loyalty to our Jewish duties which flow from more concentrated Torah study. This determination is expressed in the Kaddish to which the memory of the dead obligates the surviving sons.

Kaddish is not a prayer in the usual sense. It is certainly not a "mass for the dead". On the contrary, it is a dramatic call for action to the congregation which concludes every major part of our Tefillot. The Kaddish draws the consequences of the awareness we gain through our Tefillot and of the positive intentions they create in us. In the Kaddish the Chazan expresses the strong hope that ultimately God's Name "will be recognized in all its greatness and sacredness by a world which He has created in accordance with His Will". This means that all God-willed goals will find their realization in a world formed by the free will of the creator, a world which will ultimately recognize the sole authority of the Divine will and Divine rulership. Every ounce of human energy must serve the realization of this goal. Thus the call of the Chazan to the congregation: Help hasten the attainment of this goal — help "bless the Name of God". The congregation answers this call with Amen.

The Kaddish on the lips of the survivors constitutes a blessing for the departed. For only he has truly lived who served God's Will on earth — only he has lived up to the true meaning of life. His failures and mistakes may have been due to human frailty and misjudgment — the good that he has striven for and accomplished in his life time secures for his existence on earth lasting significance and meaning in the eyes of God. This is true all the more if he succeeded in inspiring others to live up to the Divine demands or if the survivors, in honor of his memory, elevate their spiritual life towards the fulfillment of the Divinely-appointed tasks of life and thus, in a sense, continue his life whose earthly shape has long ceased to exist.

According to this conception, Kaddish is also able to produce atonement. Those who continue living wish to complete that which the departed has failed to accomplish. His life was not lived in vain if it serves to inspire those who come after him to fulfill their God-willed tasks of life. This aspect bestows upon the Kaddish a moving quality especially when it is pronounced by the stumbling lips of children's mouths. By standing before the congregation and by calling upon the congregants to bless the Will of God with ever greater fervor and thus cause God's Kingdom to become a reality, the educators of the child proclaim the sacred vow that this child will be reared in such a manner that he will dedicate his full adult strength toward the realization of this task.

Thus the dead live. The light that is lit in their memory (a custom which also seems to date back to talmudic times, comp. Kesuboth 103) directs the silent admonition to the living to take care that the life of the departed should not be extinguished in their midst.

Even the visit to the "House of the Living" (as Jewish thoughtfulness describes the cemetery to emphasize its character as a symbol of eternal life and ultimate resurrection) should not be devoted to melancholic thoughts of death. For the dead wish to help us appreciate life. Our graves are not marked by elaborate monuments (Shekalim 7). Woe to the dead whose memory is preserved only by way of such material reminders. It is the simplicity of the headstone which is designed to arouse awareness of the lasting significance of every earthly life, however modestly lived, which was dedicated to the fulfillment of its Divinely appointed task on earth. The simple stone over the grave renews the memory of the life and striving of the departed and ties closer the bond that unites the living with the dead and obligates the living to continue the work to which the departed had dedicated their lives.

It is in this sense that the dead help the living to life and pray before the Throne of God for the life of the living (Taanit ff.). For the dead desire that the living may live.

THE CHANUKAH MIRACLE IN OUR TIME

"Blessed be God, who has performed miracles for our forefathers, in those days, at this time . . ." — We have truly witnessed miracles — miraculous is the road of Torah; — the historical road of the Jewish people, from the very beginning, is an unending chain of Divine miracles safeguarding our existence. Do we have the right to expect to witness similar wonders in our days, the miracle that we long for with hearts full of pain?

Thrice daily our Tefilla teaches us to pronounce these words of blessing and gratitude:

> "In gratitude we recognize that You, God, are our God and the God of our fathers, through all eternity. Rock of our lives, shield of our salvation, are You through every generation. Gratefully we pay homage to You and recount Your praise: that our lives are committed unto Your hand, that our souls are entrusted to Your charge; that Your miracles accompany us daily, Your wonders and benefits at all times, evening, morn and noon — You are the Good, for Your mercy has never ended, the Merciful, for your loving deeds have never ceased — we have always placed our trust in you . . ."

This is a proclamation of overwhelming impact which bestows upon its adherents the victorious crown of heroic invincibility. Is there still need for a motivation? Here, we witness the incredible sufferings of a people writhing in agony under the brutal blows of the enemy and shedding the life-blood of innumerable men, women, children and aged — and there, thrice daily, morning, noon and night, this confession!

This is the credo of a people, of every individual who counts himself part of this people, gratefully paying homage to God for being *his* God as He was the God of our forefathers in all eternity. God, whose loftiness heaven and earth can not contain, is to him *his* God, who bends down and extends His fatherly hand to all who long for His nearness and guidance. God bears for him His Torah, messenger of His sacred Will, to lead him through a life that could not be lived without Divine direction. God calls his life into His service in order that he dedicate himself, through faithful realization of the demands of Torah, to the solution of those tasks which God alone comprehends. This Divine leadership is the object of his overflowing gratitude, morning, noon and night . . .

To each Yehudi God rises as the "Rock of his life" to whom he may cling, who is a source of invincible strength and power, at a time when the seemingly bottomless abyss threatens his very existence. Divine guidance elevates his temporary and insignificant life above human frailty and allows it to take part in the work for salvation which the creative will of God secured also for the world of man. This salvation will come to its ultimate undoubted fruition, as true as God is the Creator and Master of the Universe, of heaven and of earth. The Jew's whole life is dedicated to the realization of this salvation, a salvation which can never be jeopardized by irresponsible, criminal, self-defying human conceit. For to him God is "shield" of his "salvation" the realization of which is guaranteed for him by God's infinite might. And this Jew should not confess his gratitude to God, morning, noon and night?

From God's hand he receives his existence; to God and His sacred Will his life remains forever dedicated. Unto God's hand he entrusts his life leaving its course to Divine wisdom. Unto God's charge he commits his soul which finds security only under God's eye. His life is ruled not by the mood of accident, not by the injustice of an unpredictable fortune, and certainly not by the cold hand of an inevitable fate. Whenever human arrogance revolts against the Divine rule; whenever, as a consequence, the human mind collapses miserably under the crushing burden of that which it cannot comprehend and, shaken by nocturnal terror, appears to fade away into nameless darkness — there the path of the Jew is illuminated by the Divine light of Torah, through night and death. This is the Divine light of Torah, which the enemies of God, the enemies of the light, have sworn to extinguish, a light that can never cease to burn — for it is Divine. God has called His people to be bearers of this light. On His people he bestows immortality as long as it realizes its immortal task as bearer of the eternal light.

"TRENDS" WITHIN JUDAISM

The future of Judaism and thereby of Jewry in this country is frequently the object of intensive scrutiny in the American Press. The discussion is spurred by the increasing number of mixed marriages resulting from a combination of lack of interest in Judaism and the strong desire to assimilate. Two additional motives, the spread of materialism and the considerable deterioration of morality, are generally not considered in relation to the problem of mixed marriages; but their impact should certainly not be underestimated.

As for us, let us never lose sight of the truth that only historically validated Divine Judaism will endure, for its future, and thereby its immortality, is guaranteed by God. God, Creator and Master of the realm of nature, is also the Creator and Master of the realm of men. In the same measure in which every immeasurably mysterious law of nature, from the gigantic to the minute, proclaims the Lawgiver by its very existence, God reveals to men His Divine Will to which they must dedicate themselves in free obedience in order to give meaning and timelessness to their human existence.

In the folly of their arrogance men have at all times attempted to oppose the precepts of the Divine Will. Although life confronts them as an impenetrable mystery they have always attempted to fashion their own version of the purpose of living—and have always had to pay for their reckless conceit with the unending misery which threads through the history of mankind.

In His infinite mercy God decreed from the very beginning, that there be always a select circle of men who, lead by God and His Almighty Will, conceive of their whole existence as Divine Service and who help guide an erring mankind on the only possible road to ultimate redemption. Therein is founded the God-willed creation and convocation of the Jewish people. As a unified people we witnessed God's Divine proclamation at Sinai and received His Law in oral teaching and with it the Torah as its concisely written formulation.

From generation to generation, in unbroken continuity, our nation transmits these historic testimonies which it witnessed in its entirety. We are God's nation because we are the bearers and champions of His Divine Will. This bestows distinction and responsibility upon the life of every individual who considers himself part of the people of God.

While it is certainly true that Jewish history throughout the millenia is filled with tragedy and instability, it is equally true that our people has always emerged victoriously, inspired and strengthened by the Divine Will, the eternal spring of its never-ceasing rejuvenation. Indelibly, Moshe Rabbenu has inscribed the "you are the few in number" (in the midst of the nations) in his nation's history (Deut. 7). Isaiah (Ch. 51) deeply implants the great truth in the souls of the "few" who uphold their God-willed convocation in uncompromising loyalty even when their lives are battered by the onslaught of degradation and assimilation: "Look to Abraham, your forefather, look to Sarah, who gave you life, for when he was but one I called him, and rich blessing was his share".

Materialism, sensuality and the resulting striving for assimilation were the great dangers envisioned by Moshe Rabbenu as he, dying, guided his people to the land promised to it by God. Twice it buried the State which rose in this land; but the remnants of this people (two-tenths were left) never relinquished for a single instant the inner strength which is nourished by the miraculous source of Divine Judaism and which secured its survival of a sheer unending martyrdom during its Galuth journey in the midst of the nations of the world.

That which calls itself reform and conservative Judaism in our days is just another variety of the types of "Judaism" (kussitish, hellenist, sadducee, and finally, karaite) which nibble at the roots of our Jewish tree of life since time immemorial. Our Divine Judaism has triumphantly surmounted them all. This certainly also seals the fate of these "religious establishments" in our time. They will struggle in vain against the increasing assimilation and mixed marriages. Why should not young men and women breathe in deeply the free air of the American mode of living; why tear hearts apart whom love has brought together? Does not this "Judaism", as proclaimed by its "religious founders", with its dogma of the "unity of divinity", with its demands of ethics (surely a historic credit of true Judaism), as a "purified Judaism", forcibly and inevitably lead towards a "purified"— Protestantism? Therefore, why not—mixed marriages? Is there not one father above us all, has not one God borne us all? (Mal. 2). Should not these words of the Prophet—actually uttered with chilling irony—bless every performance of a mixed marriage?

We do not fear for the future of our Divine Judaism, not even in America. Yet, in the spirit of self-respect and responsibility towards God and His Divine Judaism of which they are adherents, it is imperative upon orthodox rabbis and orthodox organizations to refuse to join those organizations which, as unfortunately quoted in the press time and again, embrace the three "trends" within Judaism, reform, conservatism, and orthodoxy. Divine Judaism categorically refuses to be labeled a "trend" within Judaism. The contrast between Catholicism and Protestantism is far less pronounced than the abyss which separates Divine Judaism from non-Judaism and yet the former would never consent to join in an organized religious union.

It is of vital importance that it be clearly stated before the general public and also in the representation towards the Government that there is but one Judaism: the historic Judaism, witnessed and proven by the entity of our people, the Judaism as entrusted to us by God.